Praise for *Align and Refine*

Align and Refine accomplishes something very important. Abstruse and highly technical teachings are explained and discussed in an extraordinarily easy to read, accessible, and highly interesting way. Concise chapters make the book easy to digest and useful to a broad range of readers. At the same time, the scope and range of ideas, concepts, and teachings presented are actually very large, representing essentially all of the most important teachings that form the basis and foundation of an understanding of the many streams of Yoga and yogic practice. The end-of-chapter contemplations and exercises make the book even more useful to any interested reader. The personal and warm voice throughout, sharing experiences, reflections, and insights, enlivens the experience of reading. The added materials in the appendices are also very useful and helpful. In short, I love the book! May this book help many more people locate that place of the Heart where wonder, bliss, soberness of high and wise vision, devotion, compassion, and love all eternally dwell!

—Paul Muller-Ortega, PhD.
Founder, Blue Throat Yoga

Reading this book is like talking with a friend who shares their experience and understanding patiently, compassionately and with the kind of wisdom that invites you to your own. Cindy has dedicated her life to the yogic journey. Her passion for the teachings, the practices, and for helping others shines through her writing like a beacon of possibility for those who are easily swept up into the currents of our fast-moving, turbulent, and anxiety-producing times. She makes no false claims and promises no quick fixes. She simply outlines a path that each one of us can take from the surface of our lives to the depths of Life itself. Newer practitioners will find practical guidance to get started, experienced practitioners will delight in having found a trusted companion, and yoga teachers from all traditions will find clear, accessible explanations for esoteric, and often-times confusing, philosophical distinctions. I recommend this book wholeheartedly.

—Christina Sell, author of *Yoga From the Inside Out: Making Peace with Your Body Through Yoga, My Body is a Temple: Yoga as a Path to Wholeness,* and *A Deeper Yoga: Moving Beyond Image to Wholeness and Freedom.*

Align and Refine

The Journey of Yoga and Meditation

Cindy Lusk

lila

Lila Press

Published 2023

Book design & composition by Wendy Holdman

ISBN 979-8-9895586-0-5 print book
ISBN 979-8-9895586-2-9 eBook

Library of Congress Control Number: 2023922570

Printed in the United States of America

10 9 8 7 6 5 4 3 2 1

For my parents, my first gurus,
who each in their own way helped me be
the person who could write and publish this book.

Contents

Gratitude

As I write this, my journey on the path of yoga comprises nearly forty years, and along the way I have been blessed to have some of the greatest living teachers. Without them, I would not be who I am today, and this book would not be possible. I mention several here, but there were many more who have shaped my experience and understanding of yoga. I send so much gratitude to all the teachers I encountered in workshops, courses, and trainings. From each I learned something, and their impact is reflected in my work. I mention the most influential below, and you will find relevant resources for their work in appendix IV.

My very first yoga teacher, Ann Barros, planted a seed when I was an undergraduate at the University of California–Santa Cruz, and Chris Berntsen nurtured my early practice in Boulder, Colorado. Richard Freeman guided me into a serious investigation of yoga *āsana,* where I learned the value of dedicated practice. He supported me as I became a new teacher, whetted my thirst for yoga philosophy, and supported my first attempts at teaching. Richard introduced me to John Friend, who showed me how to align my body to be free of pain. John opened up the world of Tantric philosophy and introduced me to many other teachers. I was impacted by Krishna Das, whose kirtans at Inner Harmony Retreat Center and elsewhere had a heart-opening effect, and by Sally Kempton, whose presence and words always awakened something in me.

Douglas Brooks ignited in me a deep love of the teachings of yoga through its stories, culture, and philosophy. Many of the stories in this book came through him. Not a day goes by when I don't think of something I've learned from Douglas, and his teachings have had a profound effect on me, my life, and my teaching. I am forever grateful our paths came together.

My studies with Paul Muller-Ortega fulfilled a call of my heart that was clearly clamoring for something more, and they produced a more expansive shift in my being than I thought possible. In a word, the greatest gift he has given me is *sādhanā*. He taught me effective practices, the value of a regular meditation practice, and self-sufficiency, the result of which has been a profound realignment in the core of my being with the pulsations of the Highest. Paul fed my appetite for a systematic understanding of yoga philosophy (particularly the Tantras) and for honoring Patañjali's teachings about meditation. Much of this book reflects what I have learned from him. And Paul bestowed upon me the gift of becoming a meditation teacher, allowing me to serve in an even greater capacity.

I must thank all the scholars and authors who have brought forth translations of traditional texts that have been languishing in homes and libraries. Of particular note is Christopher Wallis, whose book *Tantra Illuminated* helped clarify many of the concepts I am articulating in this book. In addition, his translations of the traditional texts have been incredibly useful to me personally, and they are upleveling the availability of the teachings of Tantra into a world that desperately needs them.

I am extremely grateful to those who have walked the path with me—my sādhanā sisters and brothers—in the different communities in which I've been involved: Ashtanga, Anusara, Rajanaka, and Blue Throat Yoga. I hold you dear in my heart and appreciate the many ways we have interacted and shared the practices and teachings.

I cannot overstate my gratitude for the students who have studied with me, who encouraged me, and who helped me deepen my knowledge in so many ways. This book is a culmination of their participation in the many courses and study groups I've offered. Thanks for showing up in my living room, various studios, and online.

The journey of writing this book has been supported by many people, and primary is Cynthia Morris, who has been my coach, cheerleader, and midwife. I could not have done this without her. Also I must acknowledge the skill of Laurel Kallenbauch as editor. She helped shape this book in innumerable ways. Finally, gratitude to Wendy Holdman for her unwavering persistence and artistry in designing and combining the various components of this book to optimize its usability.

So much love and gratitude go to my partner, Peter. He has supported me in so many ways on the path of yoga and in my teaching career, as well as with writing this book, including both technical and emotional support—and everything in between.

From all of my teachers I repeatedly heard an honoring of their own teachers, a remembrance of those who helped them on their paths. So, finally and foremost, I honor with a deep bow the great lineage of teachers, all those who have held the teachings, kept the practices alive, and passed them on for the benefit of all beings.

INTRODUCTION

Welcome to the Journey of Yoga and Meditation

One summer in my late twenties, I found myself heartbroken and lost while touring with the Grateful Dead. My partner of ten years, whom I had moved to Colorado to be with while attending graduate school, fell in love with someone else and left me on the spot. When I returned home to school and the reality of this breakup, I turned to yoga. I had taken a series of classes previously, which planted a seed that had lain dormant for several years. Now I felt a strong inner impulse to pursue yoga as a means of self-care. Little did I know that honoring that impulse would lead not only to caring for and healing my shattered self, but as well to an experience and understanding of a deeper Self that I had intuited throughout my life.

In those days (the 1980s) yoga was not cool; it was on the periphery of society and considered strange by most. Yet something in the practice soothed me and set me on a long journey of self-discovery and transformation. That journey was not a straight line. It was full of confusions, twists, and turns. As a Westerner, the culture around yoga seemed mysterious and weird. As I experienced yoga more deeply, I tried to understand what it was all about. What is yoga? How does it work?

I had so many questions, and I dove in wholeheartedly. I attended every workshop and training in my area and eventually traveled to India. What I found continued to consternate me. The messages were contradictory. Different teachers said different things, and what I learned from the texts on yoga had little to do with what I was doing on the yoga mat or in my life in general—let alone the worldview I had grown up with.

Yet I persevered. Something kept pushing me to know more, and slowly I came to some understandings through the help of many teachers and lots of practice and study.

Simultaneous with my personal journey, yoga in the West exploded in popularity, and since then, yoga as an industry has experienced unprecedented growth. Yoga appears in the news, on the internet, and with social media influencers. As it has become more popular, contemporary yoga seems to have divorced itself even more from its roots, so the disconnect between the traditional yogic teachings and the current yoga scene is even greater than when I began. For some people, this may be an appropriate and positive development, but not for me or for many others who are attracted to yoga and its deeper teachings—even if unaware of that in the beginning.

Like so many people, my journey started with the practice involving yoga postures, called *yoga āsana*. Āsana taught me a lot, but as I studied more, I found there is so much more to yoga than "stretching in Sanskrit" as one of my teachers characterized it. I learned that much of what the tradition calls "yoga" is not only about our bodies but about other aspects of our being, including the mind, the nature of ultimate reality, and the meditative process. As I continued to practice and eventually became a teacher of yoga āsana, I sensed I "should" be meditating, but again I had to confront many misunderstandings about meditation and its underlying teachings.

This book reflects my journey from āsana to meditation, including how the yoga of meditation works. As we will discover, there are many yogas. So here is a focus on the streams of yoga with which I'm familiar, have found most useful, and are also quite prevalent in the modern yoga world. Presented herein is a combination of the foundational teachings from the Classical Yoga of Patañjali and the nondual Tantric perspective. Specifically, "Tantra" in this book refers to what scholars have labeled "Kashmir Śaivism."

This approach reflects my personal path of yoga and the path of many serious, modern-day yogis. And in some ways, it reflects how yoga in the West was initially dominated by more classical approaches and how more recently the teachings of Tantra have become increasingly available. My goal is to honor this great tradition by providing authentic and traditional interpretations of the teachings, but I interpret them to make them applicable to our everyday lives as twenty-first century yogis. In this way, we will begin to clarify many of the confusions in the modern-day yoga marketplace and explore the promise of yoga.

I am approaching this book as a journey—for us together—the reader and the writer. It's reflective of my own experience, which is both idiosyncratic and illustrative of what many go through as modern-day yoga students. Because yoga is a huge topic, our journey together is an introductory, guided tour through the major landmarks. We make selected stops along the way, considering teachings more or less deeply as we progress. At times it may seem like a whirlwind tour. My hope is that hitting some of the representative places along the journey will pique your interest in exploring the territory of yoga in more detail.

I have been lucky to have some of the greatest living teachers as my guides, whom I acknowledged at the beginning of this book. Their wisdom has been essential in my journey, and I hope what I have written begins to represent some fraction of what I've had the grace to receive from them. What I get right in this book is attributable to my teachers; any inaccuracies are my own.

This book is an attempt to provide some context for those who are sincerely interested in the deeper teachings of yoga—those who have a sense that there is something profoundly valuable to be learned but are confused (as I was) about the contradictory messages and the disconnect between the ancient texts and the images of skimpily dressed models twisting in knots in some exotic location. This is the book I wish I'd had as a young yogi. It is based on more than thirty-five years of practice, study, and teaching. I take a long story and make it much shorter and more accessible, while striving to keep it authentic to the teachings. A major emphasis of this book is to make yoga applicable to the modern practitioner, whether you're interested in Eastern spirituality or you've been on the path for a while but are confused about yoga's "spiritual" aspects.

If you are reading this, some seed has been planted in your life, the way it was in mine. Something inside wants to know more, to understand more of what yoga and meditation have to offer. For anyone new to yoga and wondering what it is all about, this book will explain. If you have been practicing for a while, or even if you're a teacher, there is plenty in this book to augment your knowledge and provide you with applicable themes for your life and teaching. In short, if you've had a sense there is more to yoga and meditation than how it's portrayed in popular culture and/or if you have an inner yearning for a deeper understanding, then reading this book will be a powerful step along your path.

May it be of service.

Orientation to the Journey of This Book

I want to share yoga's wisdom and teachings because I believe yoga helps change human consciousness, which can result in changes in our personal lives that could resonate throughout the world. From my own experience I know the challenges of exploring the original texts. My goal in this book is to make the teachings of yoga and meditation authentic, accessible, and applicable. I truly believe yoga's teachings are as relevant today as they were thousands of years ago. To make them authentic, I draw from original source texts and from what I've learned during decades of study with my teachers—along with my personal experience and insights. I've made necessary choices in order to make the teachings relevant to contemporary yogis.

I see myself as a guide for those who are curious about the deeper understandings of yoga. As a guide, I have walked the path just a little farther, and I turn around to offer others a hand to help them along the way. Before setting out, we must pause to orient ourselves and gather important tools that will support the journey—including some foundational definitions and concepts that will aid us in our continued journey of yoga.

Learning and Study Is an Iterative Process

One of the biggest challenges in writing this book has been deciding how to order the teachings, as the teachings are multilayered and interconnected, and they require background information to unpack. It's a chicken-and-egg thing. So sometimes I mention a teaching without elaborating on it until later. I also present a given teaching at multiple places in this book as it relates to other teachings and contexts. At the point I most fully explain a Key Teaching, it will be indicated in **bold print**, as in the following paragraph.

Studying the authentic source teachings from the original Sanskrit texts requires one to unpack meaning in a variety of ways. At first, there is a lot of new vocabulary and technical terms. This in and of itself can be valuable and illuminating. Just learning a new word or phrase can open up avenues of understanding. And as we will see, each time we pause to consider a word, phrase, teaching, or text, our understanding will shift. **Study is an iterative process in which teachings are considered again and again to discover nuance, deepen comprehension, and understand their application.**

Given all of this, it can be easy to get lost in the process, especially in these beginning sections, where foundational concepts are presented. Therefore, the key teachings will be summarized at the end of each part, and in addition the table of contents could also be useful for this journey.

Because these teachings have been transplanted to the West, a major pitfall for Western students is that incomplete or superficial comprehension has yielded many common misunderstandings. Usually there's some truth to such assertions, but they can lead to unfounded conclusions that become perpetuated in the yogic milieu and that are sometimes divorced from their original meaning. This book addresses some of the common misunderstandings currently prevalent in the yoga community.

Sanskrit Is the Language of Yoga

In a time when cultural appropriation is a big and important topic, especially in yoga, I have insisted on presenting yoga's foundational teachings and primary aphorisms, or *sūtra*s, in their original Sanskrit. I understand that the profusion of Sanskrit terminology will be daunting for some readers. There is no avoiding this because to be authentic we must grapple with the original formulations. The truth is we're learning a new language, and that requires effort, practice, working with the vocabulary, and contemplation. These are practices discussed in this book as part of the process of yoga.

To help alleviate a sense of overwhelm, I've done several things. First, each Sanskrit word or phrase is defined the first time it appears. Then, when those Sanskrit words appear later in the book, their Sanskrit with the English translations are combined, separated by a forward slash:

for example, *karuṇā*/compassion. Exactly how the words appear varies, depending on the context, but the purpose is to remind the reader of what the Sanskrit terms mean. Second, appendix V includes a few notes on Sanskrit that may alleviate some confusion. Finally, there is a glossary of key Sanskrit terms at the end of the book.

I employ a fairly traditional approach to understanding the original Sanskrit teachings. First, I've provided a word-for-word English definition. Second, I often break Sanskrit compound words into their component meanings. And third, I sometimes refer to the verbal roots of Sanskrit words to unpack their meaning.

Words in Sanskrit, like those in many languages, have different meanings depending on their context. For example, the word *śiva* literally means "auspicious," or it can be the name of a god (Śiva) from the different stories and myths of the tradition. Also, *śiva* is used to designate the undifferentiated ground of being. As we shall see, in this latter context, *Śiva* is not a god but a word for Absolute reality. I have taken care to define terms relative to the context of the teachings being elaborated.

As mentioned, I present many source teachings drawn from the traditional texts. Again I had to take a middle path so as not to overwhelm the reader. In most cases I present teachings from the texts themselves, using the original Sanskrit along with my translation. On occasion, I provide a reference. Sometimes I simply make statements that are pervasive in the tradition, and/or that I've learned from my teachers without providing a reference. This latter instance is generally because I do not know of published translations of material I have learned orally.

It is important to note that I am not a Sanskrit scholar, though I have studied Sanskrit and the textual teachings presented in this book for many years. I understand scholars will likely find my treatment and translations of individual terms and *sūtras* superficial or sloppy. This book is intended for lay practitioners, not for scholars, so I err on the side of keeping it accessible. My apologies to the scholars out there, to whom I am greatly indebted. It is my hope that this book will encourage readers to turn to translations of source texts from actual Sanskrit scholars to further their understanding.

In my references to the source teachings, I provide abbreviations as follows. The teachings presented are primarily drawn from four Sanskrit texts: the *Bhagavad Gītā* (BG), the *Yoga Sūtra* (YS), the *Śiva Sūtra* (SS), and the *Pratyabhijñā-hṛdayam* (PH). I have included suggested English translations of each of these four texts in Appendix IV: Recommended Texts and Resources.

In my translations and discussion of these source teachings, I've focused on what I feel is relevant and applicable at the introductory level. First I provide the more "traditional" meaning, as intended in the context of the source text, in keeping with the goal to stay authentic. And then I often interpret the teaching as it evolved through later iterations and as it can be applied to the modern practitioner. Each teaching has depths of meaning, so I by no means provide an ultimate explanation. Any teaching is subject to interpretation, as one can quickly discern by reading a few translations and commentaries on a given textual teaching. At first, as a student, it is important to try to understand the teaching in its original context. However, any teaching will ultimately have its greatest impact when we make it our own. In truth, these teachings are to be explored over and over again, and I hope that by making the teachings herein accessible, students will later seek out the source teachings in their original context.

Yoga's History and the Value of Stories

One of the most confusing things about yoga is its long history. This compounds as one tries to sort through all the teachings. They seem to be saying the same thing—but are they? Different texts seem to argue with each other, contradict, or proclaim their superiority. A question that has consistently arisen for me and for students concerns the timeline of yoga. When did different teachings emerge? What are all the different schools, and how are they different or the same?

Answering these questions is beyond the scope of this book. But to briefly address them, I have included two resources. First is appendix II, which outlines the history of yoga, particularly as it pertains to the teachings in this book. This will be useful to read on its own and/or to consult whenever you need a little context about a mentioned text or school of yoga. I also offer some recommended books for further study in appendix IV.

Among the source teachings I present are a variety of stories drawn from the Indian epics and Purāṇas (sacred texts containing the stories of the tradition). In the Hindu tradition, and certainly in my journey of yoga, these stories have been a primary and effective way of transmitting particular teachings and making them accessible. It is important to note that from within the Hindu tradition, these stories are *itihāsa*, which literally means "so it was," and they are taken as actual history. From a Western scholarly perspective, they are labeled as myths. Please note that the same stories occur in many different places in the tradition with different details, emphasizing different teachings. I have learned the stories from my teachers, who also emphasized their particular perspective, as well as what they learned from *their* teachers.

As you will see, these stories are extremely useful in illustrating teachings and making them relatable and applicable to our lives. I learned from my teacher, Douglas Brooks, that **although myths may not literally be true, they teach a greater truth. When studying the stories of the tradition, consider yourself to be every character in the story.** You will see how this allows for a richer and deeper understanding of their teachings and how it makes them more applicable to your life.

Make It Your Own

You will find suggestions to Reflect and Explore throughout this book. These are opportunities to consider your experience and understanding of the teachings. They include writing exercises, and the contemplative practice of *bhāvanā* is outlined as an aid in chapter 12. Sometimes these exercises involve practicing certain concepts and/or observing your life. So these serve several purposes. In part II, I explain that such explorations are actually part of the practice of yoga and serve to deepen the understanding and experience of yoga. To the degree you are willing to pause, reflect, journal, and explore, your understanding will be enhanced. Equally important, the opportunities to explore help make the teachings applicable to your life. I cannot overemphasize the value of pausing to reflect on the teachings as you go, using the practice of bhāvanā. Your experience will be optimized by going slower, giving space in awareness for the teachings to reverberate, and working with them to further understanding and make them useful in your life.

However, notice that the Reflect and Explore prompts for a given teaching are sometimes quite numerous. This is by design. It is not intended that every one needs to be considered before moving on, although certainly one may. Instead, read through them and pick the ones that feel juiciest at that reading. You may then return and explore other prompts at a later point. It is important to note that sometimes what doesn't initially speak to you—or perhaps it even rubs you the wrong way!—is exactly what you could most benefit from considering.

This Is Not a "How-To" Book

For the majority of people, the journey of yoga requires practices of some sort and spiritual seekers in today's world can simply turn to phones or computers and find a plethora of offerings. It is beautiful that so much information is widely available for anyone to access, yet it can give the false sense that it is all equally good and that one can mix and match to suit their personal preference at the moment. I will repeatedly argue that it is important to seek a qualified teacher.

There are many meditative techniques and practices that have been labeled as "meditation." So to be clear, in this book **meditation is a process wherein awareness is turned inward to penetrate beyond the surface toward your essence—the heart of who you are.** While meditation is the core practice addressed in this book, there are many other ancillary practices, which together comprise what is called *sādhanā*. **Sādhanā is an assemblage of practices utilized over time as one moves along the path of yoga and meditation.** Though this book focuses on meditation, some of the theory and results of practices discussed actually concern the wider spectrum of sādhanā. However, detailed differentiation of these many different practices is beyond the scope of this book, and the primary teachings are relevant to either the core practice of meditation or the larger gambit of sādhanā.

This book describes a journey of yoga and meditation: how the process works, involving movement through the layers of your being, which can present many challenges, as well as delights, and which ultimately ground you in the center. Like any journey, at times it is smooth, exhilarating, and sweet; at other times it can be difficult, which could derail the process if one does not have a guide. Ultimately, **it is important to have personal contact with a qualified teacher to teach the practice, explain how the practice works, what to expect, and for support on the journey** as you negotiate all that comes up. Considerations about teachers and about selecting a teacher are included in chapter 13 and in appendix III.

Therefore, this book is not a "how-to" book. It will not provide meditative techniques. Instead, this book is intended to give general teachings from the tradition about yoga and meditation. This could clarify the process of meditation for those who already meditate, and it could address some common experiences, teachings, and misunderstandings that students may encounter in today's yoga world. After reading about the process and benefits, you may be inspired to seek a qualified teacher.

Align and Refine outlines the complete journey of yoga, exploring it at the level of the individual, in the context of many esoteric teachings. The book is divided into nine parts, each reflecting the journey of yoga and containing several short chapters relevant to particular teachings. Each chapter builds upon the previous one, so reading in sequence could be useful—even ideal. However, if you hit a chapter that is annoying or unapproachable, feel free to skip to the next one.

I have intentionally created shorter chapters, which serves several purposes. First and foremost, the teachings are rich in both their meaning and in their potential to impact your yoga journey. I recommend moving slowly, reading a chapter at a time and utilizing the Reflect and Explore questions and practices to bring the teachings alive for yourself. In addition, the short chapters allow you to easily find a particular teaching you might be most interested in or wish to revisit. Feel free to roam around accordingly.

KEY TEACHINGS FROM THE INTRODUCTION AND ORIENTATION

- Study is an iterative process in which teachings are considered again and again to discover nuance, deepen comprehension, and understand their application.
- Although myths may not literally be true, they teach a greater truth. When studying the stories of the tradition, consider yourself to be every character in the story.
- Meditation is a process wherein awareness is turned inward to penetrate beyond the surface toward your essence—the heart of who you are.
- Sādhanā is an assemblage of practices utilized over time as one moves along the path of yoga and meditation.
- It is important to have personal contact with a qualified teacher to teach the practice, explain how the practice works, what to expect, and for support on the journey.

PART I

Beginning the Journey

The teachings of yoga are vast and deep, presenting a quandary of where to start. So we begin with teachings from two of the seminal texts of yoga to provide a context for our journey: the opening scene of the *Bhagavad Gītā* and the first aphorism of the *Yoga Sūtra*. We consider our *saṃkalpa*/intention for our journey and the foundational teaching of the Seed and the Tree. The last chapters in this section explore my process of awakening, confusions, and the definition of yoga from the *Yoga Sūtra*.

CHAPTER 1

The Conversation on the Battleground

To ease into our journey together, let's begin with the *Bhagavad Gītā*, one of the most beautiful and revered texts of the Indian tradition. It starts with a rather dramatic scene, which is actually in the middle of a much larger epic, the *Mahābhārata*. Due to long and complicated circumstances detailed in the *Mahābhārata*, two armies have lined up to do battle. As described in the first chapter of the *Bhagavad Gītā*, their flags are waving, their horses and elephants await, and there is a clamor of the drums beating and conches blowing. As they prepare to fight, the warrior Arjuna asks his charioteer, Kṛṣṇa (commonly spelled Krishna), to pull their chariot into the middle of the battlefield. Among those gathered on both sides to fight are Arjuna's relatives, teachers, and friends. Both Arjuna and Kṛṣṇa know most of these people will perish.

This moment is what Arjuna, a warrior, has trained for his whole life. And what happens at this instant, which should be the pinnacle of his career? He freaks out; he has a meltdown. He drops his weapon and refuses to fight. What ensues is a conversation between Arjuna and Kṛṣṇa that lasts for eighteen chapters, with the armies seemingly in freeze-frame, during which most of the teachings of yoga extant at the time are summarized. The teachings are exquisite and varied, and this opening scene is a beautiful teaching in and of itself.

Remember that you are every character in the story. You are Arjuna the warrior—struggling to do the right thing, stuck between a rock and a hard place—as is the case so often in life. Like Arjuna, one can be confused and loathe to enter into challenging situations that don't seem to have an optimal outcome. As well, you are Kṛṣṇa, an incarnation of the Highest, patiently pausing to answer Arjuna's many questions, providing perspective and the guidance of a trusted counselor.

These two characters can be thought of as different parts of ourselves: the confused and searching human, and the wise higher Self. Arjuna and Kṛṣṇa—our individuality and our Heart essence—stand in the midline between a place of confusion and wisdom. The battlefield itself can represent any situation in our lives. Everyone faces challenges; we all have battles we must fight. There will be times in life that are extremely intense and chaotic. There are times when the optimal choice is simply not available, yet one needs to forge ahead in the best way possible. And this is exactly the time to engage in yoga.

One of the most important teachings from this scene before a battle is that of a sacred pause. When facing a challenge, do we rush in, follow an urge to gain power, or act out of anger? Or can we pause and seek counsel from a deeper part of ourselves? Do we act from unconscious conditioning, or can we stop, take a few breaths, and listen to the guidance from a higher place within? Sometimes there is time to contemplate the options before responding to a challenge. And sometimes one must act in the heat of the moment.

It is our refined being and alignment with the highest Self, cultivated through the practice of yoga, that guides us. Yoga practice allows us to connect with a deeper part of our self, our Kṛṣṇa self. Each time we step onto the mat and begin to watch the breath, each time we close our eyes for meditation, is an opportunity to access greater wisdom that will provide answers if we pause and listen. With repeated practice and by stabilizing that connection, the guidance comes more instantaneously. Yet, like any conversation, we have to truly listen.

Arjuna and Kṛṣṇa journey together through the eighteen chapters of the *Bhagavad Gītā*. Through deep listening, Arjuna receives many teachings and practices from Kṛṣṇa, whom he accepts as his teacher early in the conversation. By the end of this discourse, Arjuna has undergone a transformation. He learns that he must align himself with Kṛṣṇa as the Highest, and he must refine his awareness in service of the Highest. He learns about the practice of meditation as a means of yoga. He learns that he cannot withdraw from his duty, his *dharma*. He must act, and he learns about skillful action, which must come from the highest possible place he can access within himself.

Like Kṛṣṇa and Arjuna, our journey together will be a conversation of sorts, studying the teachings from the tradition to show how we, too, can access the Highest in ourselves to guide our actions in the world. Kṛṣṇa teaches that yoga means a lot of different things in different contexts. Here, yoga is outlined as a process by which we refine our individual awareness and align with the highest Self. This alignment grants access to the Heart, unleashing innate wisdom so that one's actions in the world reflect the highest. As your consciousness becomes refined, the condition and experience of life will shift, as will your impact on those around you. As you change your consciousness, you begin to change the world in which you live.

This is my highest vision for our yoga: as we change our consciousness, we have a positive impact on the world. To manifest this vision in our lives requires stepping onto the path of yoga, sincerely submitting to what can be an arduous journey. It starts with a willingness to transform, to open to possibility, and to sometimes stand in the fiery process of personal evolution.

REFLECT AND EXPLORE

- How are you like Arjuna? What are the biggest battles in your life right now?
- How are you Kṛṣṇa to yourself? How do you converse with your highest Self, your Heart?
- How do you work through your challenging situations? To whom do you listen?
- How are you Kṛṣṇa to others?
- Practice and note your experience(s): When you encounter a challenging situation, try taking a sacred pause to listen to some deeper guidance. This could be as simple as taking a few breaths. Or you could choose to delay action and give yourself time to consider how best to respond.

CHAPTER 2

Atha: Now We Begin

It is hard to know where to begin to address the questions of what yoga is and how it works. Yoga has a long history of evolution and refinement. Like any domain of knowledge, each successive wave of investigation incorporates what is useful from the previous wave and offers refinements based on the latest developments. And so it continues on and on.

We are forced to step in midstream and, in fact, there is really little choice but to dive right into the deep end of yoga's philosophy. Anywhere one starts is not really the beginning, and there is really no end. Yoga itself is always evolving, and so are we, as is our understanding of it. We evolve and refine our understanding, much like the tradition refines itself as it moves through different teachers, morphs and clarifies, rejects certain archaic or inadequate suppositions, and incorporates new developments.

As we begin exploring, it is important to understand that we are not at the beginning; and are, in fact, in the middle. It is necessary to learn a certain vocabulary and concepts foundational to moving forward. Because the material is quite deep, it can feel overwhelming. So remember that we are involved in an ever-unfolding process of experience and understanding. One must start somewhere, even while knowing that everything will continue to shift as the journey unfolds.

Learning the deep teachings of yoga can be quite confusing, given that we are dropped into a modern-day stew that combines perspectives from Hinduism, Buddhism, and other traditions with both traditional and modern interpretations. As I began to explore the deeper teachings of yoga, I was invariably directed to the *Yoga Sūtra* (YS), the seminal text codified by the sage Patañjali on what is known as Classical Yoga (see appendix II: A Selective History of Yoga for more information). You may be familiar with this text if you are a yoga teacher, as it is included in most yoga teacher trainings. If you are a student of yoga, you've likely heard some of the teachings from this text articulated to some degree in class. Every text that follows the *Yoga Sūtra* in the yoga tradition assumes one is familiar with it. So for all these reasons, it is a good place to start.

YS 1.1 *atha yoga-anuśāsanam*
atha: now
yoga: yoga, union
anuśāsanam: teachings, instruction, exposition
Now let us study the teachings of yoga.

The very first sūtra of the *Yoga Sūtra* literally means "Now the teachings of yoga." We invoke this sūtra now (*atha*) at the beginning of our studies together (*anuśāsanam*). As you can see, the *Yoga Sūtra* begins with the word *now*, but the "now" of Patañjali and the "now" of modern practitioners in twenty-first-century culture are separated by many centuries and by many innovations, shifts, refinements, and advances in the teachings of yoga. So from this point **now let us study the teachings of yoga (YS 1.1).**

The overall feeling I get from this sūtra is of a threshold, an invitation into the teachings of yoga. You are being invited to begin the journey. It implies that something in the past has led you here, now. And that from "now" the future will unfold. All times—past, present, and future—are folding into the now. Every moment is at least in part a result of the past and will affect each moment that unfolds into the future. So we begin now, knowing there is a vast history leading to the present moment, and there is a lot to yet unfold.

One implication of this sūtra is that you are ready *now*. Maybe yesterday you weren't ready, but now somehow you are, the prerequisites have been met. Something has brought you this far; otherwise, why would you be reading this book right now? And there's a sense of urgency: Today, not tomorrow. Don't put it off any longer.

Each person has their own trajectory, and it is important to pay attention to that. I share my own trajectory as one example—the struggle of a modern-day yogi—in hopes that I can shed some light, having walked on the path for many years. At the end of this chapter, you are invited to contemplate your journey and what has led to this moment.

While unpacking how yoga works, we will see how each now, each moment, contains a choice that will affect the later unfolding of life. So "now" in this sūtra can indicate that each moment is an opportunity for yoga. In each moment we can bring to bear a heightened awareness that is a result of our yoga practice.

Anuśāsanam is usually translated as "exposition," "instruction," or "teaching." The Sanskrit prefix *anu* is akin to the English prefix "co-," meaning "together." There's a sense that these teachings are meant to be studied with others, alongside a teacher at least. They weren't originally intended to be read independently in a book, as one might do today, and that's one of the reasons it can be so difficult to understand these ancient texts.

Patañjali is also indicating that these teachings are part of a long, continuous lineage that he is bringing together in this text of the *Yoga Sūtra*. It also means that many subsequent teachings will flow from this text.

And what about that word *yoga*? Patañjali defines *yoga* in the famous second sūtra we will consider later. In the fullness of the text, he gives a wide variety of definitions and techniques, including a three-fold path of *kriyā-yoga* and the famous eight-fold path of *aṣṭāṅga-yoga*. This is one of the important teachings for students of yoga: **There are many yogas.** Various definitions are outlined in the *Yoga Sūtra*, the *Bhagavad Gītā*, the Upaniṣads, the Tantras, and many other places.

So now, atha, we begin our study of yoga. It would be nice to have one clear definition and path of yoga with a beginning, middle, and end. But this is not the case with these teachings. They are not novels or stories. Like many of the yogic teachings, texts, and myths, they are instead like road maps, pointing in a direction and indicating the landmarks along the way. But as the saying goes, the map is not the territory. And our experience of that territory is heavily influenced by what we bring on the journey: our previous experiences and knowledge.

I have studied the teachings presented in this book for many years. Each time I consider a teaching in the "now," I bring it into my current awareness, which is different than my past awareness. So, what I take away will be different and, hopefully, more clear and refined.

To traverse the territory of yoga and meditation, there are several teachings and tools that will aid in the journey and make the map more comprehensible. So the first sections of the book build a foundational framework, gathering the necessary tools that will allow for more success on the journey. Patañjali has to begin somewhere, much as this book must begin somewhere. But anyone who has studied the *Yoga Sūtra*, or just about any of the yogic texts, knows it is not a beginner text. It presumes some previous knowledge. The "now" assumes some prerequisite has been met in the past. So to begin, we must build a foundation of background material, to create a common framework in the present "now."

And each of us, now in this moment of absorbing these words, has a different past, which comes with a different set of understandings and presuppositions. So for some, the teachings presented herein will seem elementary or even dumbed down. For others, these teachings will seem "woo-woo," esoteric, unfamiliar, or ostensibly indiscernible.

Yet everyone will benefit, as I have, from taking some time to consider each teaching. If it is brand new, just allow the teaching to enter your awareness and percolate inside. Try to maintain an open mind. If more experienced, this "now" is an opportunity to visit anew or to refresh or reframe your understanding in a deeper way. Perhaps you might hear it differently when stated with a different nuance or context, in part because who you are "now" has shifted from when you studied previously.

REFLECT AND EXPLORE

- Consider your own journey (from your childhood until now) into yoga and meditation—or into spirituality in general.
  - ~ What has brought you to this point *now*?
  - ~ How has it unfolded?
  - ~ What have been the significant events?
  - ~ What has your path looked like?
  - ~ Who or what have been your teachers?

- Why are you here right *now*?
- What do you wish to unfold
  - in the future?
  - with this study?
  - with your spiritual journey?

CHAPTER 3

Saṃkalpa: Intention

The questions in chapter 2 about why you're here and what you wish to unfold—particularly when exploring the teachings in this book—are related to the notion of *saṃkalpa*/intention. If you are a student of yoga āsana, at some point a teacher might have asked you to set an intention for your practice. In that context, it could be that you simply want to stretch your hamstrings, breathe more deeply, or have some pain in your body that needs to be addressed. Or perhaps there is something a little deeper: a need to relax, to release some anxiety, or to sleep better. Sometimes the teacher might suggest you dedicate your practice to someone or something in need. These intentions can take many forms.

The Sanskrit word for "intention" is *saṃkalpa*, and it's related to one of the deepest aspects of the underlying ground of reality itself: the *icchā-śakti*. Icchā-śakti will be considered more thoroughly in chapter 25, but for now, icchā-śakti is the power of desire or will. It is the highest impulse that moves everything into manifestation. Without it, nothing would happen.

Intention, will, and desire are complicated and paradoxical concepts in yogic literature, especially as we attempt to apply them to our everyday lives. For example, from the renunciate yoga perspective, desire is seen as a problem that is to be obliterated. The contrast between renunciate and householder is discussed in more depth in chapter 8. Basically, a householder is anyone who lives in the world rather than withdrawing. For those of us who are householders, the practice of saṃkalpa allows us to consciously set in motion the transformation of our life on many levels. Your intention is a promise to yourself, a taking note of what is meaningful and important to you. **Saṃkalpa/intention makes conscious, and sets in motion, the desires one wishes to manifest.**

These concepts have been expressed in the West in many diverse and related ways, including prayer as well as New Age and self-help visualization and manifestation techniques. As explained in this book, the success of intentions depends on many factors.

Like many concepts that have been morphed so much as to become laughable to some, the practice and concept of saṃkalpa can be profound. For now, pause to consider your intention with this book. Then we will spiral back to this concept later in this journey. When considering these questions, remember that something has led you here now, consciously or unconsciously. So stop, take the sacred pause, and listen to your Kṛṣṇa self, the deepest place you can access inside so that what emerges and coalesces as saṃkalpa/intention is a gift from the deepest Heart.

REFLECT AND EXPLORE

- What do you need or want from this book?
- Why are you reading this book?
- How do you want to engage with this book?
- What are your expectations? How willing are you to be open, to listen, and to receive?
- Why do you practice yoga/meditation?
- What are your deepest desires for your practice of yoga/meditation?
- What is the most auspicious purpose for your life?
- Write out a specific saṃkalpa for your journey through this book. Highlight and/or keep this somewhere handy to refer back to.
- To what must you commit in order to fulfill your saṃkalpa?
- What must you let go of to fulfill your saṃkalpa?

For myself, I have a deep desire to bring forth the teachings and practices of yoga so others may benefit from them. My intention for this book is to present foundational teachings of yoga in an authentic, accessible, and applicable way. My intention is to plant seeds of understanding, and in doing so address some of the fundamental misunderstandings I've personally experienced and that I see prevalent in the popular culture.

CHAPTER 4

The Seed and the Tree

A beautiful teaching in this tradition and many others is that of the seed and how it holds the potential for a tree to sprout, grow, blossom, fruit, and create more seeds. The *Chāndogya Upaniṣad* has a story of a father who asks his son to bring him a fruit from a giant banyan tree. The father asks the son to break open the fruit and then to cut into one of the tiny seeds. He then asks his son what he sees inside the seed, and the boy, looking at the viscous material, says that he sees nothing. Then his father explains that this apparent nothingness holds the potential of a giant tree.

Think of a fig, whose seeds are very tiny. Yet somehow within each seed, there is potential for a giant tree. The seed can barely be seen—it is almost invisible—and looking inside, it looks like nothing. Yet when nurtured, the seed will ultimately sprout and yield fruit. **The seed contains the potential for the tree.**

This teaching applies to many aspects of the journey of yoga. A yoga class I took in college planted a seed that laid dormant for several years. Then when my life was blown apart, somehow I intuited that yoga could be of use, and I began to nurture that seed.

Here at the beginning of the journey, we are planting seeds. And being here now—as in the first aphorism of the *Yoga Sūtra*—is likely to be a result of some seed already planted within that is waiting for a bit of nurturing in order to sprout and grow into a full recognition of yoga. Throughout this journey of considering the teachings of yoga, we are planting seeds into our awareness. Those seeds are nourished with the nutrients of sādhanā/assemblage of practices, including the study of the teachings, as they reverberate and grow in awareness.

REFLECT AND EXPLORE

- Contemplate the teaching of the seed and the tree.
  - ~ How have you experienced it manifesting in your life?
  - ~ Can you relate this teaching to your contemplations regarding your path of yoga thus far?
  - ~ Can you discern how "seeds" you planted later sprouted and bore fruit?

CHAPTER 5

Stepping onto the Path: Awakening and Initial Explorations

When I was in graduate school, I took up yoga āsana after I suffered a life-shattering romantic breakup. I had taken a yoga class as an undergraduate, and somehow I sensed that at this juncture in my life, it could be useful to me. I sought out a teacher in the same lineage I had experienced in college, and that teacher eventually led me to his teacher. I ended up in a form of yoga that was extremely physically demanding. I found the challenge a great distraction from the combined emotional roller coaster of heartache and the stress of graduate school.

This form of yoga āsana was physically demanding, and it required fierce mental concentration. With a prescribed sequence of yoga postures, the mind is freed of some of its executive functioning, allowing for a movement of the mind internally on the breath.

I distinctly remember one day as I was practicing when I noticed a part of me I hadn't experienced before. I noticed that amidst the movement and straining, the effort and sweat, deeper than the breath, there was a still, quiet place. In the center of it all, some part of me was watching everything on the surface unfold. It felt like home.

I was so intrigued by, and attracted to, this place. What was it? And how do I experience this more? I began to realize that there was much more to this practice of yoga than I had thus far learned. Perhaps you too have had this sense that yoga has much more to offer beyond its physical benefits. Or maybe you've sensed that there is more to life itself than our physical existence.

I began to pay more attention to my state of being as I moved through the physical postures. Sometimes waves of emotion surfaced amidst my āsana practice—sometimes sweet and blissful, but sometimes anxious and sad. It felt like the practice was touching into something deeper within me that needed to be healed or that wanted expression.

I began to ask questions of any teacher who would listen. What is this place inside? And what about those feelings coming up? What are we doing in this practice? What is yoga, and how does it work? As I sought an explanation, I found myself looking wherever I could for answers. I attended workshops, I read magazines and books—this was before the internet was fully developed—and together these provided disjointed and contradictory information. Every piece of new information I learned only led to more questions. If I thought I'd found an answer, I realized that each time I considered it, there was even more to it.

In part, this is the nature of the teachings: one thing leads to another and circles back to the former. It is all interconnected. The linear mind wants it to be laid out nice and neat, but any nice-and-neat explanation is inevitably just the beginning of an answer that has many nuances, twists and turns, and further questions embedded within it.

My seeking yielded some answers and even more confusion. A large part of the confusion is that there is no one "yoga." There is no one path, but there is *our* path, a journey each of us takes that admittedly can be long and winding. My journey has yielded an understanding that I suspect will be useful to many who are trying to understand what these ancient teachings have to offer us.

But along the way, there will be much confusion. And learning to live in, sit with, and still practice with that confusion is part of the journey, and it relates to some of the teachings explored in this book. One of the most confusing aspects as a modern-day consumer of the teachings was discovering so many different and apparently contradictory perspectives from different schools of thought, and then sorting out what, if any, were the implications for me on my path.

One thing I discovered is that although scholars have differentiated and labeled various streams of teachings, these streams originally interacted to a great degree. As a result, there was an intersecting, overlapping, and intermingling of the teachings. In fact, there remains a great deal of historical uncertainty about the evolution of the teachings.

In the marketplace of yoga, I also encountered several very different levels of teaching. On one end of the spectrum was fluffy, New Age stuff I found first in magazines and later on the internet. On the other end of the spectrum were very heavy, almost impenetrable scholarly renditions of the texts themselves. Then there were the seemingly exotic lineage streams from India embodied in swamis, ashrams, and such. None of these provided very much context.

The fluff seemed ungrounded from the original teachings, and the academic texts seemed inapplicable to my modern life and practice. And the Indian teachers were intriguing but initially seemed unapproachable. Nonetheless, I imbibed all of this to some degree, yet I had a really hard time integrating it into anything coherent or applicable to the āsana practice I was involved in or to my life in general.

Before going any further, it will be useful to pause and assess your understandings and confusions about what yoga *is*, particularly regarding anything beyond a physical practice.

REFLECT AND EXPLORE

- What is yoga?
- What is meditation?
- How does yoga work?
- How have you learned about the deeper teachings of yoga?
- What does it mean to be a yogi?
- What messages have you heard about how your mind works?
- What are other predominant messages from the yoga culture?

As I began to answer these questions for myself, the easiest and most readily available information came from popular yoga culture. But fairly soon I found it confusing, and unsatisfactory. Consummate with my training as an academic, I sought recommendations for background material to read. I suppose, like many of us, I was looking for some kind of introductory textbook that laid it all out in a nice linear way.

What I found is that the field of yoga is vast and not particularly organized. Somehow it seemed related to Hinduism and the Indian culture involving gods, iconography, and ritual. Hinduism didn't seem to have any central text like the Bible or the Koran. But from both the popular yoga culture and my teachers, invariably I was pointed to a handful of texts, including the *Yoga Sūtra*, the *Bhagavad Gītā*, and the Upaniṣads. Later I discovered this was probably in part a historical matter because these were the texts that had been translated by scholars early on. I chose first to consider the *Yoga Sūtra* of Patañjali since it had "yoga" in the title, which is what I was particularly interested in.

CHAPTER 6

Core Teachings of Classical Yoga

In chapter 2 we considered the initial sūtra from the *Yoga Sūtra*, "Now we begin the study of yoga" (YS 1.1). In the next sūtra, Patañjali gives his famous definition of yoga: *yogaś citta-vṛtti-nirodhaḥ* (YS 1.2). In short, it means "Yoga is what happens when the mind settles down."

YS 1.2 *yogaś citta-vṛtti-nirodhaḥ*
yoga: yoga
citta: mind
vṛtti: fluctuation, modification
citta-vṛtti: movement of the mind; whatever thoughts or emotions move through awareness
nirodhaḥ: restriction, control, restraint, cessation
Yoga is restraining the movements of the mind.

Citta is the mind, and the *citta-vṛttis* are the turns and movements and fluctuations of the mind. They are everything we experience in our psychophysical consciousness: all our thoughts and feelings, everything that passes through awareness. And *nirodha* basically means "stopping." So this sūtra says that yoga is restraining the movements of the mind.

When I first approached this teaching, I wondered: *How is this possible*? Could one actually stop the mind? Had I already had a taste of this? I seemed to have experienced some settling of my mind during moments in yoga, and certainly a quieting of my whole nervous system due to my practice.

YS 1.3 *tadā draṣṭuḥ sva-rūpe-avasthānam*
tadā: then
draṣṭṛ: seer
sva-rūpe: literally "in own form" or one's own essential nature
avasthānam: abiding, standing, dwelling
Then the seer abides in its essence.

The *Yoga Sūtra* goes on to say that when the mind is *nirodha*/controlled (YS 1.2), the seer abides in its essence (YS 1.3). *Draṣṭṛ* refers to the seer (the "see-er"). So when we calm our mind, as in the previous sūtra (YS 1.2), the seer abides in its true essential nature (YS 1.3). These two sūtras encapsulate a primary teaching of the *Yoga Sūtra*, which very basically says: yoga is settling the mind. Then you experience your true nature.

Is this what I experienced that day practicing yoga āsana when it seemed that part of me was simply watching or seeing everything else happening in my mind and body in an unattached way? Was I abiding in my essence?

REFLECT AND EXPLORE

- Describe any experience you've had of the seer/see-er/draṣṭṛ.
- Practice and note your experience(s): For some period of time (it could be a day, a week, a month), notice your citta-vṛttis/ movements of your mind.
  - ~ Particularly note any habitual ways of thinking.

As I continued trying to understand the *Yoga Sūtra*, I discovered a lot of teachings, many of them mysterious and some of them downright weird. (At that time, there were very few translations available, and most of them were quite scholarly.) The first thing I noticed was that the yoga of the *Yoga Sūtra* and other texts did not seem to have a lot to do with my life as a female Westerner or what I was practicing in yoga class. This disconnect set up some fundamental confusions for me and, I suspect, for any modern-day practitioner who has attempted to understand the deeper teachings of yoga beyond the mat. Many people give up and simply reject the deeper teachings, sticking to the physical practice, but I had a deep yearning for more. And it's likely that you do too, since you picked up this book.

I found out quickly that yoga historically has very little to do with āsana, the bodily practice I knew and loved. In fact, yoga had more to do with the mind. Furthermore, the foremost commentary on the *Yoga Sūtra* says about YS 1.1: "Yoga is *samādhi*."

This *samādhi* thing was one of the most puzzling aspects to me. It seemed important because Patañjali devoted a lot of his text to it. Indeed the first chapter of his text is titled "Samādhi." From my limited exploration, the word appeared to refer to some kind of mystical state. I found the whole concept of *samādhi* rather mysterious and complicated, and somewhere I picked up the idea that it was some kind of alien state of awareness. It brought to mind the stereotype of yogis sitting around contemplating their navels.

As I continued my studies of the *Yoga Sūtra*, I found the means to yoga in Sūtra 1.12: *abhyāsa* and *vairāgya*. (This sūtra will be addressed in more detail in chapter 37). The thoughts can be quieted through practice, or abhyāsa, and dispassion, or vairāgya. Given the rigors of my āsana practice, I understood the value of abhyāsa. But the vairāgya aspect was perplexing. Here, and in other sūtras, Patañjali is clear: the yogi should be free from all desire. Later on, when I studied the *Bhagavad Gītā*, I learned one must act but relinquish the results of action (See, for example, BG 5.12). Yet I certainly wanted to see the results of my āsana practice as I worked toward progressively more advanced postures. I found this message of dispassion and nonattachment hard to swallow because I had many attachments—like a job for one. However, I kept getting the message that to be a yogi, one must withdraw from the world into an ashram.

So one of the things I was most confused about was an overall tone that yoga practitioners must control all desire and somehow overcome many of the innate human tendencies to achieve this samādhi. I was so torn. I had found a practice that was clearly helping me, and I wanted to explore it more deeply. But the message I got was that one had to remove oneself from all of society, sit on your butt, and zone out in this indescribable state of samādhi.

After trying to explore the deeper messages about yoga in the texts, I was even more confused because it was hard to see a connection between what was in the texts and what I was doing in my yoga āsana practice. When I studied the *Yoga Sūtra*, it seemed to be about controlling the mind and states of consciousness, yet what I was trying to do in my practice was put my foot behind my head.

I found these teachings so perplexing, and I repeatedly asked anyone and everyone: We are born into these bodies and this world, which seems like a gift, so why does the path of yoga seem to deny all the world has to offer?

These confusions played out in various ways for many years on my path, and ultimately I found answers and some reconciliation. Similar confusion plays out in the yoga world at large, which during the course of my career has grown into a multibillion-dollar industry. I sometimes interact in an online group for yoga teachers, in which there are frequent "discussions" (to put it nicely) reflecting the tension between those who express more traditional views of yoga and those who want to remove all of the underlying teachings and stick with a biomechanical practice.

However, I've set up a bit of a false dichotomy, because the truth is that yoga can hold all of these things. And to reconcile it for myself, I discovered that there are teachings of yoga that are more applicable to those who wish to proceed along the path of yoga while being productive members of society. My journey moved through a sequential process of transforming my life through practice, as I increasingly understood the "why" of yoga and how it works. While my journey is idiosyncratic, it mirrors both the evolution of the modern yoga scene and to some degree the history of yoga. So like the tradition itself, I intermix teachings from different sources to build an intelligible framework to describe the journey of yoga.

KEY TEACHINGS FROM PART I: BEGINNING THE JOURNEY

- Now let us study the teachings of yoga. (YS 1.1)
- There are many yogas.
- Saṃkalpa/intention makes conscious, and sets in motion, the desires one wishes to manifest.
- The seed contains the potential for the tree.

PART II

Preparing for the Journey: Foundational Concepts

I spent many years in a yoga āsana tradition that infamously ascribed to the idea of practice only, with very little information on theory, which led to numerous injuries. Yet as I attended workshops to learn biomechanics, I found myself impatient when teachers took time to discuss and demonstrate poses. As I look back now, from the perspective of decades of practice and study, I better understand the wisdom of proper preparation for the journey. As the guide on this journey of yoga, I lay the groundwork for our exploration of the teachings of yoga in the following chapters. You may find yourself getting impatient with this introductory material and want to just get on with it. But taking the time to attend to these foundational understandings will serve you immeasurably as you progress through this book, and as you move through your own journey of yoga and life.

The preparation starts with the story in the Tillai Forest, which describes a yogic journey and therefore illustrates many concepts. Then we turn to how Naṭarāja encodes the contrasting paths of renunciate and householder yogas. Next, the concepts of *jñāna* and *vijñāna*, intellectual and experiential understanding are differentiated. Aspects of *svādhyāya*/self-study, *vikalpa-saṃskāra*/the refinement of knowledge, and the contemplative practice of *bhāvanā* are explained. This leads to a discussion about gurus and teachers. Part II finishes with a consideration of how to think about the gods, and as we transition from preparing for the journey to stepping onto the path, we invoke Gaṇapati.

CHAPTER 7

The Story of the Tillai Forest

This is a lovely story of a journey, with its challenges, awakenings, and discovery. I am deeply grateful to my teacher Douglas Brooks for this version of it, much of which takes place in the Tillai Forest. (*Tillai* is a Tamil word for a particular shrub). The story involves several characters, but central is Naṭarāja. *Rāja* means "royal," and *naṭa* is "dancer," so Naṭarāja is Śiva as the Lord of Dance, a symbol that resonates in the heart of Tantra and is treasured by many.

The story begins with the god Viṣṇu reclining on his couch of Śeṣa, the serpent. Viṣṇu seems unusually weighty and excited, so Śeṣa asks him, *What has happened to cause this agitation, this ecstatic vibrating?* Viṣṇu replies that he has seen the Lord of Yoga's blissful dance, his *ānanda-tāṇḍava.* He has seen the beautiful self-expression of the Divine, Naṭarāja's dance.

Śeṣa then asks Viṣṇu if he, too, could see the dance, and Viṣṇu replies that he can but that he must become embodied to taste the experience. So he is born as Patañjali, a being who is part human and part snake. Śeṣa, now Patañjali, burrows into the darkness, into the depths of the earth. He is now part snake, after all. And, eventually, he emerges in the forest of the tillai trees, where he begins searching for the Lord of Dance, Naṭarāja, whom Viṣṇu has experienced. For a long while he searches for Naṭarāja, he perseveres, as he knows the dancer is somewhere in the forest of the tillai trees.

One day, Patañjali comes upon a *liṅga,* a statue that has a single pillar or column and signifies the unmanifest Absolute reality, also known as Śiva. It signifies everything but appears as nothing. It holds all possibilities; it represents potentiality prior to manifestation. This liṅga has obviously been worshipped, as it is adorned with sandalwood paste and *kumkum* (the red paste that people put on their foreheads and on statues and such). Seeing this adorned liṅga, Patañjali realizes he is not alone in this forest—there are other seekers as well. Others have been seeking longer than he has.

Also adorning the liṅga is an exquisitely beautiful flower, unlike anything Patañjali has ever seen before, and he wants to make this flower an offering to the liṅga. So he searches and searches the forest for the flower, but to no avail. Each night he falls asleep not finding the flower, and then every morning he wakes up to see the liṅga adorned with a new flower. Finally, Patañjali decides to make an offering he *does* have: a particular seed from the earth where he burrows. So he makes his own unique offering from the ground he inhabits.

And then from the trees descends a being who is mostly human but with the paws of a tiger. This is Vyāghrapāda, whose name literally means "tiger paws." Vyāghrapāda was given the boon of paws, which allow him to climb high up into the trees to gather the exquisite flowers no one else can touch. He has been watching Patañjali all the while, and as Patañjali sleeps, he brings beautiful flowers down from the treetops and does his *pūjā,* his worship. Vyāghrapāda has been watching Patañjali carefully and has realized he is sincere and devoted.

Patañjali and Vyāghrapāda sit together at the liṅga. They learn that they each know *mantras* to chant, so they teach each other what they know, and they chant together. As they chant, the liṅga starts to twist and turn. And from the liṅga—that form of potentiality—Śiva emerges as the Lord of Dance, Naṭarāja. In his blissful dance they see all of creation, manifestation, and dissolution. They see revelation and concealment, and they see the *abhaya-mudrā* gesture of the upturned hand, signifying "no fear." They receive and share these teachings from Naṭarāja's dance, and they each also receive individual teachings. Naṭarāja bestows upon Patañjali the gifts of the teachings of Ayurveda, of grammar, and of yoga. Then Patañjali departs, having seen the dance and received his gifts. His text, the *Yoga Sūtra*, reflects a yoga of effort and ascetic discipline required of him on his journey.

Vyāghrapāda stays, as he lives in the forest as a householder with his wife and daughter. After Patañjali has gone, Vyāghrapāda asks Naṭarāja: *Is there more*? Together Patañjali and Vyāghrapāda saw the *ānanda-tāṇḍava*, the dance of bliss, yet there are several more of Naṭarāja's dances that Vyāghrapāda witnesses because he asked for more. Eventually Naṭarāja resumes his potential form as the Śiva liṅga.

There are many teachings held in this story, which has much to teach about the path of yoga. Several points are reiterated here and will be related to other teachings later. And, as always, remember that you are every character in the story: you are Patañjali, you are Vyāghrapāda, and you are Naṭarāja.

At the beginning of the story, Śeṣa gets a hit of something Viṣṇu has experienced, and he wants to experience it himself. He becomes a seeker, searching for more in life. It's like when you're around someone who has an attractive energy so compelling that you want to be around it and learn more. In different ways, many of us have a sense that we want more out of life—and that is why we turn to yoga and meditation.

So Śeṣa asks how he can experience the dance, and he learns that one must embody to experience more. Human embodiment allows one to engage the journey of yoga, discover what life offers, and hopefully experience the bliss of the Divine. So in this story, Śeṣa embodies as Patañjali.

Patañjali works hard to burrow through the ground and into the Tillai Forest, where he finds the liṅga and then searches for his offering. Patañjali is no slacker. He doesn't give up, and he is unrelenting on his path. So in his teachings, there is an intense studentship (*adhikāra*) in the form of a yoga of effort and discipline.

Patañjali sees the lovely flower someone else has offered, and he searches the forest for the flower to no avail. The flower is not his gift, it is the gift of another. We each have our unique offering to make, and it may take us time to discover this. Sometimes we try to copy someone else's offering and it just falls flat. And it takes Patañjali a while to discover that his offering is that of the seed, which comes from the earth.

Vyāghrapāda has seen the evidence of Patañjali's devotion and comes down from the trees to worship with him. They teach each other what they know, and then chant together. Naṭarāja has always been there; he is hiding in plain sight. So as they practice and worship, something shifts, there is a change in perspective, and Naṭarāja's dance becomes manifest from the potential of the liṅga. When they finally do see the dance, they learn the *pañca-kṛtya*s, Śiva's five acts, and they learn abhaya-mudrā, the gesture of fearlessness.

Next, they each receive their individual teachings. Patañjali receives the wisdom of the *Yoga Sūtra* with its emphasis on samādhi and a path of renunciation. He leaves the forest and elucidates these and other teachings. Vyāghrapāda stays in his forest home with his wife and daughter, and he learns there are more dances—more stages in the path of yoga.

This story provides many teachings about the path of yoga. I've referred to several of them, and we'll continue to unpack this story as we move along in our journey.

REFLECT AND EXPLORE

- Outline the teachings of this story, making note of what resonates most for you.
- Consider how the teachings apply to your life.
- Have you had the experience of trying to offer someone else's gift? What are *your* unique gifts?

CHAPTER 8

Naṭarāja and the Two Paths of Yoga

The image of Naṭarāja, Śiva as the Lord of Dance, encapsulates many beautiful teachings, some of which are presented in this chapter and later in the book. Take a moment to pause and consider your impression of Naṭarāja.

REFLECT AND EXPLORE

- Look at an image of Naṭarāja. You may already have one, there is one on the cover of this book, or it's readily available on the internet.
  - For a few moments take in the feel of Naṭarāja —not so much the specific details, but the overall presence of the image and how it resonates with you.
  - Write about your general sense of this image.

Whatever you see is what you see, but one of the main things the image elicits is, of course, a dance. Naṭarāja is dancing, but there is also a sense of serenity. His face is serene; he is very steady and aligned along a central axis. Yet this is a wild dance, and Naṭarāja's hair is flying about. So here there is a representation of both the wild dance and a serene center.

One way to think of these two qualities relates to the meaning of Śiva—which is explored in more detail later—as the ground of being, the unmanifest, quiet and centered, stillness itself. This is explicitly expressed in the liṅga. Yet in the image of Naṭarāja, Śiva is dancing the world into manifestation. From the center of his dance, everything begins to pulsate, and all of manifestation occurs. He's starting the whole wheel turning, from which all that is manifest is created. So there is an aspect of the cosmic dancer dancing life itself into existence.

These two aspects of Naṭarāja are related to a thread that runs throughout yoga philosophy and is mirrored in the modern yoga scene: the contrast and choice between what are termed *nivṛtti* and *pravṛtti* paths of yoga. The term *vṛtti* relates to turning or revolving. Nivṛtti is turning *away from* the world. This path requires renouncing the world and all associated desires. Pravṛtti is turning *toward* the world. This path involves engaging in the world. So **there is a general contrast between two paths of yoga: the nivṛtti, or renunciate path, and pravṛtti, the householder path**.

Many modern-day yogis struggle on the path because so many teachings seem to say that they're supposed to turn away from the world and become monks or nuns or swamis in order to do yoga properly. As considered earlier, this is the path of Patañjali's *Yoga Sūtra*, which says to stop the mind (YS 1.2). The nivṛtti path asks us to withdraw from the world and focus entirely inward. This impetus of asceticism that runs throughout yoga is the origin of many images of yogis—and of Śiva—withdrawing into a forest, sitting on a mountaintop or in a cave, or becoming a wandering mendicant without possessions, home, or family. This concept of how to be a yogi seems impossible for modern-day practitioners to fulfill, if one even desires to do so.

When I first began my yoga journey, the perceived push toward asceticism in the yoga world was very confusing to me. I began my practice in a very rigorous yoga school that emphasized breath, a steady gaze, and a prescribed sequence of postures. It required immense discipline, focus, and dedication. Through that practice, I got a glimpse of the quiet mind, a still point, that part of me that was watching, the draṣṭṛ/seer, that serene center reflected in Naṭarāja's face and centeredness.

At that time, I was practicing yoga āsana for at least two hours a day, six days a week. I developed a very strong, toned body and a disciplined demeanor. I also suffered a variety of physical injuries as my teachers and I worked to contort my body into the prescribed postures. It felt rather harsh and controlling.

Because of all of this, I began to have larger questions about the path of yoga and started exploring the philosophy underlying the practice. At that time, there weren't many texts or books on yoga, but one that was available was the *Yoga Sūtra*, which, as I've already said, delineates an ascetic or renunciate path, turning awareness inward and away from the world. I began to understand how such a philosophy could lead to a strict and controlled approach toward the body and mind, which was what I was experiencing in my āsana practice. I was so perplexed by this perspective, which didn't resonate with me. Again and again, I found myself asking, *If the goal of yoga is to subjugate the body and withdraw the mind from the world, why are we born into these bodies, into this world, with the gift of such active minds?* I was not interested in being a renunciate, even though I had an intense desire for greater spiritual awareness.

When I encountered a different yoga āsana school that honored the body, mind, and all of manifestation as part of a divine pulsation, it drew me in. It resonated with what I sensed intuitively. It was such a relief to hear teachings such as "Life is a gift to be enjoyed and savored." It felt right to begin practice with a softening, an opening, and an emphasis on play, beauty, and delight. I found out that this approach was based on Tantric yoga philosophy, a development that came later than the Classical Yoga of Patañjali's *Yoga Sūtra.* And Tantra acknowledges a householder path for those who choose to function in society and all that entails.

It was then that I started learning more about Naṭarāja, including his myths and related teachings. I delighted in the idea that our lives were a dance and that we were here to enjoy the gift of embodiment. Dance wildly; share your gifts. These were the messages I was hearing, which reverberated deeply within me.

Though Tantric yoga was music to my ears and resonated deeply with my heart, I often felt uncomfortable in that school, with its emphasis on play and delight and dancing on the surface of life. It felt ungrounded and too undisciplined compared to my previous experiences with a more orderly practice.

The first very stringent school taught me to turn inward and connect with a deeper part of myself. It taught me the power and beauty of disciplined practice. A prescribed āsana sequence forced me to do poses that were challenging, and I learned how practice over time can slowly bring transformation and results. I learned to be like Patañjali, persevering despite all the challenges.

The Tantra-based school taught me to honor and delight in the gift of my embodied life. There I learned about Śiva as Absolute Consciousness and that everything was a manifestation of that Absolute Consciousness: me, you, and all of the material world. I discovered that the journey of yoga was intended to reveal this to us. I realized that, like Vyāghrapāda, I could live in the world yet still honor the path of yoga.

I felt lucky to have experienced both of these schools, and it felt that each had a piece of the truth, yet I struggled to reconcile them. This is the paradox represented in Naṭarāja, the serenely quiet yogi and the wild dancer. Eventually I realized what was missing from these schools of yoga āsana was the practice of meditation. In both, there was a sense that one should be meditating, but no method was explicitly integrated. So when I saw the opportunity to begin practicing and studying a Tantric-based meditation method, I dove right in.

Along with receiving a meditation practice for householders, I learned how the practice worked, which allowed me to assimilate my previous experiences. I came full circle back to the teachings of Patañjali's *Yoga Sūtra* with its emphasis on meditation and practice. And as I began studying Tantra, I confirmed that there was more than the ascetic path, as I'd always intuited. The meditative state is not the end but the beginning. Through meditation, we connect to the ground of being, which supports us as we then move through everyday householder activities.

I am belaboring this point because as modern-day yogis within the marketplace of yoga, all of this is very mixed up. It is important to keep this distinction of renunciate and householder paths in mind, because many of the teachings out there are, in fact, renunciate teachings, which can be a problem for those of us who are householders. Householders don't need practices that require negation of the world because they can decrease one's efficacy in the world.

Please note that I'm not dismissing the renunciate path. It is a legitimate and noble path of yoga. However, it is not for most people, and if you *were* cut out for that path, you would long ago have gone to pursue it in some isolated setting.

It is important to clarify that the householder path of Tantra is not simply being an everyday householder who attends a few yoga classes without ever going any deeper. The householder path is also very often misunderstood as fulfilling every desire one has at the surface of life—desires that are not tied to the *source* of desire. The Tantric householder path often involves an esoteric spirituality, with practices to help create a connection to the deepest parts of consciousness. Yet, unlike the renunciatory path, which ends with an immersion into the depths with no return to the surface, the householder path utilizes that connection with Source to feed the surface, everyday activities of life.

Patañjali's *Yoga Sūtra* tells us the ultimate limb of yoga is samādhi, that state of enstatic, or internal, awareness. In the story of the Tillai Forest, Vyāghrapāda stays to see more of Naṭarāja's dances, and in doing so he represents a path that leads to more stages of yoga beyond samādhi. These further stages allow one to live a fully embodied life from a place of expanded awareness.

The story of the Tillai Forest is a powerful exposition of our path as yogis in the world. We will learn the power of Patañjali's teachings, a yoga of discipline and inward-turning. But like Vyāghrapāda, we will also explore how there's more to yoga than the samādhi of the *Yoga Sūtra*. One can experience the Divine while embodying the householder life. Yoga can be a support in the many dances in life. And like both Patañjali and Vyāghrapāda, we must each learn to offer our own unique gifts and to dance our unique dance.

REFLECT AND EXPLORE

- How do you see the relationship between practices that move you inward and living your life fully as a householder?
- Have you experienced any conflict regarding these two paths of nivṛtti/inward-turning/renunciate and pravṛtti/outward-turning/householder?
- How have all your yoga practices supported your householder life?

CHAPTER 9

Jñāna and *Vijñāna*: Intellectual and Experiential Knowledge

The story of the Tillai Forest alludes to important concepts on the path of yoga: *jñāna* and *vijñāna*. Before unpacking these concepts, please note that these Sanskrit terms have many related and diverse meanings in different traditions. For our purposes, *jñāna* refers to intellectual understanding and rational conceptualization of the teachings, and *vijñāna* relates to experiential understanding. In the story, Śeṣa (who embodies as Patañjali) heard about Viṣṇu's experience and gained some intellectual knowledge about Naṭarāja's dance, but it was only when he experienced it for himself that he truly understood.

Consider how this works with the practice of yoga āsana, or with any skill or sport. It isn't enough to just look at books and read about the postures; you have to get on the mat and practice. And consider how much the practice is enhanced when a teacher pauses to explain some bit of theory or insight into the intricacies of a pose to gain both a deeper understanding and experience of it. **The path of yoga requires an intellectual understanding, jñāna, as well as an experiential understanding, vijñāna.** Experience grants a deepening of knowledge, and knowledge grants a deeper experience.

An example of the concepts of jñāna and vijñāna is knowing a mango. If someone has heard of a mango or seen a picture of it but hasn't tasted a mango, they can't fully understand what a mango is. One must actually taste and experience it. Or, tasting a delightful fruit or hearing some piece of music or seeing an amazing work of art, may set in motion a desire for more knowledge about that experience.

Anyone who is a teacher understands this interaction between knowledge and experience. For example, textbook descriptions of chemical reactions come alive when students mix together chemicals and see the results in the lab. This is why many subjects require both lecture and labwork to fully learn them. This whole process is even more true regarding spiritual practice and experiences. Intellectual study without practice is barren and superficial. Practice without study is unrooted and potentially superficial. So to more fully understand, one must take the teachings of yoga texts into the "laboratory" of our practice.

Traditional texts, especially sūtra texts like the *Śiva Sūtra*, *Pratyabhijñā-hṛdayam* and the *Yoga Sūtra*—all of which we will be exploring—are given in very pithy aphorisms. These sūtras can be likened to a framework, a map, or a guidebook. This framework is the intellectual knowledge. It can give some things to look out for or curious places to visit on the yogic journey.

Anyone who travels knows there is a big difference between reading about something in a guidebook and personally experiencing it. So it is with the texts and teachings of yoga as guidebooks. They are pointing to spiritual mappings and experiences that you someday may encounter, or maybe already have. Sometimes studying these teachings helps you understand something that has already happened or that is in progress in practice or life. Sometimes it isn't until you receive the teaching and then return to practice that you start to see the connection. Or you see how the teaching is manifesting after you've been alerted to the ideas, like an enhanced experience of some locale you're visiting with the aid of a guide or a guidebook.

As we traverse this path and consider these teachings, it's important to remember that the initial exposure to a teaching may be unclear and confusing. It may require some work as we refine our knowledge to increase understanding. These aspects of the path will be further explored as we continue the journey together.

REFLECT AND EXPLORE

- Write down your definition of jñāna and vijñāna.
- Contemplate your experience of jñāna and vijñāna.
- Think of examples of jñāna and vijñāna
  - ~ from different subjects or domains of knowledge in your life.
  - ~ from your practice and experience of yoga.

CHAPTER 10

Svādhyāya: Self-Study

Our understanding of experiences on the path of yoga is facilitated by exploring the teachings of yoga through study. This is what you are doing right now: engaging in what the tradition calls *svādhyāya.* **Traditionally, *svādhyāya* refers to recitation and study of the yogic texts, but it can also refer to a mindful exploration of everyday life, as well as the innermost Self.**

You may be familiar with svādhyāya from studying the *Yoga Sūtra*, where it is listed as one of the three components of kriyā-yoga (YS 2.1) and also as one of the five *niyamas* (YS 2.32) in the eight-limbed/aṣṭāṅga-yoga system (YS 2.29). Svādhyāya is also mentioned in the *Bhagavad Gītā* (see, for example, 16.1 and 17.5) and many other yogic texts. So obviously study is something very integral to yoga.

Svādhyāya is a lifetime practice for any serious yoga practitioner. I am a teacher, but foremost I am a student. One cannot be a teacher without first walking the path of the student, and for me, continuing to learn and grow as a student is a qualification for being a good teacher. As I said, I see myself as a trail guide, someone who has been just a little way farther up the path, and I'm reaching back to give you a hand. But we walk the path together, hand in hand, as well. As any teacher knows, teaching a subject deepens understanding of the topic.

The Sanskrit word *svādhyāya* is usually translated simply as "self-study." Several different suggested etymologies of this word give insight into its varied meanings. There is a general agreement that *sva* means "self," and it also means "own." So *svādhyāya* means one's own study, or self-study.

As for the rest of this word, there are several different explanations. Some say *dhyāya* comes from the verbal root *dhyai*, which means "to contemplate, think on, recollect, call to mind." So *svādhyāya* can mean one's own contemplation of a teaching. Or to broaden the definition, it could even mean contemplation of *sva*, your own self.

Some say *svādhyāya* is from the word *adhyāya* which is a lesson or lecture. Here, a meaning would be one's own lesson, as taught by a teacher, similar to what you are receiving right now. Another interpretation is *i* as the verbal root, which means "to go," so *svādhyāya* could mean, literally, "one's going into."

So this word svādhyāya has a rich variety of related meanings. As we study teachings from the texts we will consider many "lessons" the tradition has to offer. And the Reflect and Explore exercises are an invitation to "go into" deeply, to apply the teachings to your own life, and to discover ways to deepen your practice. All this is the process of svādhyāya.

Svādhyāya is a practice, like any other practice such as meditation, *japa* (repetition of mantras), the āsana practice in a typical yoga class, or even practicing a musical instrument. You may have already discovered that trying to study any of the yoga texts is a pretty daunting proposition for a variety of reasons. First of all, they're written in Sanskrit. Second, they're filled with a lot of assumptions about what you already know, and they contain many technical terms that have to be unpacked. That's why it's so useful to have a guide on the path. That is exactly why I wrote this book!

Traditionally, svādhyāya also means reciting the texts themselves. For example, memorizing and reciting the Vedas, the oldest of the yogic texts, was how these texts were passed down from generation to generation in the oral tradition. These ancient texts were preserved by people who memorized them and chanted them, syllable by syllable, long before they were ever written down.

To make the texts applicable to our lives, consider another layer of svādhyāya/self-study: literally studying ourselves. We watch, listen, and observe ourselves mindfully as we live our lives. For example, when practicing āsana or any physical practice or hobby, pay attention to the body. Study what happens when moving an arm, a leg, a finger, or the ribs in a certain way: what is the effect? What brings one into greater alignment? For me, my practice of yoga āsana taught me to listen carefully to my breath. As I observe my breath, I notice when I over-effort or when my attention wanders.

In addition, one can study the mind and how it works. Are there habitual thought patterns? Do particular situations evoke particular thought patterns, desires, or impulses to react in a particular way? And, of course, we study ourselves by looking at our actions and their effects. Start by observing the impulses and look at the effects of acting on those impulses. How does it feel when imbibing certain substances? What happens when reacting to another person in a certain way? When meditating on a given day, or for a week, a month, a year, what effect does that have?

This is an important part of svādhyāya—of studying ourselves. Many times we don't make these connections between our choices and the condition of our lives. We're not fully aware or not studying ourselves carefully enough to realize, for example, that after meditating in the morning, the day unfolds more smoothly.

By connecting the dots, the relationships between thoughts, actions, practices, teachings, awareness, and life as a whole can be identified. A Sanskrit word for "relationship" is *sambandha.* This word has a variety of meanings in different contexts, but here a definition is "association," "relation," or "connection." The Reflect and Explore exercises included in this book are intended to encourage discovery of the connection between the teachings and our lives.

There are many levels to sambandha. For example, discovering the effects of our practice can sometimes be quite clear—other times not so much. Changes can be very incremental and subtle, so we must study ourselves to see them. Seeing the longer-term effects requires even more conscious svādhyāya/self-study. In the first year I started meditating, it seemed that absolutely nothing was happening. Yet when I looked back and compared my life to that of a year prior, I realized several things had shifted. For example, I was so much more relaxed and less reactive about many things. I felt I could get out of my own way more readily and allow teaching to flow through me more easefully and with greater insight.

In our modern society that seeks and expects immediate gratification, we often fail to make the connections. Sometimes we can't see the long-term effects or changes. It is easy to forget where we started and hard to see how far we've progressed. For instance, there is a lag between actions and their effects in our āsana practice. Perhaps we couldn't touch our toes in a forward bend or straighten our arms in Downward Dog at the beginning, yet looking back a year later we see the progress. Similarly, we may not perceive the connection between our behaviors and long-term health. For instance, imbibing certain substances or engaging in particular activities can create consequences we're not aware of until several days or years later when the effects fully unfold. One may feel depleted, anxious, depressed, congested, or sick, and wonder: Why am I feeling like this? This process of studying ourselves is a means to understanding how to bring all the pieces of life into the light, refine our being, and move into greater alignment.

Ultimately, the highest meaning of svādhyāya is the study of the highest Self. This is what a lot of the teachings are directed at, which brings us back to the original meaning of svādhyāya, the study of the texts. Through our studies, we begin to consider the Heart of who we are and the essence of everything.

In some ways, all of yoga is encapsulated in this highest aspect of svādhyāya relating to the study of the highest Self. Observing our day-to-day actions and habits, we can then adjust our behavior, watch for the effects, and notice what keeps us more connected to Source essence and make refinements accordingly. All this happens as we continue to deepen our understanding and experience of our innermost Self, our Heart, through practice and study.

REFLECT AND EXPLORE

- List and contemplate the different meanings and ways svādhyāya can be practiced.
- Why do you think svādhyāya is important on the path of yoga?
- Studying yourself, name some benefits you have accrued from yoga practice(s).
- Consider how you are progressing with any intention/saṃkalpa from part I of this book.
  - ~ What is helping and/or what is hindering?
  - ~ What refinements (if any) do you need to make?

- Practice and note your experience(s): For some period of time (it could be a day, a week, a month), observe the connection/sambandha between your yoga practice(s) (including study/svādhyāya), and your everyday experience.
    - ~ When experiencing something negative, can you identify any of your actions that contributed to it?
    - ~ Make similar observations regarding positive experiences.

CHAPTER 11

Vikalpa-Saṃskāra: Refinement of Understanding

The practice of svādhyāya allows for a progressively deeper understanding of the teachings of yoga. And, as already said, this is an iterative process of considering the teachings over and over again to refine understanding. We learn through repetition and refinement.

When studying the texts, keep in mind that the teachings come through the sages and the seers who bring them forth from their experience and insight, then put them into words. In a way, they are trying to describe the indescribable. Our understanding of the teachings which come from the sages in their deep states of awareness, is facilitated by the state of *our* awareness. To the extent our awareness is clear, we are better able to understand these profound teachings of yoga. We have to stretch and strengthen and expand our awareness through practice, particularly meditation, much like stretching and strengthening physical muscles to move into deeper yoga poses.

One of the greatest teachings from the Tantric sage Abhinavagupta is that of *vikalpa-saṃskāra* from his *Tantrāloka*. The discussion here (and later) is particularly informed by Paul Muller-Ortega's teachings in "'*Tarko Yogāṅgam Uttamam*': On Subtle Knowledge and the Refinement of Thought" (referenced in appendix IV). ***Vikalpa-saṃskāra* is the refinement of understanding, including both understanding of the teachings and the refinement of the place of awareness from which that understanding arises.**

Vikalpa is one of the five types of citta-vṛttis/thought fluctuations that Patañjali delineates in the *Yoga Sūtra* (YS 1.6). One translation of *vikalpa* is "conceptualization." Vikalpas are concepts held in the mind, including concepts about the yoga teachings, others, your relationships, yourself, and even your general worldview. Concepts are how information, correct or incorrect, is organized in the mind. Traditionally in the *Yoga Sūtra*, vikalpa is considered a "problem" because it's one of the citta-vṛttis the yogi is trying to stop. However, vikalpa as a concept, idea, or thought is neutral. Whether it's problematic or not is dependent on the nature of its content.

From a Tantric perspective, thoughts are regarded as part of the manifest world, and as with everything manifest, they can have an aspect of concealment or limitation. As the bumper sticker says: "Don't believe everything you think." Often our knowledge—our concepts—are not quite right. They could be unclear, fuzzy, or just plain wrong. And then we live our lives in accordance with these incorrect concepts. So you can see how more clarified concepts in awareness would enhance life experience.

Saṃskāra, the second part of vikalpa-saṃskāra, is another example of a Sanskrit word that has many different meanings. One meaning of saṃskāra is that of a residual trace or latent impression of past actions. This meaning will be explored in more detail later in this book, but *saṃskāra* has a different meaning in the context of vikalpa-saṃskāra. Here the idea is one of working with something, a process of refining, like any raw material that needs to be refined or processed to separate out the impurities. An example is raw ore from which minerals are extracted through a process of refining out the impurities to yield pure gold.

So vikalpa-saṃskāra can be defined as the purification or refinement of conceptual understanding. It is the process of refining understanding, thoughts, concepts, assumptions, and even the general state of awareness. The teachings and concepts have multiple layers of meaning and application. So, important to svādhyāya/self-study is the idea that vikalpa-saṃskāra is the uncovering of the depth of meanings, particularly the progressive refinement of understanding the teachings of yoga and how to apply them to our lives.

At the first encounter, a teaching may seem very mysterious, complicated, or weird, not unlike some new yoga pose. So we may not understand it initially—and even get frustrated—but understanding will deepen as one works with the material in various ways, including listening, reading, contemplating, and writing, all of which are techniques to deepen understanding. And like the practice of yoga āsana, there's always more! When a teaching is considered again—voilà!—there's an even deeper meaning or understanding or different nuance or application, just like there are deeper and more complex variations in the yoga postures. Someone wouldn't do a yoga posture once and then say "Okay, been there, done that, don't need to consider again." Instead, they try the posture over and over again, discover its nuances and benefits, creating greater understanding.

Practically speaking, how does it happen? On one hand, it is a natural process that occurs throughout life. Approaching any topic repeatedly—whether it's a body of knowledge or a skill or a worldview—deepens understanding. We get more information, use it, and work with it. This is the process of refinement/saṃskāra. But it isn't just about more information or more facts—though more information certainly helps in many cases. Ultimately it's about increased comprehension and understanding.

Over the years, I've taken and taught many courses on yoga philosophy, often studying the same texts over and over. Students continue to sign up for courses on the same topic because they know that each time they study a teaching, their understanding of that teaching deepens. The process of writing this book and working with the material has yielded more insight into the teachings of yoga. This deepening of understanding is the process of vikalpa-saṃskāra.

Yet there's a broader way to think about vikalpa-saṃskāra, which relates to why we experience an increased understanding of teachings with repeated study. Through continued practice, we are changing our awareness. Due to the practice of meditation, awareness itself becomes more purified, so the intellectual field into which the teachings are placed also undergoes vikalpa-saṃskāra. It becomes more refined and thus better able to penetrate into the meaning of the teachings. There is a lot more to say about this as we continue our journey.

As we repeatedly revisit teachings from new perspectives, and to the extent we work with them, this process of vikalpa-saṃskāra will unfold. That is why you are encouraged to reflect and explore the teachings as an aid for deepening understanding.

REFLECT AND EXPLORE

- Write down your definition of vikalpa-saṃskāra.
- How does vikalpa-saṃskāra relate to other topics we've considered thus far? (These could include the topics of saṃkalpa/intention, jñāna/knowledge, vijñāna/experience, and svādhyāya/self-study.)

CHAPTER 12

Bhāvanā: The Practice of Contemplation

What aids this whole process of integration and refinement of understanding called vikalpa-saṃskāra? All of the practices contribute, but particularly *bhāvanā*, the practice of contemplation, is integral to study/svādhyāya, increased knowledge (both jñāna and vijñāna), and the refinement of our understanding/vikalpa-saṃskāra. The word *bhāvanā* comes from the verbal root *bhū*, which means "to be or become." Here, *bhāvanā* means to manifest or bring about, particularly in the mind. It is a practice, one that is useful for svādhyāya. Essentially, bhāvanā is a practice of contemplation that aids the process of vikalpa-saṃskāra. Chapter 41 will address how both vikalpa-saṃskāra and bhāvanā become a naturally arising, spontaneous gift from the practice of meditation.

With bhāvanā, we are seeking input from a deeper or higher place within awareness—the wisest part of oneself that can be accessed, the draṣṭṛ/seer (YS 1.3), the place that is closest to Source. We are seeking guidance from the Highest for the clearest possible information. One of the qualities of the Highest is *sat*, which has a sense of true reality or being, associated with "truth." At the highest level of reality, the Truth is known. The Highest is omniscient, all-knowing. But often humans are not, even though some would like to think they are.

Everyday waking awareness has an aspect of limitation or concealment, and the path of yoga leads one toward revelation. So one way to think of vikalpa-saṃskāra and bhāvanā is as means toward revealing what has been concealed. We are moving from concealment toward revelation. The practice of bhāvanā is explicitly aimed at accessing that highest, wisest, clearest part of ourselves to refine conceptual understanding, and reveal what is concealed for us in the teachings.

The success of bhāvanā depends on several things. First, it depends on actually doing the practice. It also depends on the degree to which one has created an "access ramp" to the wisest self, along with how well refined one's general state of awareness is due to the practices of yoga.

The practice of bhāvanā, along with the resulting refinement of understanding/vikalpa-saṃskāra, relates to the different ways of thinking about svādhyāya, including both svādhyāya as studying the texts and studying oneself. We must grapple with the material and engage with the process of refining our understanding. Again, this isn't just about passively listening or reading to gather information—that is just the beginning. Instead, it's about taking the time to go deeper and to make it real for ourselves. In this way we can live our yoga, applying it to our life with increased understanding.

Often a teaching is approached with the surface mind only, as with so many other subjects or any problem. On that level, there is no end to recursive thought and argument, especially about these more esoteric yoga concepts that are hard to think about analytically. Bhāvanā asks us to go deeper within, seeking and receiving guidance from a clearer place of wisdom. It is our Arjuna self pausing to listen to our Kṛṣṇa self.

In the practice of bhāvanā, the analytic mind is temporarily released in order to settle into a quieter, pre-thought awareness. We are recruiting a different part of our self as a guide. Then insight is brought out from the depths and into thought and language. That's where the writing piece of the bhāvanā practice comes in. It is often through articulation that we see whether our understanding is still limited or that, in fact, more has been revealed. We are "working" ideas and information through the refinement process of vikalpa-saṃskāra.

In addition, the process of placing a teaching in a deeper part of our selves, taking it out of the analytic mind and into a quieter place where it can reverberate, can lead to shifts in our general state of awareness. We are planting the seed of the teaching under consideration into a deep place within ourselves. The truth in it begins to be a part of our awareness, which will allow the teachings to begin to guide us on the surface of life. **The practice of bhāvanā presumes a willingness to consider the teachings seriously and to work with them, allowing their wisdom to saturate our awareness, so that anything that seems impenetrable begins to soften, sprout, and reveal itself.**

The practice of bhāvanā is *the* practice of study, svādhyāya. With it, one goes beyond just gaining more information or data. As the teachings resonate in our awareness, the higher Consciousness emanates a deeper understanding so that the teachings become more real and meaningful.

Another benefit of bhāvanā is that it allows you to discover to what degree a teaching, or any concept, resonates with a deeper part of you. An idea is placed in awareness and allowed to reverberate in order to discern the thrust or truth in a teaching. There may be some discomfort with a particular idea. For example, when contemplating a decision, you could sit with one of the possible alternative solutions, see how it resonates, and then write about it. With regard to the teachings of yoga, it's entirely possible that a particular teaching may not resonate at a particular point in time. That is absolutely fine, but don't dismiss it outright, because at some later time it might be exactly what you need. One word of caution, however. What emerges from bhāvanā is dependent on the clarity of the awareness field it moves through. So although bhāvanā can generally yield greater understanding and insight, it may not instantaneously give the ultimate truth.

The contemplative practice of bhāvanā is different from meditation, though a meditation practice creates a more clarified field of awareness for contemplation. A question can be placed into awareness after a brief meditation, then after allowing time for it to steep in that deeper place, the contemplation is brought to the surface of the active mind. Finally, writing about it brings it even more clearly to your awareness and your life.

I highly recommend this wonderful practice of bhāvanā as an aid to increased understanding of the teachings. Remember: this is not an intellectual or logical exercise. We're not listening to the surface minds or emotions. We are attempting, to the best of our ability, to access a place closer to our essence for guidance. To the extent an access ramp to our highest Self is established through practices like meditation, the answers will come from that place, rather than intellectual reasoning alone.

The beautiful thing is that there is no limit to this process. There is always more. Just like one hasn't mastered a yoga āsana or a piece of music by practicing it just a few times, so it is with the teachings of yoga. As we contemplate and grapple with the teachings, our understanding becomes more and more refined. As time passes and the teachings are revisited, the wisdom gained in the intervening time helps us understand the teachings more deeply. That's why svādhyāya/studying these teachings is a practice in and of itself, and bhāvanā is a wonderful technique to aid the process.

STEPS FOR THE CONTEMPLATIVE PRACTICE OF BHĀVANĀ

- Clearly formulate and articulate what teaching, phrase, issue, or question you'd like to contemplate and thereby gain a greater understanding. For example, you may seek a deeper understanding of a sūtra from some text. Begin by writing it down or repeating it, in Sanskrit or English (or both), whichever resonates most with you.
- Sit quietly in meditation for a few minutes. If you don't currently have a regular meditation practice, you may simply watch the breath and allow the mind to settle.
- Place the topic of contemplation into that meditative space. Don't try to actively think about it or problem-solve intellectually; simply let the contemplation be in awareness. Sometimes it is good to set a timer for five to ten minutes.
- After that period of time, free-write in a journal or a notebook. Do not plan the writing, try to be artistic about it, or otherwise manipulate it. Don't worry about punctuation, spelling, or even making sense. Just let the words flow from the hand(s) onto the page. Again, a timer could be useful for this part. Sometimes the most interesting stuff emerges after fifteen minutes. The process of writing is very important. Insights from the contemplation arise from a deeper awareness like a tender seedling that has to be planted to fully grow and blossom. When we articulate the teaching in our own words, we assimilate it even more deeply, make it our own, and are better able to integrate it into our life.
- Review what was written and see if there is anything more to add. It could be helpful to consider specifically how to apply what came out of bhāvanā to your life and write this down.

Bhāvanā as a practice is important for understanding the teachings, but it can be applied to anything you are struggling with or wish to gain more insight into, be it intellectual, emotional, or interpersonal. If you are having a personal dilemma, for example, sit down and do bhāvanā. As in the opening scene of the *Bhagavad Gītā*, it is useful to pause to ask for information from the highest place one can access for this practice. Going forward, use the practice of bhāvanā in all the Reflect and Explore exercises. Try it now on the question below.

REFLECT AND EXPLORE

- How does bhāvanā relate to the teaching of the Seed and the Tree (from chapter 4)?

CHAPTER 13

Teachers, Gurus, and Guides

The considerations of svādhyāya, vikalpa-saṃskāra, and bhāvanā signal the importance of an active participation in creating an increased understanding of the teachings. The teachings are a gift from the lineages of yoga, which we honor by applying ourselves to them. Through this process, understanding and insight arise from our awareness, which becomes increasingly clearer as we continue our journey of yoga.

The whole process of study, as well as guidance in all the practices, is supported by teachers. Spiritual teachers are among the most venerated professionals in the world, and rightly so. A teacher is a necessary component for progress on the path of yoga and meditation because having walked the path already, they can guide us in the right direction, help us avoid pitfalls, and generally make our journey more efficient and effective.

That said, gurus and teachers who abuse their power and engage in exploitation have been unveiled and widely denounced by the yoga community and elsewhere. In response, some people are inclined to entirely reject gurus and the notion of needing a teacher at all, relying solely on inner guidance. This is unfortunate, as human teachers who hold the wisdom and practices of yoga are an invaluable resource on the path of yoga and meditation.

Before going any further with this topic, take some time to consider your current beliefs about gurus and teachers.

REFLECT AND EXPLORE

- When you hear the word *guru* what comes to mind?
- How do you define *guru*?
- What messages have you received about gurus?
- What role have teachers played in your life?
- How have teachers helped you on the journey of yoga and meditation?
- Have you been harmed by a teacher?
- Who or what have been your greatest teachers, and why?

On my own journey, and in the yoga community at large, I've heard a range of contradictory messages about the role of, and the necessity for, the guru. These include:

- No awakening can occur without the guru.
- The whole idea of the guru is a sham; they are all corrupt.
- The guru is within, you are your own guru.
- The community is the guru.
- Life itself is the guru.

When one thinks of a guru, it can bring to mind an exotic person in robes—a spiritual leader with many followers. Memes of their wise words appear on social media. On the other hand, many so-called "gurus" have recently been exposed for their inappropriate conduct.

Near the beginning of my path of yoga, I desperately wanted a guru. In retrospect, what I really wanted was someone to just do it for me, or at least tell me exactly what to do. In some ways, I wanted to relinquish my power and my own discernment and have someone take charge of my life for me. I didn't want to have to think for myself. With this rather childish attitude, I left for India to study with the head of the lineage in which I was involved. I had seen my teachers and many others bow at his feet, so I did too. In addition, I consciously brought an attitude of submission to the guru. I wanted to completely relinquish my individuality, and along with it, any need to think for myself.

That yoga lineage has a long tradition of exacting discipline. Guruji, as my teacher was called, put me through the wringer, as his teacher had done to him. After two months I developed an intensely focused practice and made a lot of progress with the yoga āsanas. I came home physically strong, muscled, and flexible, but also painfully injured with a torn hamstring and low-back issues that I deal with to this day. Luckily my injuries were mostly physical. Sometimes the damage is way deeper.

Despite pain and injuries, I continued in the lineage for many years and returned two more times to India to study with this teacher for even longer periods. Injuries were a norm in this lineage, considered to be part of the process. Unfortunately, I didn't have any other reference point. Eventually, I realized this was not beneficial to me, and I found other teachers. Still, it took quite a while for me to think about the role of the teacher in a healthier way.

As I continued on my path, I repeatedly received the message that the guru holds a special status in the tradition. For example, from a root text in the Tantric tradition, the *Śiva Sūtra*, the teaching is *guru upāya*: "The guru is the means" (SS 2.6).

SS 2.6 *gururupāyaḥ*
guru: guru
upāya: method or means
The guru is the means.

What is a guru really? What is their role on the path of yoga? An often-given definition of *guru* is whatever takes one from the dark to the light. The guru is that which takes you from ignorance to knowledge, concealment to revelation. The guru is whoever or whatever guides you in the journey of yoga. The tradition differentiates between different types of gurus, and the ultimate is the *sadguru* or *sat-guru*, referring to the "true teacher." Some define *guru* as an enlightened spiritual master, but another way to think of the sadguru is as the underlying higher

Consciousness that can guide us, if and when we choose to listen to it. This is where we get the idea that guru is within—because ultimately it is.

The one primal guru that is Consciousness itself appears in many forms. Human teachers who can access this Consciousness act as conduits for the highest knowledge. A teacher is valued in any field of knowledge as someone who takes a student from a place of not understanding to a place of knowledge. This applies to everything from cooking to car repair to art and, of course, any academic field. We rely on experts to educate us. As SS 2.6 clearly states, teachers are a primary means to knowledge. We can certainly teach ourselves to some degree—and there are rare cases of spontaneous knowledge, such as child prodigies—but it's generally more effective and efficient to learn from a teacher.

Because some gurus have been revealed as charlatans, power mongers, and/or sexual predators, some students have reacted by completely rejecting spiritual teachers. Some declare, "I am my own guru." Although there is some degree of veracity that the true teacher is within, the problem is whether one has access to that wisest place. And the rub is that this is acquired primarily through practice as taught by a qualified teacher.

A potent teaching on the guru comes from the *Bhagavad Gītā*, where Arjuna seeks the counsel of his charioteer Kṛṣṇa, a metaphor for the whole process of yoga. First off, it points to the grace (*anugraha*) of having a teacher. It is interesting to note that earlier in the *Mahābhārata*, the epic from which the *Bhagavad Gītā* is extracted, both armies in the battle had the opportunity to choose Kṛṣṇa for their side. Arjuna chose to have Kṛṣṇa, while the other side chose Kṛṣṇa's troops. Arjuna sensed his need for guidance on his journey of yoga. He chose a connection with a teacher and with his higher Self. It is like when we decide to commence a practice of meditation, intuiting there is something there that can support us down the road when one chooses to align with the Highest.

Instead of rushing into battle when he still feels hesitant and unsure, Arjuna pauses to consider what he is doing. And in that pause, Arjuna and Kṛṣṇa converse. Early on in this conversation, Arjuna asks Kṛṣṇa to be his teacher (BG 2.7), and the conversation between them continues for the eighteen chapters of the *Gītā*. He asks question after question, and he gives his full attention to the guidance dispensed. Arjuna is engaged in svādhyāya: he is studying himself and, with Kṛṣṇa's help, the teachings of yoga. He experiences vikalpa-saṃskāra as he refines his understanding with each question that Kṛṣṇa patiently answers.

This conversation can be seen as a metaphor for the different aspects of the guru. Kṛṣṇa is indeed Arjuna's physical teacher, his trusted counsel, his guru. And he gives Arjuna many teachings. But in this story, Kṛṣṇa is more than a charioteer dispensing teachings and wise counsel. As is revealed in chapter 11 of the *Bhagavad Gītā*, Kṛṣṇa is God incarnate. So when Arjuna pauses with an inquiry for Kṛṣṇa, it can be seen as turning inside to the counsel of his highest Self. So, in this sense, he seeks the guru within.

But let's be clear: Who are you consulting when you turn within? We can't delude ourselves into thinking that our everyday neurotic self is the best counsel to seek because this has the potential to reiterate all of our old patterns and ways of being. It is not moving us from the dark to the light and could simply reinforce our ignorance. So before relying solely on insight, we must first clarify our being to create access to the wisest self. And usually, the means to do so (such as practices like meditation) come through a teacher.

***Guru* can be thought of in three ways: the external teacher, the teachings themselves, and the highest Self.** (This is addressed in Abhinavagupta's *Tantrāloka* 4.78). Ultimately, it is most potent to access all three of these for optimal results. And which of these is more useful and reliable depends, in part, on where you are on the path of yoga.

At the beginning of our path of yoga, it is generally more reliable to have a guide, as with any new domain of learning. (For more about this, please refer to appendix III: Choosing Yoga Āsana and Meditation Teachers.) Yet, as my experience indicates, this is also when we are most vulnerable. Begin by finding someone who can accurately dispense the teachings. This is part of the traditional interpretation of the sūtra: "The teacher is the means" (SS 2.6). One generally needs a teacher to unpack the teachings, explain them, and help apply them. And we definitely need a teacher to initiate us into practices like meditation that clarify and create access to the wisest Self.

The teachings from the texts of yoga are just as important as the teacher. The texts reveal the insights of the most astute seers who have access to the deepest parts of Consciousness and bring to light information from that place. Also, texts collect together, organize, and/or synthesize existing knowledge. However, the teachings are often in cryptic and seemingly undecipherable forms. They are like seeds or bullet points that must be unpacked by a knowledgeable teacher. And, as already discussed, students must take the information from a teacher and from the texts and plant them, bringing them into our awareness through the practices of svādhyāya and bhāvanā in order to create refinement of our understanding/vikalpa-saṃskāra.

Eventually, as we move farther along the path of yoga—and especially as we meditate more—our access to, and clarity of, the inner Self becomes greater and is, therefore, a more reliable guide. In the meantime, we must be careful not to delude ourselves. This is why it's suggested that in addition to consulting the inner guru, to verify insights with both the texts and teachers.

It would be so much easier to simply be told what to do, which is what I first desired. And in the beginning, a certain amount of that may be necessary for the effects of yoga to blossom within a new practitioner. Yet both student and teacher are human beings with more or less associated psychological baggage. So we must always bring discernment to bear, and balance that with messages from teachers and the texts.

Ultimately, the three aspects of the teacher, the teachings, and the inner wisdom all have at their source the guru, in the different facets just discussed. The teachings come from the *ṛṣis*, the seers and sages of the past. They were teachers; they were gurus. Some of the teachings are said to be a direct download, if you will, from the absolute Consciousness itself. For example, the *Śiva Sūtra* is said to come directly from Śiva, via the sage Vasugupta.

So many have taken the journey and walked the path before us, as explorers of consciousness. Some became teachers, who gifted us with guidebooks outlining the journey. They speak of the rarified air of the high mountain peaks that are unimaginable to those of us who are deep in the shadows of the valley. We are indebted to the lineage stream, the *paramparā*, the succession of teachers who have passed down the practices and teachings. They were practitioners and students who became teachers. We would not be here discussing yoga were it not for the paramparā, the many teachers of the tradition who articulated and passed on these teachings.

A beautiful example of this is the great Tantric sage Abhinavagupta. He begins his magnum opus, the *Tantrāloka*, by acknowledging all of his teachers, including his parents, who are truly our first gurus. Throughout his text, Abhinavagupta calls forth the teachings from the texts he has studied, which he honors and reveres, even as he challenges and innovates. And then his student, Kṣemarāja, takes what he has learned and synthesizes it into his own teachings. For example, he writes the *Pratyabhijñā-hṛdayam*, a text we will be studying later in this book.

What I write in this book is a result of this same process. Like those before me, I am synthesizing what I have learned from my teachers, from my own svādhyāya/self-study, from bhāvanā/contemplation, and from vikalpa-saṃskāra/refinement of understanding. Of course, this book reflects my current state of understanding. What I've gotten right is entirely thanks to those who walked the path before. Any errors are my own.

A consistent message I've received from my teachers is that the time of the mega-guru is over. Instead, what is now emerging is a larger number of teachers, each working with smaller groups, quietly creating shifts in consciousness that eventually will reach a critical mass. And in this context, the journey can be supported by fellow community members.

In the story of the Tillai Forest, Patañjali and Vyāghrapāda each share the teachings they know. This sharing teaches us the beauty of companionship and of a spiritual community, called the *kula* or *saṅgha*. Fellow practitioners are each a *kalyāṇa-mitra*. *Kalyāṇa* means "beautiful," "virtuous," or "good," and *mitra* is a "friend," so kalyāṇa-mitra refers to a spiritual friend, companion on a spiritual path, a friend of virtue, or a good counselor. And the kula, the collection of spiritual friends, is greater than each of our individual selves. Each brings the gift of their own experience, their spiritual knowledge.

For this to be successful, of course, the community members have to be actively practicing and studying, not just being passive recipients of the teachings. Each must make the effort required to produce vikalpa-saṃskāra/refinement of understanding so that what they offer each other has authenticity.

The story of Patañjali and Vyāghrapāda shows how fellow seekers are a blessing to each other and how they learn from each other. Vyāghrapāda and Patañjali teach each other what they know, and it is when they chant together that Naṭarāja emerges from the potential form of the liṅga to manifest his dance. This is emblematic of the paradigm shift happening in the world today. Power isn't embedded in a few charismatic teachers or gurus but is dispersed among a lot of different individuals.

REFLECT AND EXPLORE

- How have you learned about yoga and meditation? Consider what has influenced you, including particular teachers, lineages, other people, books, etc.
- Write down your definition of the three components of the guru. How have you experienced each of them?
- Do you favor learning from teachers, the traditional texts, or looking within? How has that worked?
- How do these three components relate to jñāna/knowledge, vijñāna/experience, svādhyāya/self-study, and vikalpa-saṃskāra/refinement of both conceptual knowledge and of awareness itself?

CHAPTER 14

About the Gods and a Traditional Invocation

Moving forward in this book, some of the most esoteric teachings of yoga as they appear in a variety of texts are presented. As we will see, it is customary to invoke the Highest first, and the god Gaṇapati is traditionally honored in the beginning. But first let's briefly consider how we might think of these Hindu deities, as they are some of the more confusing aspects of yoga's cultural environment.

The first time I went to India, I remember being so amazed and confused by the plethora of Hindu gods and goddesses, including the interaction of worshippers with them. First of all, the variations are endless, and each deity has numerous different details, including what they're holding in their many hands, their different vehicles, and so on. It was all quite exotic, confusing, and foreign, and it still is in some ways to me as a Westerner. It's a complex matter, and there's no one way to explain it, as the worship of deities can be approached both exoterically and esoterically with different emphases in different lineages.

A more exoteric approach is treating the gods as deities to be worshipped in a religious manner. The whole domain of popular yoga can seem to have these religious overtones, which some people may feel conflict with their personal religious beliefs. But rest assured, the practice of yoga and meditation is not tied to Hindu religion.

One way to think of these deities is as different aspects of the Highest, of the ultimate Reality, or whatever you want to call it. **Each of the gods is a representation of some aspect, attribute, or flavor of the Highest.** Consider these forms as a gateway or current of the divine energy, which teaches us something about the nature of the Divine and also about how to live as humans.

For example, a prevalent teaching is the trinity of Brahmā, Viṣṇu, and Śiva, which represents creation, sustenance, and destruction. You may have heard of the Goddess Lakṣmī representing wealth and beauty, or of Sarasvatī's connection with art and knowledge. You may know of Hanumān as embodying the love of the Divine and of service. And then there is elephant-headed Gaṇapati, also known as Gaṇeśa or Vighneśvara. He is quite popular in the West, likely because of his exotic and somewhat jolly demeanor. Gaṇapati is known as the remover of obstacles and is traditionally invoked at the beginning of any undertaking. Standing on the threshold of this journey together, let us invite the blessings of Gaṇapati.

Oṃ gaṃ gaṇapataye namaḥ.

Gaṇapati's story can help us understand why he's often invoked at beginnings, at thresholds, and as the remover of obstacles. When he was a boy, his mom, Śakti, asked Gaṇapati to guard the door of her boudoir as she bathed. His dad, Śiva, returned after a long absence and did not know Gaṇeśa was his own son. Gaṇeśa boldly guarded the door as he was told to do and put up a valiant fight, but naturally Śiva prevailed—by chopping off the boy's head! Śakti, quite perturbed, insisted that Śiva make it right. So an elephant's head was used to restore the boy.

In this much-condensed version of the story, Gaṇeśa literally stands in the doorway, blocking access to Śakti. So, he is known as the god of thresholds of many sorts, including beginnings, entrances, obstacles, and challenges. Traditionally, he is invoked at the beginning of events and he stands at the thresholds of homes and temples.

So we invoke him now at the beginning of our journey together. Every journey has challenges, no more so than when we look into our hearts to see what is standing in the way of the pure, full, and free luminosity of the essential Self. The path of yoga involves the removal of all that obscures our heart, and Gaṇeśa is invoked for that reason too. He also represents that which stands in the way of our understanding and our ability to fully imbibe these challenging teachings that sometimes seem strange, obscure, esoteric, and/or paradoxical. We call on the grace of Gaṇapati to clear our minds so we may penetrate into a deeper understanding to support our journey on this path of yoga.

As mentioned, he has many names, including Vighneśvara. *Vighna* means "obstacle," which explains his popularity as the remover of obstacles in one's life. Because life is always about transitions, and obstacles are common, we need the wherewithal to address them gracefully, and Vighneśvara represents that quality of Consciousness to call upon for support to do so. He is the Lord of Obstacles because there are often aspects of our selves and of life that must be dealt with and moved through, rather than avoided. So in many senses, we must experience these obstacles and do what is necessary to remove them in order to progress in life and practice. So Gaṇeśa can be thought of as actually placing the obstacles that must be addressed.

We summon Gaṇapati for support in the beginning, and as we continue to move through the inevitable and unavoidable thresholds and obstacles in life. Gaṇapati is part of us, and this capacity to meet every challenge is already within each of us. We need only to connect, align and unleash it to gain access to the innermost sanctuary of our heart. Creating the connection that allows us to cross this threshold is what yoga and meditation are all about.

Oṃ gaṃ gaṇapataye namaḥ
Oṃ gaṃ gaṇapataye namaḥ
Oṃ gaṃ gaṇapataye namaḥ

REFLECT AND EXPLORE

- What obstacles, challenges, thresholds, beginnings, or transitions are you currently facing?
- Practice: Repeat or chant aloud *Oṃ gaṃ gaṇapataye namaḥ*. (Various versions of this chant can be found on the internet, which will help with the pronunciation.)

KEY TEACHINGS FROM PART II

- There is a general contrast between two paths of yoga: the nivṛtti, or renunciate path, and pravṛtti, the householder path.
- The path of yoga requires an intellectual understanding, jñāna, as well as an experiential understanding, vijñāna.
- Traditionally, svādhyāya refers to recitation and study of the yogic texts, but it can also refer to a mindful exploration of everyday life, as well as the innermost Self.
- Vikalpa-saṃskāra is the refinement of understanding, including both understanding of the teachings and the refinement of the place of awareness from which that understanding arises.
- The practice of bhāvanā presumes a willingness to consider the teachings seriously and to work with them, allowing their wisdom to saturate our awareness, so that anything that seems impenetrable begins to soften, sprout, and reveal itself.
- The one primal guru that is Consciousness itself appears in many forms. Human teachers who can access this Consciousness act as conduits for the highest knowledge.
- Guru can be thought of in three ways: the external teacher, the teachings themselves, and the highest Self.
- Each of the gods is a representation of some aspect, attribute, or flavor of the Highest.

PART III

The Nature of Consciousness

This section articulates a vision of the Highest reality, along with some of its characteristics. The Tantric tradition acknowledges a Sourceplace from which everything manifests into different levels of reality in the physical and psychological worlds. This process is encapsulated in the teaching of the Ocean and the Wave, which helps us understand how to think about the paradoxical teachings in the following chapters, as well as the different agendas of the householder and renunciate paths. Following the teaching of the "highest first," we consider the first aphorisms from two Tantric texts declaring how the absolute Consciousness manifests as our very own Self.

The middle chapters of part III include descriptions of the highest absolute Consciousness, which is free, whole, and has unlimited power/*śakti.* We end with a consideration of the five powers and the five acts of the Divine to conclude the description of the indescribable highest Consciousness.

CHAPTER 15

Consciousness Is the Divine Heart Source and the Ground of Being

In this chapter, we jump right into the deep end. There is really no other way to do it but to directly confront the most profound, mysterious, and multifaceted questions that seekers have considered for millennia. So many traditions grapple with explanations of the origins of the universe and our place in it. One of the more challenging aspects of writing this book has been what to name this Highest reality. The tradition itself uses many different names, and in addition, I've used several different labels, including the Divine, the Heart, and the highest Consciousness. This is intentional—so as not to hang you up on any preconceived notions—though it could cause dissent or discord within you. For some, this will activate notions of God from other traditions that are not applicable to what is considered here. For some, learning about these concepts yields a lot of confusion. For others, it will seem like home. Any of these reactions are okay.

You do not have to believe anything, just keep an open mind. The last thing we want to do is to throw out our discriminative ability, which the tradition, in fact, reveres. If you have a sincere interest in penetrating the layers of your being into the heart's essence, then don't let terminology bog you down. You are not being asked to convert to some religion or belief system. And remember that however you initially come to grips with these teachings is just the beginning of a long process of refinement and growing understanding.

What follows is an explanation of some of the most esoteric teachings in the tradition. They are landmarks on a map that outlines the journey of yoga. It is important to know the general lay of the land. Before going any further, however, consider your current beliefs and understandings about highest Consciousness.

REFLECT AND EXPLORE

- What is Consciousness?
- Do you think there is a higher Consciousness? How do you conceptualize it?
- Is it necessary to believe in a higher Consciousness to do yoga or meditate?
- Does the idea of "God" or "Higher Consciousness" turn you off, or is it attractive to you? Why?

Some teachings regarding Śiva, Naṭarāja, and Kṛṣṇa have already been considered, and they point to different depictions of the Highest. When speaking of the Heart, or Highest in the Tantric tradition, it may sound like God, but it is not how we think of the God of many cultures. The Highest is the Sourceplace that permeates everything and is not separate from us. It can be thought of metaphysically, but it also helps to think of our physical and psychological realities.

As always, where to begin? Let's start by considering the everyday world. In that world, there are objects: our bodies, furniture, other people and animals, pens, trees, all the objects that make up the physical world. These are each comprised of several layers of reality, which present themselves in awareness to the degree you turn attention to them and have the appropriate means to observe.

When one penetrates inside apparently solid objects, one finds much beyond the surface presentation. With the right instruments to observe, like a microscope, one can see that objects are comprised of different layers such as molecules and atoms and even smaller particles. Science has also revealed that what seems solid is actually comprised of a lot of space.

Turning in a different direction, looking up at the night sky, there are stars, planets, even galaxies, all more or less revealed with the appropriate conditions and instruments. The stars and planets are all there during the daytime as well, even though they can't be readily seen. The whole reality of outer space is revealed only when the conditions are right.

Physics indicates that the universe is mostly empty space and that matter comprises only a small part—so what is in that space? Is it the same or different from matter? Modern science has taken quite a while to penetrate these questions.

Philosophers and scientists have intuited and theorized there is more to the universe than is readily observable. It wasn't until advanced instruments were developed that we could peer into space and beyond the boundaries of our galaxy and into the greater universe—or that we could observe the minutiae of matter with a microscope.

Throughout human history, we've known there's more than meets the physical eye, and scientists have spent a great amount of effort investigating the physical world, from the microscopic to the boundaries of our universe and beyond. When I listen to popular science explanations of the cosmos, it often reminds me of what Tantra says about the nature of the universe. Science has explored the human body in amazing ways, yet it has made much less progress in investigating consciousness.

Nonetheless, there are well-developed theories and philosophies of Consciousness elaborated by those who spent time investigating it. These are the *ṛṣis*, the seers, the see-ers—those who have turned their awareness inside to their own consciousness—exploring and investigating its makeup to describe the nature of reality. And what some of these seers discovered—not unlike what modern science has discovered—is that there is a unifying energy, a source that underlies, unfolds, and enfolds all of the material world. This Sourceplace has many names and descriptions, some of which will be explored in what follows.

The Tantric tradition articulates that beyond the physical reality and our everyday bodily existence **there is a Sourceplace that is the ground of being, which pulsates everything into existence as part of Itself.** This statement is such an extraordinary and paradoxical teaching that it is challenging for us to understand within the limited perspective of our body-mind.

Some traditions simply say "it" cannot be described and refuse to do so. And they are right to some extent, because any words will inevitably fall short of fully representing the highest reality. To be clear: at the very highest level, the absolute Consciousness is qualityless, and therefore indescribable. But the Tantric tradition reveres knowledge, the process of refining our understanding, and the human capacity for language. In fact, speech is revered and even worshipped. So this section tries to describe what is seemingly indescribable, the absolute Consciousness, both as manifest and unmanifest.

The unmanifest sourceplace has been given many names in the different streams and traditions of yoga. The Upaniṣads speak of Brahman, and the Tantric tradition speaks of Śiva, Śiva-Śakti, Cit, and Citi, among other names.

CHAPTER 16

Layers and Levels

On the journey of yoga, when turning inward to examine consciousness and how yoga and meditation work, we inevitably face some huge considerations that the Tantric tradition does not shy away from. Considering ourselves as human beings: who are we? When you introduce yourself to others, what do you say? You may say your name, how old you are, where you live, what your occupation is, maybe your relationship status, and whether you have kids or hobbies—and so on. But is this who you are? Are you the sum total of your physical characteristics and your accomplishments, your personality, and your actions? What is beyond, above, or beneath all of that?

In my journey, these questions began to percolate within me: Who am I? Am I who I thought I was? And what about that silent part of myself, that witness self I experienced in my āsana practice? These are some of life's biggest questions. It could be useful to contemplate them for yourself at this juncture.

REFLECT AND EXPLORE

- Ask yourself: Who am I?
- What animates your everyday consciousness? Where does your moment-by-moment awareness come from?
- What does "spiritual" mean?
- What is beneath the surface awareness?
- What is the nature of reality?

- Do you think of a higher consciousness as separate from you, or part of you?
- Is it possible that you are God incarnate?

Completely diving into the deep end to answer these questions is beyond our scope at the moment, but we will get our feet wet on these questions regarding the nature of reality and consciousness. Consider first the ordinary, everyday awareness that you are using to read this book. This everyday awareness is utilized to function in the world, without generally examining its deeper aspects. But even a quick consideration will reveal that when awareness is turned internally, the field of consciousness includes sensations, perceptions, thoughts, feelings, and memories. This is part of your reality, but it's less tangible than the physical body. You can't touch or see the thoughts, yet they are part of you.

In college, as a psychology major, I studied various psychological theories, including that famous image of the iceberg. Our conscious functioning—what is in the awareness at a particular moment—is the tip of the iceberg that is the totality of individual consciousness. Because below the surface is so much more. What is it that's there? Where do our anxieties and habits and temperament come from? Modern psychology tries to address this, but much of it is also addressed to some degree in the yoga tradition. First, the notion that there are levels to our everyday reality must be acknowledged. There is more than meets the naked eye. There is the iceberg readily seen, and there is all of that iceberg below the surface.

Another useful analogy is to think of an animated film that starts with a view of the biggest space of our universe, then moves into our galaxy, then into our solar system, planet, continent, country, city, street, home, and finally to us. Then penetrating into the body, into a given system like digestion and into the individual digestive organs, until arriving at the atomic level. And then there's even more at the subatomic level.

These are all layers of reality that we more or less know about. Yet before these physical realities were observed and measured, they were theoretically posited by those who studied these domains. And so it is with consciousness. The sages and seers have been exploring the territory of consciousness for thousands of years, reporting their observations and theoretical considerations.

Classical Yoga and Tantra both posit layers of the human being, including the "gross" (tangible) body, the sense and perceptual capacities, as well as deeper psychological processes including the thinking and analyzing capacity of the mind, and our sense of identity. And they go further to discuss even more subtle aspects of the individual akin to what is commonly called the soul or the spirit.

These aspects of reality were outlined in the Sāṃkhya school, one of the major traditional philosophies of India. They are part of the *tattvas*, which are the primary ingredients of human existence. The tattvas enumerate these categories which span from the elements (like air and earth) to the senses, to the mind and its components, to the higher Self. Classical Yoga imports these ideas from Sāṃkhya into its system, and then Tantra goes even further with more tattvas describing a universal Consciousness that is the ground of being and the source of everything.

CHAPTER 17

The Ocean and the Wave: Absolute and Relative Reality

In my early days as a yoga student, I heard a pervasive message indicating that the spiritual path required renouncing all worldly desires. This was reiterated in the lineage I first landed in, which required severe discipline of body and mind and commitment to the method, which confirmed the notion that to be a yogi required great effort and negation of any individuality. It did not matter if my particular body was amenable to putting my foot behind my head, and I pushed through difficulties to achieve all sorts of yoga āsanas. All of this did not sit well with either my body or my heart. So I kept searching until I found a path that honored the journey of embodiment and living as a householder.

I learned, as the story of the Tillai Forest indicates, there were different paths in the tradition. Patañjali symbolizes a renunciate path for those whose destiny was to withdraw from the world—and note that many of the early proponents of yoga in the West were renunciates. But in addition, there is the householder path of Vyāghrapāda for those committed to living fully embodied in the world.

A wonderful teaching relevant to these paths is that of the Ocean and the Wave. The concept of an ocean or lake and its waves is used in the tradition in many different ways. For example, in the Classical Yoga of Patañjali, the definition of yoga is the calming of the fluctuations of the mind (YS 1.2). An analogy often used regarding this definition is settling the waves of our turbulent awareness. Individual awareness can be thought of as an ocean or lake, and the waves are the citta-vṛttis, the fluctuations of thoughts and emotions that inhabit our awareness. Here the goal of yoga is to calm the waves of thoughts and emotions so the lake is smooth and clear (YS 1.2). When this is accomplished, one can see the reflection of the purest self (YS 1.3), like the reflection of a mountain on a smooth lake.

From a Tantric perspective, the ocean can symbolize the highest Consciousness. In this view, individuals are each a wave that emerges from that ocean of Consciousness. As our individual wave arises from that ocean, we look around and see the other waves of manifestation, and we tend to think that surface reality is all there is. This represents a forgetting, a lack of recognition of the oceanic source from which our individual life arises.

So the Tantric path of yoga seeks to remember or recognize that we are nothing but the ocean of Consciousness, manifested as our particular, individual life wave. Everything manifest is an expression of absolute Consciousness. **Individual life waves arise from the ocean of Consciousness.**

Renunciatory traditions have the goal of subsiding into the ocean. Their aim is for the individual life wave to merge back into the ocean. From this perspective, withdrawal from society helps eliminate anything that creates waves in one's consciousness. In the Tantric householder perspective, the energy of the ocean is harnessed as a resource to support the activities of the individual wave. We are successful to the degree that we have clarified our awareness such that the ocean of Consciousness is revealed. The means to this understanding is the practice of yoga, particularly meditation. In this way, we recognize that we are nothing but the ocean of Consciousness.

The yogic practices connect us to, and align us with, the oceanic sourceplace, which allows us to channel the energy of the ocean. We utilize that connection as householders to live to the fullest in a way that is aligned with our highest desires. Our work and our relationships are positively impacted. We become conduits for the attributes of yoga like nonharming, truth, compassion, and so on. It also allows us to bring forth our unique gifts. In this way, we can be of the greatest service, whether it is through something we bring into the world or by simply shifting the energy in our everyday realm through our demeanor and actions.

REFLECT AND EXPLORE

- Contemplate the teaching of the Ocean and the Wave.
- How have you experienced this teaching?

There are many ways the tradition teaches about the arising of the individual life waves from the oceanic sourceplace. We've already considered this sourceplace as Naṭarāja, the dancing Śiva. Naṭarāja dances everything into existence. In that dance, all of manifest reality emerges, including our individuality.

Scholars and philosophers often use the terms *absolute* and *relative* to differentiate these levels or aspects of reality. **The oceanic sourceplace is called the "Absolute Consciousness." It creates all of the waves of existence, known as "relative" reality.** Each of us as relative, individual life waves forget that we are nothing but the absolute ocean of Consciousness. We will explore how the tradition describes some of the mechanisms that create this sense of separation and differentiation. And then, having asserted all of this, the tradition describes how we can remember or recognize that we are each nothing but the oceanic consciousness.

The idea that there are layers to reality means that **reality is different at different levels**. This statement relates to a lot of confusion in the popular yoga milieu and is important to keep in mind when completing the contemplation exercises. While many of the teachings describe the Absolute transcendental reality, the contemplations often ask about your experience of them in your relatively limited world. Misattributions of aspects of the highest absolute Reality to relative reality create a lot of misunderstanding. We have already encountered this regarding the idea of "You are your own guru." This is true when one has access to a deep level of awareness within the highest Self. However, it would be folly to rely only on your surface (relative) reactive patterns to guide you through life.

Likewise with many of the teachings that follow. The highest Sourceplace will be described, which to a large degree is also descriptive of our highest essential Self. Yet at the level of the relative manifest world, these qualities of the Absolute can be cloaked to such a degree that they seem not to exist. The path of yoga involves uncovering the highest Self in order to bring these qualities into the manifest world.

Moving forward, it is important to remember the foundational notions of svādhyāya/self-study, vikalpa-saṃskāra/refinement of conceptual knowledge, and the tool of contemplation/bhāvanā. Working with the teachings is a practice. Our understanding initially might be quite unclear. Don't worry about that. It is hard for our surface thinking mind to grasp notions about a subtle reality that can't be directly perceived with the senses. Ultimately we have to experience them for ourselves. This is the play of intellectual knowledge/jñāna and experience/vijñāna.

CHAPTER 18

Highest First

When I began studying the Tantric tradition, one of the first things I learned was a reiteration and amplification of the teaching of "highest first," which like many teachings has a plethora of meanings. First, and fundamental to the Tantric tradition, is the unequivocal acknowledgment of the concept of the Highest, the Heart of Consciousness, the Source that underlies everything. This idea differentiates Tantra from the Classical Yoga of the *Yoga Sūtra* explicitly through those additional tattvas (elements of reality).

Another way the idea of "highest first" is reflected in the tradition is that the highest teaching is often given first in the texts, in the first aphorism, teaching, or even the first word. For example, in the *Bhagavad Gītā*, the first word is *dharma*, which is a primary teaching in the text, particularly for the warrior Arjuna, who is in a quandary about what his duty is. In the *Yoga Sūtra*, yoga is defined at the beginning of its first chapter, and the rest of the text can be thought of as an elaboration of this teaching. So the idea is that these first teachings are the key to everything. If you get it, you get the essential point of the entire text, and you'll see how everything flows from that initial statement.

Additionally, as a prelude to many texts, there is often an invocational verse that explicitly invokes the Highest in some words of praise. You may have noticed that many yoga classes or courses of study also begin with some sort of invocation of the Highest. Near the beginning of this book, we invoked Gaṇeśa as we stood on the threshold of what could be a challenging journey of understanding. Invocation calls out for the support of the Highest, and brings a dedication to the Highest front and center.

"Highest first" asks one to turn toward the Highest in the first moment of an endeavor and in each moment throughout life. This teaching asks us to pause and summon the highest possible response we can access in each and every situation.

REFLECT AND EXPLORE

- Contemplate the teaching of "highest first."
  - ~ What are different ways it manifests?
  - ~ How do you turn to the highest in your life?
- Why do people chant at the beginning of yoga class?
- Practice and note your experience(s): For some specific period of time (a day, a week, a month), consciously pause to access the highest, most heart-connected space within, before acting. You may simply take a deep breath to remember the Highest. It may involve some contemplation and journaling to sort out the highest response.

CHAPTER 19

You Are Divine Heart Consciousness

The trajectory of my yoga journey in some ways reflects the evolution of yoga philosophy from Classical Yoga to the later teachings on Tantra. The severe bodily discipline, the injuries, and the accompanying renunciate flavor in the initial school within which I practiced didn't sit well with me. I felt it didn't honor my body, mind, or the gift of embodiment. Something was missing. Then I took a workshop from a teacher who spoke to my intuitions. He spoke of how life is a gift to be celebrated. He indicated that life was a dance to bring creative beauty into the world. This was something that resonated so deeply with me. I learned these ideas were from the yoga tradition of Tantra. So again I started to ask: What could I read to learn more? Again I was sent to a core sūtra text of the tradition: the *Śiva Sūtra.*

I tried reading an extremely scholarly edition and was again completely lost. However, as I moved into a Tantra-based āsana school, my practice changed, so I experienced a little less dissonance. The messages I was getting about the meaning of yoga from a Tantric perspective were articulated in the classes themselves and related to the practice and my life in general. Eventually, I discovered the shadow side of this particular method of modern postural yoga, but much of it served me well for quite a while. And I learned a lot about yoga and about myself.

The Tantric tradition asserts that **everything emanates into existence from Source, including you. You are not separate. You are Consciousness.** This profound and core teaching requires a willingness to sit with paradox. For now, simply allow these ideas to permeate your awareness. Consider how *you* think about it, or at least consider some common and different ways to think about it.

This teaching is encapsulated in the first sūtra from the *Śiva Sūtra*, the core text of Tantra that I first studied: The highest reality, Caitanya, is the self, ātmā (SS 1.1). The first word of this first sūtra, *caitanya*, comes from the word *cit*, meaning "Consciousness," pure eternal intelligence. As already noted, this Highest Consciousness has many names including Śiva and Cit, which can be confusing. Here, Śiva is not the god Śiva. There are exoteric religious streams that worship these gods as deities, but here Śiva has a more esoteric meaning.

SS 1.1 *caitanyam-ātmā*
caitanyam: supreme Consciousness
ātmā: Self
Consciousness is the Self.

This sūtra indicates that Cit, or Śiva, is the nature of the Self, here called the *ātmā*. *Ātma* or *ātman* is a word used in many of the older texts, particularly the Upaniṣads, to name individual Consciousness, that spark of divinity or spirit within each of us. SS 1.1 is simply translated as: "Consciousness is the Self." The full, free, perfect Consciousness is the true Self and the essence of the individual self. This is so important to remember: in Tantric philosophy, when discussing the Highest, we are not talking about something separate or out there but, instead, that which is our own innate consciousness.

And this sūtra can be turned around to say: the Self is Consciousness. The individual being is one with the universal being. And as we will see in the next section, the reality of the whole universe is Consciousness.

The tradition of "highest first" is reflected first thing in the texts, often in the first sūtra or even the first word. So it is in this first sūtra from the *Siva Sūtra*. Word order is important in these sūtra texts, and "Consciousness" is the first word of the first sūtra, indicating that it is the most important and highest teaching of this text. Then the first sūtra, "Consciousness is the Self," indicates that supreme Consciousness manifests as our very own Self. Part of how this sūtra encapsulates the highest teaching is that it captures the paradox of our humanity.

There is a sense that every human being at essence is good, full, and perfect, which some call "divine." Yet, as individuals in the domain of the relative manifest reality, we don't necessarily experience ourselves and others as divine. Turning the translation around to "Self is Consciousness," this sūtra indicates there is a pathway from our individual self back to the absolute Consciousness. We'll be exploring how the tradition explains this philosophically, as well as practically, including how to begin to experience that innate essential Self. This is the journey of yoga.

Initially, it is important for us to not get too hung up on a thorough understanding of these concepts. This is especially true if this is your first exposure to these teachings. It may take some time for the process of understanding/vikalpa-saṃskāra to emerge. For the moment, you may just tuck these ideas away, suspending judgment in order to move forward on our journey toward understanding how yoga works and is applicable to our lives.

REFLECT AND EXPLORE

- Contemplate (again) the notion of Consciousness.
- Contemplate the notion of Self/ātmā.
- Contemplate the alternate translations of SS 1.1 as "Consciousness is the self" and "Self is Consciousness."

CHAPTER 20

Consciousness Manifests Everything

As mentioned earlier, the image of Śiva as Naṭarāja symbolizes how the unmanifest Absolute Consciousness dances everything into existence. This teaching is encapsulated in the first sūtra from another core text of the Tantric Tradition, the *Pratyabhijñā-hṛdayam*: Consciousness in her freedom is the cause of everything in the universe (PH 1).

PH 1: *citiḥ svatantrā viśva-siddhi-hetuḥ*
citiḥ: Consciousness
svatantrā: free, autonomous, independent
viśva: the universe, everything
siddhi: attainment, accomplishment
hetuḥ: cause
Consciousness in her freedom is the cause of everything in the universe.

Here again, is the highest teaching first, beginning with the first word, *citi*. One of the things I love about this sūtra and the text from which it is drawn is that it utilizes the feminine noun in describing the Highest. *Citi* is a feminine form of the verbal root *cit*, "to know." Here it is the creative force of the universe, mother of all creation. It is another word for the highest Consciousness.

As this sūtra says, that highest Consciousness manifests everything in the world. As noted earlier, this highest Consciousness is called the

"Absolute" Consciousness, while the manifest is termed "relative." **The Absolute Highest Consciousness is known as "transcendent," and its manifestation is known as "immanent." The paradox is that the transcendent Consciousness is also immanent in everything.** The different terminology is used to distinguish the Highest from its manifested world, but remember that we as the relative waves are inseparable from the absolute ocean of Consciousness.

REFLECT AND EXPLORE

- Contemplate PH 1: "Consciousness in her freedom brings about everything in the universe."

CHAPTER 21

Svatantra: The Absolute Is Absolutely Free

The second word of PH 1, *svatantra*, is an extraordinary and important concept. Usually translated as "free," it also means "independent," in that there is no reliance on anything else. The absolute Citi manifests everything as a result of its freedom, or svātantrya. (As I noted elsewhere in the book, Sanskrit words take on different endings depending on the specific meanings. So here, *svatantra* means "free," whereas *svātantrya* means "freedom.")

At the level of the highest reality, the absolute Citi is completely free. The freedom implied in svātantrya is a much larger concept than simply liberty and the pursuit of happiness. At the level of the Absolute, it means freedom from any limiting factors, including time, space, and form. It is the ability to be anywhere as anything at any time. It seems inconceivable.

The prefix *sva* means "self," and *tantra* can mean "loom," (as in "weaving"), so another interpretation of this word is "self-weaving." She takes the strands of existence and weaves them into the manifest world as we know it. This concept of freedom, svātantrya, or self-weaving, is important to consider at all levels of reality. On the level of the relative manifest world, including the path of yoga, it is important to consider how freedom of choice is exercised in all of our actions.

REFLECT AND EXPLORE

- To what degree do you feel free (or not)?
- Under which circumstances do you feel most free?

CHAPTER 22

Everything Is a Manifestation of Consciousness

Each word in a sūtra can hold a teaching in itself. One word that seems rather innocently slipped into this first aphorism from the *Pratyabhijñā-hṛdayam* is the word *viśva*. It has many different meanings, including "everything" and "the universe." Here it indicates that the Highest manifests as everything in the Universe. You are a manifestation of the Highest—and so is everything in the manifest world. **The tradition proclaims, *nāśivaṃ vidyate kvacit*: There is nothing that is not Śiva.** [From the *Svacchanda Tantra*, cited by Kṣemarāja in SS 3.24 commentary] Nothing. No thing. Nothing is not Śiva. Or conversely: everything is made of Consciousness.

Water can be used as an analogy for how everything in the manifest world is Consciousness, though in a more contracted form. In the sky, water is present in cloud form as vapor, which then condenses into liquid water. Then it becomes even more solid as it freezes, becoming ice. The water is the same substance, but it condenses and thickens as it takes another form. This process of contraction will be considered more thoroughly in part IV (including in chapter 27).

You, me, your neighbor, the planet, and everything on it are made of Consciousness. This includes the famous, the infamous, your family, the politician, the rabbits and snakes, *everything*. This is a radical proclamation, and understanding and experiencing this can have a radically transformative effect on your life.

REFLECT AND EXPLORE

- If everything is Divine Consciousness, how do you interact with ________? (Fill in the blank with various people or things, such as a friend, a teacher, someone challenging, something from nature, or something inanimate.)
- Consider our planet. How do we interact with Earth in a way that acknowledges the Highest in the mountain, the tree, the air, the water, and all our co-inhabitants, including insects, birds, reptiles, fish, and fellow mammals? What does this interaction look like specifically?
- Practice and note your experience(s): For some period of time (it could be a day, a week, a month), imagine putting on special glasses that allow you to see the divinity in everything. Go about your day wearing these "glasses." When it is difficult to think of others as manifestations of the Highest it can help to think of them as children or elderly people, in order to interact from a place of love.

CHAPTER 23

Pūrṇa: The Divine Is Full, Whole, and Perfect

This is a traditional invocation from the Upaniṣads (See, for example, the *Īśā Upaniṣad*).
OṂ Pūrṇam adaḥ pūrṇam idam
Pūrṇāt pūrṇam udacyate
Pūrṇasya pūrṇam ādāya
Pūrṇam evāviśiṣyate
That (the unmanifest Absolute) is full and perfect
This (the relative manifest) is full and perfect
After taking from the whole, wholeness remains.

This verse from the Upaniṣads beautifully encapsulates the paradoxical teaching regarding the Highest. Notice the word *pūrṇa* is repeated. It is variously translated as "full," "whole," or "perfect." Technically, it's related to what we've been considering: how the Absolute reality is completely perfect, full, and whole—and out of that perfection comes the relative manifest world, which is full and whole. Yet the ultimate Absolute reality still remains full. Again, this idea puts us squarely in the realm of paradox, which is something we have to work with whenever notions of the absolute Consciousness are considered.

The first line of the verse, *pūrṇam adaḥ pūrṇam idam* literally means "that is full; this is full." Some translations (including the one above) indicate that "that" refers to the Highest, the Absolute, whereas "this" refers to the manifest or relative reality. The verse continues with the paradoxical teaching that when the absolutely full Reality manifests into the relative, the Absolute reality remains full. Also, because we as manifest beings come from that highest perfection and wholeness, we are also perfect and whole beings.

And yet, from our experience as embodied beings it seems that we are limited—for instance by time and space. As humans, our experience traverses the continuum of reality: from more earthy aspects like our bodies, to subtle thoughts and everyday awareness, to even more subtle depths of our consciousness, then finally to the highest Self. Just by having bodies there are physical limitations. But at essence, we are perfectly full and whole. Again, it's quite a paradox.

The Ocean and the Wave teaching is useful here. The ocean of Consciousness is vast and full, and from this perfect Consciousness, the manifest proceeds and is also at its essence perfect, full, and whole. The great ocean of absolute Consciousness is full, but from it arises all the waves of manifestation which embody that perfection. And when the wave rises out of the fullness of the Absolute, it remains full. So again, we as manifest beings are nothing but the fullness of the perfectly full and whole ocean of Consciousness.

REFLECT AND EXPLORE

- Contemplate the paradoxical teaching from this traditional verse.

CHAPTER 24

The Absolute Śiva-Śakti

There are so many ways the tradition names the Highest, and in Tantra a pervasive one is "Śiva," as in the *Śiva Sūtras*. The word *śiva* means "auspicious," and it has a sense of benevolence, happiness, and liberation. In many Tantric texts, Śiva is also one of the names of the absolute highest Consciousness.

Remember that in the first sūtra of the *Pratyabhijñā-hṛdayam*, *Citi* is a name for the Highest, a feminine noun suggesting the Highest is the generative cause of the universe, highlighting the creative energy. This idea of creativity as an attribute of the Highest is a hallmark of Tantra.

In some philosophies, this Highest Reality is conceptualized as unmoving, completely still, and quiet, which is sometimes how Śiva is characterized. But the Highest is elsewhere conceptualized as also having a creative power, called śakti. *Śakti* literally means "power," "potency," or "energy." Śakti is the creative energy of the universe. She is what animates the stillness, she is the motion, the vibration. Śakti is the potency and potential of all forms of energy.

This can be confusing because the tradition conceptualizes Śiva and Śakti, in a great variety of ways. Śiva is also the name of a powerful and ancient Hindu deity, about whom there are many myths and teachings. Even more confusing is that many of the Hindu deities each take several forms. For example, there is Śiva as the ascetic sitting on the mountaintop, Śiva as the ancient deity Rudra ("the howler"), Śiva as the teacher Dakṣiṇāmūrti, and Śiva as the dancer Naṭarāja.

Likewise, Śakti (sometimes called Devī) is conceptualized as the Goddess and can refer to a large number of goddesses you may be familiar with including Sarasvatī, Lakṣmī, Kālī, and Parā. But here Śiva and Śakti are not referring to gods and goddesses. Instead, they are two inseparable attributes of the same thing: the Highest Absolute Reality. Yet the tradition retains the sense that the Highest contains both Śiva as the still ground of being and Śakti as the pulsating potential creative energy.

It is quite a paradox because Śiva-Śakti seems like two things. But it is one thing with different attributes. When considering the Highest as the ocean, the water is Śiva but the movement—the flow—is Śakti. The whole, dynamic flow of the water of the ocean, which includes the quiet depths and the active surface, is Śiva-Śakti.

The highest **Śiva-Śakti is both the absolute stillness of Consciousness as well as the unlimited potential of power and creativity.** Śiva and Śakti coexist and co-create. They are one thing with two aspects. Śiva and Śakti are two sides of the same coin. One way I've heard this explained is that they are one by denotation, but two by connotation. The two words *Śiva* and *Śakti* connote the one highest reality: Śiva-Śakti. Together they create the "play," or *līlā*, of life. It is their relationship, the friction between them, that allows for manifestation.

So be aware that *Śiva* as a name for the highest absolute Consciousness, in general, refers to Śiva-Śakti. There are many lineages within Tantra, and they use various names for the Highest. Whether It is named Cit, as in the *Śiva Sūtra*, or Citi in the *Pratyabhijñā-hṛdayam*, it refers to the same thing: the still presence of Śiva and the creative impulse of Śakti. And again, it is important to remember that whatever label is used, we are talking about the ground of being from which everything manifests, including ourselves. Śiva-Śakti is not something outside us, but that which is our innermost nature. And the path of yoga helps us recognize all these aspects of the Divine.

REFLECT AND EXPLORE

- Contemplate this paradoxical teaching of Śiva and Śakti.
    - ~ How have you seen this manifest in the world and your life?

CHAPTER 25

Pañca-Śaktis: The Five Divine Powers

One way the Tantric tradition speaks of śakti, the power of the Absolute, is via the *pañca-śaktis. Pañca* means "five," so the pañca-śaktis are the five powers of the highest absolute Consciousness. **The pañca-śaktis/five powers are: *cit*/Consciousness, *ānanda*/bliss, *icchā*/will, *jñāna*/knowledge, and *kriyā*/action. They are different aspects of the potency of Consciousness.**

The first of these, *Cit*, as one of the words for Consciousness, asserts a supreme awareness, the ultimate knowledge of Śiva-Śakti. It is the power of awareness that illuminates, and it is the foundation of everything.

Ānanda means "bliss," absolute joy that is naturally present in the Highest. This bliss of the Highest is not dependent on anything to create it. So ānanda implies svātantrya, or freedom of the Absolute, because this highest joy does not rely on anything and is entirely unlimited.

Icchā-śakti is "the power of desire or will." It is an unlimited will, and in the Highest it is related to omnipotence: completely unlimited power.

Jñāna means "knowledge." It is a different kind of knowledge than cit, which is knowledge of the Self, or expanded awareness. The knowledge of jñāna describes ideation. It is related to omniscience, complete and unlimited knowledge, the knowledge of all things.

The last of the pañca-śaktis is *kriyā-śakti. Kriyā* comes from the verbal root *kṛ*, "to make or do," so kriyā-śakti is the power of action. As the culmination of the five powers, it is the movement into activity.

The yoga tradition has many such pentads, and they are often divided into a dyad and a triad to explore the nuances of meaning. Here, the dyad is cit and ānanda—awareness and bliss—and the triad is icchā, jñāna, kriyā: will, knowledge, and action.

The Highest is often described as cit-ānanda and this dyad represents power more internal to Śiva-Śakti. Cit-śakti, the power of illumination, is the highest awareness. The natural outcome of that state of consciousness is ānanda, bliss. It is important to consider the difference between ordinary happiness and Absolute bliss. Happiness is often dependent on something—some desired circumstance we are happy about—whereas bliss is independent of circumstance. Bliss has no object.

The triad of icchā, jñāna, and kriyā can be thought of as a description of the process of manifestation or creation. Icchā is the spontaneous, divine desire and/or will to create. At the level of the Absolute, icchā is related to unlimited will and omnipotence, the will of the Divine to do anything it wishes. Jñāna is the knowledge, the ideas of how to create. At the level of the Absolute, it is omniscience, or all-knowingness. Kriyā is the action required to create something, and at the level of the Absolute it is the capacity to assume any form.

Consider how these five powers naturally follow one from the other, starting with the highest Cit, self-revealing Consciousness. From that Self-awareness, bliss naturally flows, as heat flows from the illumination of fire. From that bliss arises the creative impulse, icchā-śakti. Then comes the ideation of what or how to create and manifest the desire, jñāna-śakti. Finally, doing or making what's desired is kriyā-śakti.

These pañca-śaktis—five powers of the Śiva-Śakti—describe the Absolute, but they unfold on all levels of reality, including ourselves, though of course to a more limited degree. In some ways, this is descriptive of our path as householder yogis, in the sense of being a practitioner of yoga as well as someone fully engaged in the world.

As we engage in yoga, especially meditation, our individual consciousness, cit, is expanded. From that expansion, ānanda spontaneously arises. We naturally find ourselves more joyful and content, even in the face of very challenging circumstances. This bliss yields an impulse for self-expression. You may have experienced this in moments of extreme joy when you want to dance or sing. This impulse is an example of icchā-śakti.

Icchā can be thought of as desire, and one way icchā is popularly described on the relative level is "What are you itching for?" As we've described in the world of spiritual teachings that have a renunciate flavor, desire often gets a bad rap. From a Tantric perspective, however, desire itself is not bad—it's a natural impulse of the Divine. As householders, the challenge is to channel desire in a way that creates more alignment with the Highest, along with greater refinement of our beings, rather than the opposite. Icchā is also related to saṃkalpa/intention. It is what you want to do.

As the saying goes, the path to Hell is paved with good intentions and the icchā-śakti can be thought of as the will to begin the process. But an intention is not enough, something must be done about it, and that is kriyā-śakti. And to make it happen you must know how to do it, and that is jñāna-śakti.

The creative process in our everyday relative lives, be it parenting, work, making dinner or art, is enlivened by Cit, by awareness, and by our connection to the Highest. As we experience greater Self-awareness, our impulse to creativity is expanded, and our ability to actually manifest those desires is enhanced. In part, they are enhanced because our individual desires become more aligned with divine will. What we "itch for" becomes an expression of the outflowing of divine will. We begin to feel like vehicles of the Divine, and our activities begin to feel effortless as we become more empowered by these five powers of the Highest, the pañca-śaktis.

REFLECT AND EXPLORE

- List and define the pañca-śaktis. Contemplate their meanings, and give examples from your life.
- Do you find any of these more dominant than others in your life?
- Contemplate the difference between *sukha* (happiness) and ānanda (bliss).

CHAPTER 26

Pañca-Kṛtyas: The Five Divine Acts

To end this part of the book on the Highest and its qualities, let's consider the *pañca-kṛtyas*—the five acts of Śiva. In doing so we will return to Naṭarāja, Śiva in the form of the dancer. Remember that Patañjali and Vyāghrapāda learned of these five acts from Naṭarāja in the Tillai Forest.

One of the most popular images in yoga culture is the figure of four-armed Naṭarāja standing in a ring of fire on one leg, with the other foot upturned. It is common to see *mūrtis*, or statues, of this dancing Śiva in yoga studios. I have one in my home studio, and it appears on T-shirts, and elsewhere—there's even one at the CERN laboratory in Geneva, Switzerland, where the dancing image relates to research on particle physics and the fundamental structure of the universe.

As we've discussed, from a Tantric perspective, Śiva is the ground of being from which all of the manifest world arises. Śiva is the ocean of Consciousness from which all the manifestational waves arise. In this image of Naṭarāja, Śiva the Absolute is dancing the manifest world into existence.

We will approach Naṭarāja first by considering some of his iconographies, looking at some of the attributes represented in the image. You may want to have an image available to look at as we go over this, and it is important to note that I will be indicating right and left, and that refers to Naṭarāja's right or left, which will be opposite to you as you look at it.

Starting with Naṭarāja's bottom right hand, its palm turned out to the observer. This gesture appears in many mūrtis/statues from both the Hindu and Buddhist traditions. This upturned palm is called *abhaya-mudrā*: the "gesture (*mudrā*) of fearlessness (*abhaya*)." It is imploring, "Do not fear." The journey of yoga can be challenging, and it takes courage to even step onto the path, so this upturned hand reassures us: *Don't be afraid. Come on in—the water in the great ocean of Consciousness will buoy and support you.*

Also encoded into the image of Naṭarāja are the pañca-kṛtyas, the five acts of Śiva. As discussed in the previous chapter on the pañca-śaktis, *pañca* means "five." And *kṛtya* comes from the verbal root *kṛ* meaning "to make or do." So these are the five acts of the Highest. The pañca-kṛtyas can be thought of as different attributes of Śiva's dance. **The pañca-kṛtyas/five acts are *sṛṣṭi*/creation, *sthiti*/maintenance, *saṃhāra*/dissolution, *tirodhāna*, *vilaya*, or *nigraha*/concealment, and *anugraha*/revelation or grace.**

Each of these will be considered in more depth, but first remember that Śiva is the Highest unmanifest ultimate reality, the ground of being, existing beyond time and space. Because of that, the description of Naṭarāja will at times be paradoxical, and one paradox is that Śiva performs all these actions simultaneously and continuously. As he dances, he is simultaneously creating, sustaining, dissolving, concealing, and revealing.

The image of Naṭarāja encodes various attributes of Śiva-Śakti as both the ground of being and that from which all the manifest world emerges. There are different interpretations of this mapping of the pañca-kṛtyas onto the Śiva Naṭarāja, which I will point out as we go. See what resonates most for you.

Moving to Śiva Naṭarāja's top right hand, which is on our left as we look at it, Naṭarāja holds a drum called the *ḍamaru*. The drum is cinched in its middle by a string with something like a pebble at the end that strikes the drumhead. As the drum is flicked back and forth, the pebble creates a "tick-tock" rhythm, like the pulse of creation giving rise to all of manifestation. This is the first act of Śiva: *sṛṣṭi*/creation. The drum represents the action of creating, of manifesting, and Śiva-Śakti is the pulse, the beat of life. The dance of life begins; the heart starts beating. The drum is a rhythm, the creative pulse from which everything flows into existence. The unmanifest ground of reality starts vibrating everything into manifestation.

The second of the pañca-kṛtyas is *sthiti*: sustenance, persistence, or maintenance. In one mapping it is represented by the upturned hand in abhaya-mudrā, that gesture of fearlessness. Another mapping teaches that sthiti/persistence is represented by the supporting leg. That steady leg supports the entire dance and therefore relates to that steadfast and persevering energy of sthiti. The sturdy leg seems to be holding everything together. It is the balancing act of life. Whatever is manifested must then be maintained. There is some persistence for a while, until of course there isn't, since all manifest things eventually dissolve.

Naṭarāja's topmost left hand (on our right) holds fire, representing *saṃhāra*, the third of the pañca-kṛtyas. Fire burns and is destructive, so this is symbolic of dissolution, destruction, reabsorption, or transformation. In the larger context of the Hindu gods, Śiva is a very fierce god, known as the destroyer. A related meaning is dissolution or reabsorption, where everything emitted is eventually reabsorbed back into the Divine.

The fourth act, *nigraha, vilaya* or *tirodhāna*, is concealment, and in one mapping it is represented by Naṭarāja's standing leg. That foot stands on the dwarf Apasmāra, the demon of ignorance, who represents cosmic forgetfulness. Apasmāra is *ajñāna* or *avidyā*, the lack of knowledge, or ignorance, of who we really are. We get lost in the wild dance of life and forget our true, essential nature, which is concealed. Here Śiva Naṭarāja stands upon ignorance, holding it at bay.

In another mapping, Śiva's fourth act of concealment is represented by the arm that crosses Naṭarāja's heart. The arm conceals the heart, and that downturned hand points to the upturned foot, which represents the fifth and last of the five acts: *anugraha*/grace or revelation. The arm crossing the heart closes off or "conceals" the heart, and that hand points the way to the antidote of the closed heart: the revelation represented by Naṭarāja's beautiful, upturned foot—his *kuñcita-pāda*.

As with most teachings, there are layers of meaning here. One way to look at these five acts is to consider the triad of creation, maintenance, and dissolution, along with the dyad of concealment and revelation. We'll first examine the triad of creation, maintenance, and dissolution in more detail.

Sṛṣṭi comes from the verbal root *sṛj*, which means "to emit, to pour forth, to let go." Śiva as the unmanifest pure Consciousness holds everything in potential form (as in the liṅga in the Tillai Forest). Sṛṣṭi is the agency within the Absolute that unfolds all the possibilities for manifestation. Sṛṣṭi can be a sense of just letting go and emitting, which infers that creation is not necessarily hard work and is, perhaps, even a sense of play. The Divine allows the manifest to flow out.

And then sthiti, the second part of this triad, is what sustains that which has been created. If there wasn't some persevering quality, whatever was created would be instantaneously gone. So sthiti is the energy that maintains things for some period of time.

Then everything manifest eventually dissolves. This is saṃhāra. Destruction is one way to think of saṃhāra, but it is also withdrawal, dissolution, or even transformation. What has been manifested and sustained for some time is now reabsorbed or retracted back into the Absolute. Saṃhāra as transformation means something old has to dissolve and change into something else. It is represented by fire, and where I live in the western United States, fire can be extremely destructive. However, when the forests burn, space is created for new growth to unfold.

These acts/kṛtyas take place on all scales, from the macrocosmic scale of the whole universe to the microcosm of individual awareness—and everything in between. So these three unfold on all levels of reality. Everything pulses into existence, persists for some time, then dissolves. It occurs in the cycle of day and night, the seasons of the year, and in our own breath. Hindu philosophy talks of even greater cycles or ages, called *yugas*.

These acts are embodied in our human life: we're born, we live, we die. I'm fond of the idea that at birth, the Divine exhales us out, and we take in our first breath. The divine act of emitting or unfolding us is sṛṣṭi, manifestation. Then at death, we exhale our last breath, and the Divine breathes us back in. This is saṃhāra, dissolution, the sense that our individual self dissolves and is reabsorbed into the Divine.

In our individual lives, this triad operates in every action we take. Sṛṣṭi is the creative impulse flowing forth, our willful self-expression through action. Sthiti is maintaining that action, and saṃhāra is allowing it to end. These three can also be considered at the level of thoughts, how they arise, catch our attention for some time, then fall away.

Then there is a simultaneous dyadic process of nigraha/concealment and anugraha/revelation, the final two in the list of the five acts. As the Absolute creates the manifest world, the Absolute itself gets concealed. The Divine moves from its unmanifest perfection into manifest limitation. In order to manifest, the Divine must limit itself. There isn't some other entity that conceals It. It creates and conceals itself. This is quite a paradoxical and mind-blowing teaching. I have heard it likened to a cosmic game of hide-and-seek the Divine plays with itself. It is simultaneously concealing and revealing itself. The Absolute limits itself by its own creative activity.

One way to think about it is that when choosing to create something, that limits you to that one thing, out of the potential of all the things you could create. So as one thing is created and revealed, everything else is concealed. Another way to think about this: as the unmanifest, unlimited, spacious Absolute takes on some form like an individual body, the very act of taking a body creates limitation. The expansiveness has to contract itself to take on the boundaries and limitations, squeezing itself into a bodily form.

In doing so, there is a forgetting of that original expansiveness. Naṭarāja stands on the dwarf of forgetfulness. His crossing arm occludes the heart in this gesture of forgetting. We forget that we are nothing but the great expansive ocean of Consciousness. Yet the hand of the crossing arm points to the upturned foot of grace, the other half of the dyad of concealment and revelation.

The heart of us, the essential Self, is covered over during the dance of manifestation into a human body. Yet our body and our embodied life is a vehicle for us to remember our essence, the heart of who we are. So the crossing hand points to the uplifted foot as a reminder of the possibility of a heart connection, to the very essence of ourselves.

That fifth act, *grace*, is a word that may have religious connotations for some of us. Yet by some circumstance, we find our way back home, so to speak, and remember the true Self. This is anugraha, vilaya, or tirodhāna, represented by Naṭarāja's upraised foot.

What is grace? You are invited to contemplate this for yourself, as there are many different ways to think about it. One way I think about grace is as anything that helps raise us up or connect us to the higher Self, to our hearts. It can simply be that which supports us in everyday life. But it is also that which leads us or opens us to that divine Source-place within ourselves.

When Śiva-Śakti contracts to embody as our individuality, we arrive on this planet forgetful of that source. Our innermost nature is concealed from us, yet by grace we can remember, and our divine Self is revealed to us. Each of us here now, when exposed to these ideas, is by grace receiving the gift of these teachings. Along with our other practices, this aids in uncovering and revealing our hearts to us.

REFLECT AND EXPLORE

- List and define the pañca-kṛtyas. Contemplate their meanings, and give examples from your life.
- How do the different mappings of Naṭarāja inform your understanding?
- How do the five acts relate to each other?
- Observe the cycle of creation, maintenance, and dissolution in some different aspects of your experience and life.
- Consider how fear works in your practice of yoga and your life.
  - ~ What do you fear most?
  - ~ How do you think about abhaya-mudrā?
- How do you experience concealment?
- How have you experienced revelation/grace?
- Consider how the teaching of the Ocean and the Wave relates to the pañca-kṛtyas.

KEY TEACHINGS FROM PART III

- There is a Sourceplace that is the ground of being, which pulsates everything into existence as part of Itself.
- Individual life waves arise from the ocean of Consciousness.
- The oceanic sourceplace is called the "Absolute Consciousness." It creates all of the waves of existence, known as "relative" reality.
- Reality is different at different levels.
- "Highest first" asks one to turn toward the Highest in the first moment of an endeavor and in each moment throughout life.
- Everything emanates into existence from Source, including you. You are not separate. You are Consciousness.
- The Absolute Highest Consciousness is known as "transcendent," and its manifestation is known as "immanent." The paradox is that the transcendent Consciousness is also immanent in everything.
- At the level of the highest reality, the absolute Citi is completely free.
- The tradition proclaims, *nāśivaṃ vidyate kvacit*: There is nothing that is not Śiva.
- Śiva-Śakti is both the absolute stillness of Consciousness as well as the unlimited potential of power and creativity.
- The pañca-śaktis/five powers are: cit/Consciousness, ānanda/bliss, icchā/will, jñāna/knowledge, and kriyā/action. They are different aspects of the potency of Consciousness.
- The pañca-kṛtyas/five acts are *sṛṣṭi*/creation, *sthiti*/maintenance, *saṃhāra*/dissolution, *tirodhāna, vilaya,* or *nigraha*/concealment, and *anugraha*/revelation or grace.

PART IV

Human Manifestation and the Human Condition

Part IV starts with the question: if everything is a manifestation of the Highest Consciousness, why do I feel bound and disconnected, and why do I experience suffering? To begin to answer this question, we look at teachings about how absolute Consciousness contracts to become our individuality and at how the mind contracts around the objects of perception so that the Source becomes concealed. Avidyā/ignorance—confusing the surface individuality with the innermost Self—is a general way the tradition speaks of the underlying cause of suffering. Tantra teaches that the *malas* (impurities) are a mechanism that taints and conceals the heart, creating a sense of separation, differentiation, and doership. This leads to *saṃsāra*, a condition in which one lives only on the surface of life, leading to transmigration. The repeated cycle of thoughts/citta-vṛttis, action/*karma*, and subliminal activators/*saṃskāras* can hold us captive and produce suffering.

CHAPTER 27

Consciousness Contracts into Individuality

The question that often comes up at this point in the journey is something like: If everything is made of a completely free and whole consciousness, including me, then why don't I feel free? Why do I feel bound or disconnected, or why do I experience suffering?

PH 5 *citir eva cetana-padād avarūḍhā cetya-saṃkocinī cittam*
citi: absolute Consciousness
eva: itself
cetana: uncontracted or expanded Consciousness
padād: state, stage
avarūḍhā: descend
cetya: object of perception
saṃkocinī: contracted, limited
citta: mind, individual awareness
Consciousness contracts from its expanded state and becomes individual awareness, conforming to objects of perception.

The fifth sūtra of the *Pratyabhijñā-hṛdayam* begins to answer this question. It says: Consciousness (Citi) contracts from its expanded state (cetana) and becomes our individual awareness (citta), conforming to objects of perception (cetya). In parentheses, I indicated four words in this sūtra that come from the verbal root *cit*, which as already mentioned means "to know." Each of these words has a teaching for us.

This sūtra begins with *citi,* the same word considered earlier as the very first word of this text, which designates absolute Consciousness. Remember that PH 1 says that the highest Citi, out of her freedom/svātantrya, contracts from its expanded state (cetana) to manifest everything. Here in PH 5, a specific result of that manifestation is given. The Highest contracts to produce the individual consciousness, citta. We as individuals are each a manifestation of the Highest, yet are limited, due to that contraction. Even so, we are at essence divine, having come from that great ocean of Consciousness.

This teaching is reflected in the image of Naṭarāja as considered with the pañca-kṛtyas in chapter 26, which describe the fundamental acts of the Highest, whether it is called Citi or Śiva-Śakti. The five acts describe how the world is unfolded from the Absolute to the relative—how the manifest world is created or emitted, then maintained, until again it is enfolded back into the Absolute. As well, in this process, one of the five acts/pañca-kṛtyas of the Absolute is concealment (nigraha). The Absolute in its expanded state (cetana) contracts from its fullness, squeezing itself into a human form. For us as individuals, this concealment is akin to forgetting who we are. It is a kind of cosmic amnesia, and the results can be devastating in this earthly realm because we have forgotten our heart essence.

This forgetting of our Heartself and our connectedness to everything can produce horrific consequences. When the primary experience is one of disconnection, it can yield results like social injustice, degradation of the environment, and so on. One of the greatest promises of yoga is the ability to recognize the divine source both within ourselves and as everything, allowing the highest qualities of awareness to pulse out through each of our thoughts and actions.

REFLECT AND EXPLORE

- Contemplate PH 5: "Consciousness (Citi) contracts to become our individual awareness (citta)."
- Consider how it relates to any other teaching, as well as your experience of it.

CHAPTER 28

The Mind Is Divine

You may recognize *citta* in sūtra 5 of the *Pratyabhijñā-hṛdayam* as the same word from the definition of *yoga* in the *Yoga Sūtra*: Yoga is the calming of the whirlings/vṛttis of the mind/citta (YS 1.2). PH 5 indicates the citta is a relatively contracted state of awareness. Remember the citta-vṛttis include all our thoughts and feelings, both positive and negative.

Technically, citta is comprised of three components: *manas*, *ahaṃkāra* and *buddhi*. Often defined as the intellect, *buddhi* is the place of judgment and discernment. *Ahaṃkāra* literally means the "I-maker." It is often translated as "ego," but it doesn't necessarily mean the ego as psychology defines it. My teacher Paul Muller-Ortega calls ahaṃkāra "the individual-identity assemblage point"—in other words, the place in which the notion of who you are assembles or where the identity coalesces. Ahaṃkāra is linked to the perceptual or operating mind, the manas. The word *manas* comes from the verbal root *man*, "to think." It is where thoughts, ideas, memories, and emotions arise. The manas receives impulses from the senses, which it refers to the ahaṃkāra and the buddhi. In addition, the manas receives information from the ahaṃkāra and buddhi. Buddhi, ahaṃkāra, and manas together constitute the citta referred to in these sūtras.

Anyone who observes the movements of the mind/citta-vṛttis knows that the mind is quite active, which, of course, is the opposite of the directive from YS 1.2 to stop (nirodha) the thoughts. The challenge in trying to calm the mind is reflected in a teaching common in spiritual circles about "monkey mind," which asserts that the mind is unsettled, uncontrollable, and full of restless mental chatter. You may perceive a bit of a rub between the idea from Tantra that "the mind is divine" and the idea of monkey mind.

When I began to study the *Yoga Sūtra*, I got the sense that thoughts are a bad thing, especially in meditation. From the perspective of Classical Yoga, one wants to squelch/nirodha the thoughts/citta-vṛttis. Early in my journey, I thought I was really messed up and couldn't meditate properly because my mind was active. But in sūtra PH 5, the expanded awareness/cetena, contracts to form our individual mind/citta. If we think of our thoughts as manifestations of the Highest/Citi, maybe thoughts aren't so bad, and perhaps they can be seen as part of a benevolent process. The mind/citta is a beautiful thing; we just need to make it an ally. We need it to function in, and maximally experience, our householder life. It allows us to live in this world. The mind is allowing you to read this book and learn these teachings.

Particularly as indicated in this sūtra, **the mind/citta is a manifestation of the Highest/Citi. Indeed, it is a gift that allows one to maximize householder life and to contact the highest Consciousness.** The mind is the instrument to return to the Divine. So from a Tantric perspective, there is an honoring of the mind that has a different flavor than is found in Classical Yoga.

REFLECT AND EXPLORE

- What are the implications of characterizing your mind and thoughts as manifestations of the Divine, even as we understand we are limited, relative beings?
- Do you see your mind as an ally or a problem? Why?
- How does the phrase "monkey mind" make you feel?

CHAPTER 29

The Mind Contracts Around the Objects of Perception

As we apply these yogic teachings to our lives, it is important to consider this last phrase of *Pratyabhijñā-hṛdayam* 5: "conforming to the objects of perception." Our citta, our individual consciousness, contracts to perceive whatever we are currently paying attention to, the object of perception/cetya. Think about that, because it has huge implications for our work with our own consciousness. **The mind is saturated with whatever one turns attention to.**

When one looks at something, the mind moves to that and becomes contracted in the sense that when focusing on one thing, other things are lost, and they aren't seen. Note that sight is used here as just one example of the senses, but this is true of all the senses and the thoughts themselves. For example, right now you're focusing on these words to the exclusion of anything else. Your mind is becoming saturated with these teachings.

From the perspective of living our life and refining awareness, where one puts attention has profound significance. For example, the object of perception, what one focuses on, can be some pattern of thought. It could be something that arises from within us like a habitual way of thinking—some reactionary, obsessive, or addictive pattern. On the other hand, it could be a remembrance of the highest perspective.

This may seem like a small point, but it has huge implications for how to live your yoga. Since consciousness is contracted according to where the focus is directed, it is important to consider where you consistently place awareness because consciousness contracts around that.

The mind is colored by what it perceives. This is why what one surrounds oneself with is so central to the journey of yoga.

A related teaching says something like: "You become the company you keep, so keep good company." Anything you surround yourself with and take into the body and awareness—people, things, images, food—affects your different levels of being. Therefore, you should consider carefully what company you keep, what is repeatedly brought into awareness through the body, senses, and thoughts, as this has a profound effect on what you become.

To summarize, this sūtra (PH 5) teaches us that one manifestation of the Highest is our very own mind. We've started to define *citta*, our own awareness, its components, and how it works. In later sūtras, some explanations of this contracting process and its results are given. Yet as we shall see, if we consistently place our awareness internally toward our hearts, for example through the practice of meditation, then the mind becomes saturated with the qualities of the Highest.

REFLECT AND EXPLORE

- Contemplate the concept that your mind contracts around objects of perception. What are the implications in your householder life?
- How does the practice of yoga/meditation relate to the teaching that your mind contracts around the object of perception?
- Practice and note your experience(s): For some period of time (it could be a day, a week, a month), watch the workings of your mind and notice what you bring into your awareness through the senses and thoughts. (This might include movies, music, news, art, spiritual teachings, physical surroundings, relationships.)
  - How does each feel? How does that affect you?
  - Does each thing brought into awareness make you feel more or less connected to your heart?
  - Does it affect your subsequent thoughts and actions—for instance how you act toward others or how you feel inside?

CHAPTER 30

Avidyā: Ignorance

This section of the book discusses how absolute Consciousness manifests into our relative being. The tradition describes this contraction in various ways, including the concept of nigraha/concealment, represented by Naṭarāja's arm crossing the heart or by his standing leg with his foot on the demon of forgetfulness, Apasmāra. From the ocean, the individual wave arises and forgets its oceanic source. It looks around and sees all the other waves of manifestation sparkling and dancing on the surface of the ocean, and it thinks that is all there is. As considered in PH 5, our awareness becomes contracted around that perception.

The omniscient, all-knowing absolute Consciousness contracts to become individual awareness and in doing so becomes limited in its knowing. We don't realize who we really are (the cit-śakti considered in chapter 25). One way this forgetfulness is expressed in the tradition is as avidyā. *Vidyā* means "knowledge," and adding the negator *a* indicates that avidyā is a lack of knowledge, generally translated as "ignorance." We are ignorant of who we are at essence.

The *Yoga Sūtra* lists ignorance as one of the five kleśas, which are impediments or afflictions that are the underlying causes of suffering. (The kleśas are addressed extensively in chapter 2 of the *Yoga Sūtra*.) Avidyā, or ignorance, is given as the primary ground from which the other kleśas are born (YS 2.4). Also, YS 2.5 indicates that **ignorance leads to a fundamental confusion. Instead of experiencing the *ātma*/Self, which is eternal, pure, and joyful, one identifies with the surface self (the *an-ātma* or "not-self"), which is transitory, impure, and painful.**

YS 2.4 *avidyā kṣetram-uttareṣāṃ prasupta-tanu-vicchinna-udārāṇām*
avidyā: ignorance, not-knowing
kṣetram: field, ground, source
uttareṣāṃ: others
prasupta: dormant, asleep, inactive
tanu: weak, attenuated
vicchinna: interrupted, intermittent
udārāṇām: aroused, activated
Ignorance is the source of the other [*kleśas*, or causes of pain], whether dormant, weak, intermittent, or activated.

YS 2.5 *anitya-aśuci-duḥkha-anātmasu nitya-śuci-sukha-ātma-khyātir-avidyā*
anitya: not eternal, impermanent, transitory
aśuci: impure
duḥkha: pain, sorrow
anātmasu: not-Self
nitya: eternal
śuci: pure, clear
sukha: happiness, joy
ātma: Self
khyāti: perception
avidyā: ignorance
Ignorance is confusing the transitory, impure, and painful not-self with the eternal, pure, joyful Self.

A related way of thinking about this is that we've forgotten *caitanyam ātmā* (SS 1.1), "Consciousness is the self/ātma." (Note the use of "ātma" in both YS 2.5 and SS 1.1). And immediately after proclaiming this highest teaching in the first sūtra, *Śiva Sūtra* 1.2, says "**Limited knowledge is bondage.**" In his commentary, Kṣemarāja points to two ways this limited knowledge manifests, which is similar to what is outlined in YS 2.5.

SS 1.2 *jñānaṃ bandhaḥ*
jñāna: knowledge
bandhaḥ: bondage
[Limited] knowledge is bondage.

The first type of limited knowledge is thinking of ourselves in limited terms, as only the wave. The contracted awareness thinks that all we are is our dance on the surface of life. We think the totality of existence is that part of the iceberg above the water. We are sucked into the daily drama of life and identify completely with it.

A second way knowledge is limited is not recognizing that we are in fact Consciousness itself. We don't know ourselves as the ocean of Consciousness. We fail to penetrate beyond the surface awareness to discover the heart of who we are at the depths.

Then further, in his commentary to SS 1.2, Kṣemarāja points to a mechanism that from the Tantric perspective is a cause of these limited identifications: the *āṇava-mala*. This will be considered in chapter 31.

REFLECT AND EXPLORE

- Write down your definition of avidyā.
- Consider YS 2.5 and SS 1.2 and the two ways ignorance is described. Put these into your own words.
  - ~ How do you see this reflected in your life?
  - ~ How do you see ignorance manifesting in the world at large?

CHAPTER 31

The *Malas*: Mechanisms and Results of Covering the Heart

In his introduction to the ninth sūtra of the *Pratyabhijñā-hṛdayam*, Kṣemarāja points out the discrepancy between the highest Citi and limited individuality and seeks an explanation of the mechanisms which create that limitation. PH 9 says: "Consciousness is covered by impurities due to the contraction of its powers and becomes a transmigrating soul."

PH 9 *cidvat-tac-chakti-saṃkocāt malāvṛtaḥ saṃsārī*
cid-vat: full of Consciousness
tat: that
śakti: power
saṃkocāt: due to contraction, limitation
mala: impurities
āvṛtaḥ: covered, impure, limited
saṃsārī: a person who experiences saṃsāra, worldly existence, transmigrating soul
Consciousness is covered by impurities due to the contraction of its powers and becomes a transmigrating soul.

"Consciousness" refers once again to Citi, the highest absolute Consciousness. As in PH 5, there is the idea of contraction (saṃkocāt). Here, the contraction of the power of the absolute Śakti, is explicitly mentioned. Then this sūtra elaborates on the process of contraction: the individual is covered by malas, the impurities (mala-āvṛtaḥ). The result is that the individual becomes a transmigratory soul (saṃsārī), which will be discussed more in chapter 32. So here, as in the fifth sūtra, is described this process of contraction which creates the individual. But PH 9 goes further by delineating some mechanisms for that contraction, as well as some consequences. Kṣemarāja specifically points to the malas to describe the limitation that hampers the freedom of Consciousness.

This contraction is described as a veiling or concealing. *Mala* literally means "taint, impurity, dust, dirt, dross." **The malas are what cover, conceal, and limit the pure, full, and free Consciousness. There are three types of malas: the *āṇava-mala*, the *māyīya-mala*, and the *kārma-mala*.** These are how the Tantric tradition explains the limiting conditions that contribute to ignorance, trap us in our surface life, and hamper the free expression of the heart.

The first, the āṇava-mala, is the primal limiting condition that reduces the absolute Consciousness to the individual, the *aṇu*. As previously discussed, the nature of the Absolute is svatantra, absolutely free, and out of that freedom the Highest chooses to conceal itself. The One becomes the many. The wave arises, as though separate from the ocean of Consciousness. We each become the aṇu, an individual, which is limited through the crimping this āṇava-mala creates. *Aṇu* means "individual," but it also means "small" like an atom, so there can be a feeling of being small, feeling less than full. This can lead to a sense of a lack of fulfillment as well as a sense of imperfection.

For the vast sky or the ocean of Consciousness to embody—to materialize—it has to shape itself and take on a covering of skin. What was unlimited is squeezed into limitation. It could feel like going barefoot all summer then having to squash your feet into winter shoes, or bundling up with clothing that's too tight, so movement that was once unlimited now feels constricted and less free.

That constriction has experiential consequences. Without the freedom to do or be anything, we have the experience of being imperfect, incomplete, unsatisfied, and incapable. We feel imperfect due to separation from the Perfect. From this root contraction of the āṇava-mala, the thought arises, "I am separate." We feel disconnected from Source. There is a sense of loss, a vague feeling that there is more, and an experience that something is lacking. We feel empty because of the separation from fullness/*pūrṇatva*. This can be experienced as feelings of inadequacy, unworthiness, or a lack of self-esteem.

As negative as this sounds, it can also be the impetus for a desire to reconnect with the Highest. Feeling a lack, we seek fulfillment. This can manifest in many ways, including how we might feed the ego or seek experiences or use drugs or sex or food to fill us up. Or we can turn toward the Highest, toward reconnecting with that which is the source of all fulfillment. It is this sense that there is something more that turns us toward teachers, teachings, and practices to help us reconnect with that Source.

Āṇava-mala is the *mūla-mala*, the "root covering," the primal limiting condition that reduces the universal consciousness to an aṇu, a limited being. This root contraction yields the two other malas. They can be thought of as progeny or consequences of the āṇava-mala. I have heard the āṇava-mala likened to an earthquake, which shifts the plates in the earth, and the other two malas are like the resulting tsunami.

The āṇava-mala is the core sense of separation, from which follows a sense of differentiation, which is the māyīya-mala. Through the process of manifestation, the one light refracts into many different colors. As a consequence, we experience ourselves as different from all the other colors or manifestations of the one Citi/Consciousness. In our individual experience this creates the awareness that "I am different" from everyone and everything. This differentiation can lead to a chronic assessment or evaluation.

The māyīya-mala is experienced as the tendency toward comparing and evaluating what is better and what is less. Consciously or unconsciously, we compare ourselves to others to see how we stack up. The individual life wave sees itself as different from all the other waves. We take measure and wonder: Is our life wave better than all the other waves? Am I bigger, more attractive, splashier?

On a positive note, this feeling of differentiation can lead us to seek connection. From the highest perspective, difference is a beautiful thing. The differentiation experienced in the relative plane allows us to enjoy the beauty of this world and other beings in it. If we can appreciate the differences as unique and beautiful manifestations of Śiva-Śakti, it can lead us toward experiencing the connectedness of all things. And on the other hand, when we focus in a comparative way on differences between ourselves and others, or between our group and other groups, we begin to act out of this sense of difference in ways that can be deleterious. For example, we may think we are better and deserve more than others who are different from us.

As we feel separated from Source and become a limited embodied being, we also experience the veil of doership, the kārma-mala. There is a sense of agency, that "I am the doer." One definition of *karma* is action. Due to the separation from the Highest, we forget the source of our actions and think instead that we are the one acting. The wave thinks it alone is creating the tide, and is ignorant of the oceanic source of all action.

On the other hand, as householders, we have to act in order to live in the world. This sense of doership allows us to fulfill our life's desires, our intentions for how we want to live this life. However, if we do not feel connected to Source, we may act in misaligned ways, reflecting the sense of disconnection and difference.

So these three malas are all interrelated, the āṇava-mala being the big pinch, the contraction, the earthquake that sets a tsunami in motion in which we feel not only separate (āṇava-mala) but different (māyīya-mala). We compare ourselves to others and feel we are lacking. From this lack, we act and we think we are the source of action (kārma-mala) and that we are in control. In all these ways, the individual life wave forgets its oceanic source. The heart of who we are, the deepest layer of our Self, is veiled. Our experience on the surface of our lives is that it doesn't even exist.

REFLECT AND EXPLORE

- How do you see the malas operating in your life?
- Specifically, consider:
    - When do you feel the most unworthy (āṇava), differentiated from others (māyīya), and/or powerless (kārma)?
    - When do you feel the most worthy, connected, and/or powerful? What helps manifest that feeling?

CHAPTER 32

The Wheel of *Saṃsāra*

The last part of PH 9 refers to the saṃsārī, which is one who experiences saṃsāra. *Saṃsāra* in general can refer to a "worldly existence" based on ignorance of the essential self. *Sāra* means "flow" and *sam* means "same," so it is being stuck in the same flow, the eddies of human existence, repeating the same cycles of suffering. It also means "transmigration," which is likened to a wheel—a wheel that turns through repeated cycles of birth, life, and death. So **a saṃsārī is one who experiences saṃsāra, including suffering, and transmigrates from one lifetime to another due to karma.**

As mentioned in the previous chapter, karma can simply mean "action," and the kārma-mala is a sense of doership. The word *karma* also refers to the chain of actions and their effects, which leads us to transmigration, of being born and reborn. This cycle of transmigration is saṃsāra. And, as we'll see below, the situation of being stuck in repetitive cycles can apply to getting stuck in patterns in our life in general.

REFLECT AND EXPLORE

- How do you think about the concept of saṃsāra?
- How do you think about karma?

CHAPTER 33

The Cycle of Thoughts, Actions, and Subliminal Activators

This part of the book examines some ways the tradition explains how the individual becomes limited, how Naṭarāja's crossing arm conceals his heart. PH 9 teaches that the malas cover the heart. The unlimited contracts into the limited individual form that is our everyday experience. Then once embodied, the sūtra goes on to indicate that we get stuck in the cycle of saṃsāra, enacting our karma.

Karma is the driving force of saṃsāra. In this and later chapters, we will consider how karma is generated, plays out, and is counteracted. It is important to remember that "karma" has many meanings. Many of us are familiar with the "Law of Karma," which is basically that for every action there is a reaction, or "what goes around comes around."

The collection of stored residues of our actions is known as *karmāśaya.* Classical Yoga posits the kleśas/impediments as the root cause of this storehouse (YS 2.12). As discussed in chapter 30, on ignorance, the primary kleśa is avidyā/ignorance—not knowing who we really are at essence.

From the Tantric perspective in PH 9, the malas work to taint our being so that we may tend toward acting in ways that are misaligned, due to the sense of separation, differentiation, and doership. Since actions can be either good or bad, so is this collection of karmāśaya. Until we clean out this storehouse of karma, we continue to be caught in the cycle of saṃsāra, or continued rebirth. The path of yoga works to refine our being, cleaning out all the residual traces of past acts, and our actions start to become more aligned with our Heart.

Recall the definition of yoga from YS 1.2: yoga is calming the "turnings" of the mind. Remember that the citta-vṛttis are the fluctuations of consciousness, everything that happens in the field of awareness, including thoughts, perception, concepts, emotions, and memory. In the West, the body, mind, and emotions are often separated. But in this tradition these are all part of the Divine's manifestation, called *prakṛti*.

If you've done the exercise of watching these movements of the mind, you know that the mind is active virtually nonstop. So many thoughts and emotions constantly move through awareness, which is why the Classical Yoga approach to completely stopping the mind seems so daunting.

As considered in YS 1.3, when the mind is calm—when the citta-vṛttis are brought to rest—we gain access to a deeper place of the Seer. The *Yoga Sūtra* goes on in Sūtra 1.4: Otherwise, we identify with the citta-vṛttis. When the mind is not calm, we stay on the surface of both the mind and of life rather than penetrating into the heart of our being. This represents the everyday state of awareness. We identify with the changing states of mind/citta-vṛttis, and we define ourselves accordingly, forgetting the deeper parts of who we are. On a day-to-day basis, we are pulled into the drama of life by the whirlwind of the citta-vṛttis, all of the experiences, memories, perceptions, thoughts, and emotions constantly spinning around in everyday awareness. Remember PH 5: Awareness contracts around the objects of perception. It's like watching a film and becoming engrossed in the main character and forgetting yourself. You become the character, feel what is happening to that character, and lose track of your own true essential self. This is how we become stuck in saṃsāra.

YS 1.4 *vṛtti-sārūpyam itaratra*
vṛtti: turning, fluctuation, modification; refers here to the citta-vṛttis
sārūpyam: conformity, identification
itaratra: otherwise
Otherwise, there is identification with the citta-vṛttis [whirlings of the mind].

A traditional example describes the essential Self as a pure, transparent crystal that takes on the color of things placed next to it, but doesn't itself change. At essence, we are each a pure crystal, but we take on bodies, experiences, and so on—all of which keep us from seeing that essential nature. That is what is described in YS 1.4: we identify with those colorings and fail to see the pure transparent crystal.

Sūtras 1.2–1.4 of the *Yoga Sūtra* go a long way toward laying the groundwork for understanding our situation as embodied humans. A very basic summary is: **Yoga is accomplished by calming the movements of the mind. Then one sees the deeper true Self, like stilling waves on a lake. Otherwise, one remains identified with the thought patterns, which are like waves on the lake.** We have a very limited sense of identity based on the fluctuations in awareness, tied only to the surface of our lives. Then it is easy to get caught in a cycle of suffering, but ultimately the practice of yoga and meditation work to free us.

So the next questions become: What is the nature of these citta-vṛttis? Where do they come from, and how can we work with them? There is a whole process by which these citta-vṛttis are generated through a cycle involving the citta-vṛttis, saṃskāras, and karma. Without going into all the technicalities of the philosophy here, we will consider the general process. Understanding this process is integral to exploring how awareness works, how meditation works, and how these teachings can be applied to everyday life.

The citta-vṛttis/fluctuations of the mind—essentially whatever is in your awareness—are said to be activated by the saṃskāras. Remember that saṃskāra is one of those Sanskrit words that means different things in different contexts (for example, in the context of vikalpa-saṃskāra it means purification or refinement). In the context of Classical Yoga, *saṃskāra* is usually translated as "subliminal impression," or "subliminal activator." *Saṃskāras* are all the impressions or imprints left by past actions, which then condition future actions. And the theory is that they are based on actions not only from this life, but from previous lives as well.

There's a cycle that involves actions (karmas), the traces they leave (saṃskāras), and the thoughts and feelings (citta-vṛttis), which works as follows. You do something or something happens to you: that is karma. Remember there are different definitions of karma, but in this context, just think of karma as an action. That action lays down an imprint, a saṃskāra, in your psyche. The saṃskāras are stored in the buddhi, that discerning part of the citta/mind. So the saṃskāra becomes part of you. It might be inactive, or when circumstances are right, it starts activating certain thoughts or feelings, which are the citta-vṛttis. **There can be a repetitive cycle when the citta-vṛttis prompt action, thereby creating karma, which lays down the saṃskāra, which causes more citta-vṛttis, and so on.**

For example, I like to have some chocolate after dinner. I love good dark chocolate, and when I have some, the experience creates an impression in my psyche of how good that chocolate is. So next time as I finish dinner, I have the thought: "Wow, some chocolate would be so good right now." So I eat some chocolate and am again reminded of how good it is.

In this example, the action of eating the chocolate is the karma. My experience of eating the chocolate yields the saṃskāra, the impression left in my buddhi. When the conditions are right (I've finished dinner) the saṃskāra is activated. This leads to the citta-vṛtti, the thought and impulse in my manas, my thinking mind, that I want more chocolate. And so I have some chocolate, further reinforcing that saṃskāric impression.

Saṃskāras are often likened to seeds. They are planted in awareness and will sprout when the conditions are right. They may lie dormant for a long time—even lifetimes. Then circumstances arise that activate them. And remember, every action creates these seeds, so they are quite numerous.

Another way to think of saṃskāras is as habit patterns. Some of the patterns aren't a big deal—like a little bit of really great dark chocolate after dinner isn't a particularly detrimental habit. But in other circumstances, these patterns can be quite debilitating. One example is post-traumatic stress, in which there are environmental triggers that elicit extreme cognitive or emotional citta-vṛttis. Drug or alcohol addictions are also debilitating habit patterns. However, some habit patterns can be positive. For example, when I get up in the morning, the impulse to meditate arises pretty quickly for me as a result of my repeated action of meditating each morning and the resulting saṃskāras embedded in my buddhi. Also, the saṃskāras differ in how ingrained they are. More traumatic or repetitive experiences will be deeply embedded. So there's a whole range of how these patterns work in our lives.

REFLECT & EXPLORE

- List and contemplate all the definitions of karma we have considered.
- Give examples from your life of saṃskāric "habit patterns." Consider those that are both positive and negative.
- How can you break the pattern of problematic habit patterns?

KEY TEACHINGS FROM PART IV

- The mind/citta is a manifestation of the Highest/Citi. Indeed, it is a gift that allows one to maximize householder life and to contact the highest Consciousness.
- The mind is saturated with whatever one turns attention to.
- Ignorance leads to a fundamental confusion. Instead of experiencing the ātma/Self, which is eternal, pure, and joyful, one identifies with the surface self (the an-ātma or "not-self"), which is transitory, impure, and painful. (YS 2.5)
- Limited knowledge is bondage. (SS 1.2)
- The malas are what cover, conceal, and limit the pure, full, and free Consciousness. There are three types of malas: the āṇava-mala, the māyīya-mala, and the kārma-mala.
- A saṃsārī is one who experiences saṃsāra, including suffering, and transmigrates from one lifetime to another due to karma.
- Yoga is accomplished by calming the movements of the mind. Then one sees the deeper true Self, like stilling waves on a lake. Otherwise, one remains identified with the thought patterns, which are like waves on the lake. (YS 1.2–1.4)
- There can be a repetitive cycle when the citta-vṛttis prompt action, thereby creating karma, which lays down the saṃskāra, which causes more citta-vṛttis, and so on.

PART V

First Steps on the Path

Our journey exploring the path of yoga so far has described the highest absolute Consciousness, which manifests everything, including us. Out of the great ocean of Consciousness, the individual life wave takes form. We take on a body; we have lives, families, and work. We get drawn into that drama, and forget the ocean of Consciousness that supports the wave. The next step in the journey will help us discover the inward-moving current that takes us back to that great ocean of Consciousness.

Part V concerns stepping onto the path of yoga, which generally involves some type of awakening, so we begin with the concept of *śaktipāta*. The importance of a teacher and practice is acknowledged, so one can move from being a seeker to being a finder. The receptivity and capacity of the student, or *adhikāra*, is an important aspect of the journey of yoga. To move along the path most people require some practice or method/*upāya*, though spontaneous enlightenment is possible for a small minority of people. This part ends with a discussion of practice/abhyāsa, and what a well-established practice comprises, along with the counterbalancing notion of dispassion/vairāgya.

CHAPTER 34

Awakening

Stepping onto the path of yoga starts with some type of awakening, whether conscious or unconscious. Looking back at your journey, you may identify turning points that have motivated a quickening of movement on the path. I described my own time of awakening, which involved a romantic breakup and its emotional upheaval. In the depths of my despair, as I hit bottom, something inside reminded me of yoga, which I had dabbled in as an undergraduate. The breakup was a call to wake up, which led me to examine what I was doing with my life in a variety of ways.

This is so often the case. Some devastating event in life wakes us up, jolts us into the heart and helps us remember there is more to being alive than the mundane life we've been enacting. So I sought out a teacher, and that teacher led me farther down the path, and then to another teacher, and so on. It was a gradual process with successive levels of awakening and awareness.

Reflecting deeper on my life as a whole, I see a pattern of seeking something more. I repeatedly experienced a feeling that something was lacking in my life, something spiritual in nature. Initially I turned to Christianity because that was what I'd been exposed to. Then I sought out various substances and experiences, as so many of us do, seeking to fill a sense of lack on the material plane through experiences or stuff.

And some of us get a taste of that "more" from yoga āsana, which was my experience. After certain poses, I would experience a "bliss hit" as energy surged through my body, and I wanted to expand that experience. Often after practice, I enjoyed some serenity and equanimity, which would persist for some time.

Ultimately, all of these openings or awakenings are due to grace/anugraha, which you may remember is one of the pañca-kṛtyas, the five acts of the Absolute Consciousness. Life provides circumstances to which we can respond in many different ways. It is by grace that one experiences these openings as an impetus on the path of yoga.

One form of grace you may have heard about is *śaktipāta.* Like so many concepts, the notion of śaktipāta has many layers of meaning and interpretation. Remember *śakti* means "power," and *pat* is "to fall or descend," so *śaktipāta* is the descent of power, or grace. It is a way that the individual experiences grace in their being.

Most of us have experienced some degree of spontaneous awakening: a hit of śaktipāta from holding a newborn baby, from experiencing art or intimacy, or by sitting on a beach or in the mountains or on a park bench. Somehow we just drop fully into the present moment, with a spontaneous realization of the Highest reality. Or it may come through some type of practice. The experience can feel like a sense of Oneness, a recognition of the connectedness of everything—with your Self as the center of it or engulfing it all. Such experiences can be a flash or a wave, and they can last a moment or for days or weeks. This is an embodied experience of *caitanyam ātmā*/Consciousness is the self (SS 1.1), explored in chapter 19. Yet for most of us, this sudden hit eventually fades, and we return to mundane awareness.

In some traditions, śaktipāta is defined as something bestowed upon a student by a teacher. You may know of gurus who distribute such blessings via a touch, a glance, or in other subtle ways. Some people report feeling an energetic transmission, while others say they've felt nothing. The student may receive or experience śaktipāta in many ways, with varying intensity. Or śaktipāta can occur without a person consciously registering an initial impression. In these traditions, this is a vehicle of awakening and movement toward greater awareness. From another perspective, however, reliance on a guru could leave a student relying on these "hits," which creates dependence rather than self-sufficiency.

One way to think of grace/śaktipāta is that it's always available and always being offered; to open to it, one just needs to cultivate the awareness and experience of it. It can be received from many sources: friends, teachers, acquaintances, or circumstances. I often sense a deeper presence and peace in certain people, including some of my teachers. In the story of the Tillai Forest, Śeṣa got some sort of hit from Viṣṇu and wanted some of what he had. The absolutely free śakti can move through us in any number of ways.

The variety of experiences regarding the wake-up call—including receptivity to a guru's śaktipāta or a sensitivity to someone's energy—points to a deeper understanding of śaktipāta. There must be some receptivity, readiness, or openness in the student to receive. This is related to the concept of *adhikāra* (discussed in chapter 35) in the sense of a student's receptivity and/or qualifications to receive the teachings.

Śaktipāta involves the initial and subsequent awakenings that propel one on the path of yoga. It entails some descent of grace into the individual, which often leads one to seek a teacher, practices, and teachings. It is said that when the student is ready, the teacher will appear, and that is precisely because of adhikāra, the readiness of the student to receive. This has certainly been my experience as each teacher led me to what I needed next. At times I wished I had met certain teachers sooner, but looking back, I wonder whether I would have been ready and receptive at an earlier time.

The importance of a teacher cannot be overemphasized. Sometimes awakening experiences can be very disorienting. They can happen spontaneously and unexpectedly, and can be quite intense and/or confusing without context or understanding. Sudden awakenings can also happen at any point on the path as practice progresses, and they can take one by surprise or be perplexing. An experienced teacher can help with moving through these intense experiences, providing the necessary knowledge and support.

The moment of initially waking up, which involves some śaktipāta, leads us to become a seeker. On some level, this impulse of the śakti has guided us toward the Highest. I was lucky, as are you, since right now you are seeking deeper teachings of yoga, turning toward yoga for deeper fulfillment. However, the initial experiences of awakening are not enough to sustain us. As one of my teachers says, one needs to move from being a seeker to being a finder. And the bridge for most is some method, some type of practice.

REFLECT AND EXPLORE

- Consider what you wrote for the Reflect and Explore questions in chapter 2, regarding your journey so far in light of the śaktipāta teaching. Or, complete that exploration now if you did not previously.
- Looking back at your life, identify moments that were a wake-up call, in which you were guided to move in a direction of growth and greater awareness.
- Have you experienced a spontaneous awakening? If so, how?
- What leads you to seek out a yoga āsana or meditation class, course of study, teacher, or teachings? What led you to read this book?
- Have you noticed an urge, subtle or strong, to seek something more at certain points in your life or throughout your life?
- Have you experienced a lack or yearning for more in your life and sensed the "more" should come from within rather than from something outside?

CHAPTER 35

Adhikāra: Receptivity and Capacity of the Student

Before students can appropriately receive practices that will move them along the path of yoga, they must be willing and ready. This willingness and readiness is related to the *adhikāra* of the student. I first learned this word as "studentship," as in the degree of aspiration one had, as well as the proclivities of the student. One could be tepid and lackadaisical, or somewhat motivated with moderate studentship, or a very intense and dedicated practitioner. One could be more open and receptive to different perspectives, or more rigid in their thinking.

In the yoga tradition, *adhikāra* relates to who is entitled, eligible, or qualified to receive a practice. For example, it was customary during earlier eras like Upaniṣadic times, that most practices were restricted to Brahmin men. Others were not entitled and seen as ineligible. A different and much less restrictive perspective is that ***adhikāra* relates to the degree to which a student is prepared, ready, and interested in receiving practices and teachings**. In part, this has to do with the capacity of one's awareness and receptivity. Adhikāra relates to how students should take the first and subsequent steps on the path of yoga, given their current degree of evolution of consciousness, which is related to the degree of śaktipāta they've received.

It is useful to think about this in other domains of practice and study. For example, the system of yoga in which I started had a well-established sequence of yoga āsanas, and one did not progress to a more advanced level until they displayed competence in the previous level, and were, therefore, ready to move forward. This is true in many domains of study, like mathematics, wherein one must first become proficient in fundamental concepts before receiving more advanced concepts. In both cases there is a sequence that is useful to follow.

Likewise, in the domain of consciousness particular practices are more or less appropriate for particular individuals, depending on the progress of the practitioner along the path of yoga. Many may sincerely wish for more advanced practices, though they are not prepared and may not have the capacity to receive the benefits, given their current state of awareness. Some say that advanced practices given to someone who is not ready for them can be harmful. More likely the practices just won't be effective, which can be discouraging to a student. Often it requires a previous practice of meditation to properly "prime" the practitioner for other ancillary practices to be most effective.

Adhikāra has a lot to do with the aspiration of the student. The student must first want to step into the journey of yoga and be receptive to seeking out a teacher. In the story of the Tillai Forest, Śeṣa was open to the energy of Viṣṇu. He then stepped onto the path, embodying as Patañjali, with a determination to experience the grace of Naṭarāja. Patañjali received from Naṭarāja the teachings appropriate to where he was on his path, while Vyāghrapāda asked for more, and received further teachings appropriate to *him*. Throughout the *Bhagavad Gītā*, Arjuna seeks guidance from Kṛṣṇa by asking progressively more astute questions, signaling his readiness and capacity to receive more. Adhikāra is reflected in students' prior cultivation of their practice and study, so that the ground of their awareness is properly prepared for the seeds of further practices and teachings to flourish.

REFLECT AND EXPLORE

- Write down your definition of adhikāra.
- How have you seen your adhikāra play out on your path of yoga?
- Consider these attributes of adhikāra: receptivity, fluidity, curiosity, groundedness, regularity, dedication, stamina, commitment, aspiration, degree of knowledge or awareness. What other attributes of adhikāra do you think are important?
- Specifically consider your own adhikāra regarding any of the above listed (or other) attributes.

  ~ Which best describes you?

  ~ Which do you tend toward?

  ~ Which do you feel you need to cultivate more?

CHAPTER 36

Upāya: Yogic Methods

One of the early books I read to understand yoga was Georg Feuerstein's book *Yoga: The Technology of Ecstasy*. I think this title is brilliant because it points to two facets of yoga: the practice of yoga and the result of that practice. Yoga results in a state of awareness, as reflected in Classical Yoga's definition of yoga as stilling the mind so the seer abides (YS 1.2 and 1.3). Also, yoga is a technology—a methodology—comprised of a variety of practices.

One of the things I found most confusing in the popular yoga world was the large variety of messages, some of them contradictory, about how to do yoga. On one hand, I heard that yoga was all about practice and effort. Then on the other, I often heard messages of allowing, of dropping it, of doing nothing. Often the latter message can come from teachers who had a spontaneous awakening of the type considered earlier.

Some people take these experiences to be enlightenment and proclaim themselves as such. If they become teachers, they proceed to teach that becoming enlightened requires no effort: it is simply a process of allowing or letting the outer layers fall away. Based on that experience of spontaneous awakening, they teach that there is nothing to do. For most of us, however, this is a transitory experience and the sense of oneness fades away and does not become our everyday reality. If the experience is fleeting, it is more of an awakening/śaktipāta, a beautiful step toward enlightenment.

The Tantric tradition acknowledges that there are some rare individuals who in this lifetime are ready for spontaneous enlightenment. They arrive on this Earth at a tipping point and are receptive to the flow of grace transmitted through some situation or teacher. They don't need practice to experience and become stabilized in the higher states of yoga. **The circumstance wherein one is spontaneously enlightened is known as *anupāya*, or "no method." The texts make it clear that this applies to an extremely small percentage of people.**

For the vast majority of people, a variety of methods or practices is available, depending on the adhikāra of the student. **Students require yogic methods, or *upāya*, appropriate to where they are on their path of yoga**. *Upāya* means "technique, method, or means of approach." The upāyas are different ways, methods, or types of practices for engaging with the journey of yoga that are appropriate to the adhikāra/capacity of the student.

As any parent knows, how one explains something to a toddler is very different than how to explain it to a preteen or young adult. A teacher in any domain knows that students learn differently. Even adult students enter any domain of knowledge with more or less background information, different ways of taking in information, and different levels of receptivity, raw desire, and commitment. This is all related to the notion of adhikāra.

As a teacher of yoga āsana, I have students who fall along a spectrum of being completely tuned in to their bodies to those who seem disembodied. Some students can readily feel alignment instructions in their bodies, while others struggle to find and move the various parts of the body as instructed. So as a teacher, I must approach each of these students in different ways. This is why I believe it is so important to teach different levels of classes, based on the readiness/adhikāra of students.

And as a student of yoga āsana, I've experienced my own inability to connect a teacher's instruction (jñāna) to my experience (vijñāna). I've been in workshops where I had no idea what the teachers were talking about and/or could not see what they were teaching in demonstrations. The instructions did not match my level of knowledge and experience.

Whether as a student, teacher, or parent, we've all experienced the necessity of connecting the level of instruction with the level of the student. So why should teaching or learning about consciousness be any different? Everyone steps onto the path at a different place, so for the teachings to be effective, a teacher should meet the student where they are. This is one reason you need an in-person teacher rather than receiving practices from a book or online.

The Tantric tradition explicitly acknowledges the necessity of different strokes for different folks through its teachings on upāya. As mentioned, the tradition acknowledges the pathless path of no method/anupāya for a few rare individuals. For the rest of us, different upāyas work with successively more or less subtle layers of awareness. Most of us start with the *āṇavopāya*, which is the path many of us are familiar with: working at the level of the body and mind.

As we progress along the path, we are better able to penetrate into, and establish ourselves in, deeper states of consciousness. We become prepared to work with practices appropriate to those deeper levels. Tantra has a well-developed theory of practice regarding how these different modes, or upāyas, can support practitioners as they progress along the path. Delineating the details of these upāyas is beyond the scope of this book, but it is important to know that different practices are appropriate according to the awareness and capacity/adhikāra of the student. To move farther along the journey of yoga, most practitioners will proceed through successively more subtle methods, under the guidance of a qualified teacher.

REFLECT AND EXPLORE

- What has been your experience of "doing" yoga? What technique was involved?
- Have you experienced the teachings of "no method?"
    - If so, what form has it taken?
    - How has it worked for you?
- What do you see as the means toward a higher state of awareness?
- What methods help you connect to your innermost Self?

CHAPTER 37

Abhyāsa and *Vairāgya*: Practice and Dispassion

At the beginning of the *Yoga Sūtra*, Patañjali gives his definition of yoga: "Yoga is the calming of the mind" (YS 1.2). Then, of course, the question is: How do you do this? Patañjali presents a two-fold path: *abhyāsa*, or "practice," and *vairāgya*, or "dispassion" (YS 1.12). **The core means to yoga is balancing regular practice with dispassion.**

YS 1.12 *abhyāsa-vairāgyābhyāṃ tan-nirodhaḥ*
abhyāsa: practice
vairāgya: dispassion, nonattachment
tan-nirodah: their restraint, control
[The mind] is restrained through practice and dispassion.

Remember that word order in this sūtra text is important, and here *abhyāsa* is listed first. Practice is fundamental to learning anything, be it yoga and meditation, the arts, parenting, or running a business. You have to actually *do* something, and doing it repeatedly is one way to think of practice. If you want to be a writer, you must write. If you want to be a painter, you must paint. And more broadly speaking, if you want to be a good parent, you must practice parenting skills, and if you want to improve a business, you must explore and implement ways to do that.

So if you want to experience the benefits of yoga, you have to do yoga. It seems obvious in some ways, yet how often does one desire the benefits of some practice, yet fail to do anything about it? You have to physically put yourself on the mat and/or meditation cushion. Before going further, pause to consider your current experience with practice.

REFLECT AND EXPLORE

- Consider the following regarding your practices, be they āsana, meditation, other practices, or even something else you're trying to learn to do regularly in everyday life.
  - ~ How long have you practiced it?
  - ~ Do you stick with it? Do you practice it regularly and continuously? Or do you alternate between doing it and dropping it?
  - ~ Do you know how to practice it properly?
  - ~ What attitude do you bring to practice?

In my own experience, I've seen the power of practice in my āsana practice, for example with arm balances. When I first saw some of the arm-balance postures in the advanced series I was learning, my initial inclination was to think, "No way!" When I first started practicing arm balances, I fell out of them again and again. Many of them seemed hopeless, yet I continued to practice. Some of them took months of practice to even begin to get, yet by persevering, I developed the necessary strength and flexibility. Even those postures I never quite "perfected" outwardly, benefitted me on my path.

In YS 1.14, Patañjali more specifically explains what constitutes a well-established practice, listing three components. (Remember word order!) First, *dīrgha-kāla*, meaning "continued for a long time." Second, *nairantarya*, meaning, "without interruption" or "continuous." In other words, the first two qualities of a well-established practice are doing it for a long time and doing it uninterruptedly or regularly.

YS 1.14 *sa tu dīrgha-kāla-nairantarya-satkāra-āsevito dṛḍha-bhūmiḥ*
sa: this
tu: but
dīrgha-kāla: long time
nairantarya: uninterruptedly, continuously
satkāra: with care, consideration, devotion, reverence
āsevitaḥ: cultivated, practiced frequently
dṛḍha-bhūmiḥ: firm ground
This [practice] is firmly established when it is cultivated for a long time, uninterruptedly, properly, and with reverence.

Then there's a third quality: *satkāra-āsevitaḥ*, which has various translations, including "right fashion," "carefully attended to," "seriously and respectfully," and "with reverent devotion." This third aspect of abhyāsa seems to have different shades of meaning. There is a sense of practicing properly, in the correct way, and carefully. Also, there is a sense of a respectful approach to the practice, even reverence or devotion. So, this sūtra says that **practice is established when done for a long time, without interruptions, and in the proper fashion—even reverently (YS 1.14).**

After considering these aspects of abhyāsa, Patañjali turns to vairāgya, the second element in YS 1.12 as the way toward nirodha/calming of the mind. *Vairāgya* is often translated as "dispassion," but also as "nonattachment."

One element of vairāgya is nonattachment toward the results of practice, especially the immediate results. Consider any physical practice, or something artistic like music. Any given practice session may be frustrating or tedious; nonetheless, you continue showing up to practice. This is abhyāsa. Then, vairāgya is about letting go of any judgment around how well you did or any attachment to a specific result.

One gift of the early days of my intense āsana practice was learning the discipline of regular practice without judging the results. The practice had a set sequence of postures, and inevitably some poses were easier and some more challenging—or even impossible for some people.

Yet, every day, regardless of how I felt, I got on the mat and went through the sequence of poses. Some days were more "successful," if one were looking at the outer form of the pose. On some days I had no problem whipping my foot behind my head and even moving into different positions from there. And other days, it just wouldn't go. And when I pushed too much, I could injure myself. So slowly I learned the vairāgya part of the equation: the necessity and benefit of nonattachment.

Likewise with meditation practice. Actually sitting to meditate is abhyāsa/practice. Yet we don't judge the specifics of what happens during our practice. Simply do the practice as instructed, allowing it to unfold however it does. Cultivating this attitude of nonattachment is one way to think about vairāgya.

From a broader perspective, vairāgya can be thought of as all that needs released in order to better walk the path of yoga. Remember that the *Yoga Sūtra* is primarily a text that teaches renunciation. It teaches withdrawal from the world, in part because that helps us move away from desire, which is fundamental in this renunciate text. Some are called to join an ashram, retire to a cave, or become a wandering *sādhu* (holy person). Then those social circumstances support a total obliteration of all desire. So vairāgya/dispassion in the context of Classical Yoga involves completely renouncing all worldly desire, including family, possessions, and so on (YS 1.16).

From a Tantric householder perspective, it is not necessary to obliterate all desire. Instead, we consider how to bring desires, intention/saṃkalpa, and actions in line with the highest, most auspicious desires. We slowly refine our lives by releasing whatever does not align us with the Highest. This is another way to think of vairāgya/dispassion.

In a greater scope of our lives as a whole, or in some particular domain of our lives, the teaching of abhyāsa and vairāgya can be even further simplified to yes and no. What do you say "yes" to in life, and to what do you say "no?" What needs to be cultivated and manifested, and what needs to be released or dissolved?

On my journey of yoga, much of this happened quite naturally. After I started practicing yoga āsana, I found I didn't want to go out and party with my friends because I wanted to attend a yoga class early the next morning. Gradually, some of my partying friends began to fade away. As I shifted additional elements of my life, I eventually found myself in a very different lifestyle that better supported my yoga practice.

This is a process many of us go through on the spiritual path: through practice, we get a hit of awareness or an experience of the benefits of the practice, and we naturally start letting go of activities, objects, and even people that hinder us on the path. And often we find ourselves simply not caring about things that previously seemed so important due to having tasted a greater fulfillment, and our whole perspective starts changing. So one way to think of embodying abhyāsa and vairāgya is making choices that are beneficial for the path of yoga, which eventually supports life as a whole.

Sometimes the greatest effort is simply starting to practice—just getting on the mat or the cushion, doing what is necessary to create the time and space for practice. This requires effort, abhyāsa, as well as some letting go of whatever is getting in the way, vairāgya. Yoga is always a combination of things, and a lot of the success of yoga depends on finding the balance, or some combination of opposing actions, without rigidly resorting to any single way. So one way this teaching can be simplified is to balance effort and surrender.

In many enterprises, it is quite easy to over-effort, if not balanced in some way. For myself, I practiced yoga āsana for many years in a very effortful and dogmatic way. This led to multiple injuries, which I deal with to this day. On the other hand, in recent years, I've found myself becoming a little lackadaisical about my āsana practice. I'm surrendering too easily into lassitude and need to put a little more energy into my āsana practice.

Consider how this teaching on abhyāsa and vairāgya can be applied to the practice of svādhyāya: study of the teachings. We have to arrange our lives to make time for study, perhaps letting go of some activities to make that happen. Then it is necessary to apply some effort toward svādhyāya, take up the practice of contemplation/bhāvanā, and actually engage with the materials.

What does it require for you to do this? Personally, I work best with some structure: for example, a course of study with a teacher or a study group with other students. I also find some commitment and accountability important. Then, to do the studies, I have to let go of some other activity to make the time. For me, this means spending less time on things that don't support my path, such as social media.

As with my āsana practice, I've had to repeatedly let go of my perfectionism, my desire to know everything perfectly as I study the yogic teachings. Because I am aware of the process of vikalpa-saṃskāra/refinement of understanding, I learn what I can at a given time and release the expectation that my current understanding must be perfect. I know some confusion may be part of the process, and I allow myself to imbibe the teachings in a way that is more open and patient.

REFLECT AND EXPLORE

- Consider a specific domain in life you want to shift or cultivate, be it some artistic endeavor, some social or physical skill, a practice, etc.
  - ~ How do the concepts of abhyāsa and vairāgya apply?
  - ~ Do you tend to favor abhyāsa or vairāgya, or are you pretty balanced? If you favor one, how is that working?
  - ~ How can you balance effort and surrender?
- Answer the above questions with regard to your spiritual practice.
- What has the practice of yoga postures/āsana and/or meditation (or any other practice) taught you about the process of abhyāsa and vairāgya?
- How do abhyāsa and vairāgya relate to the study of yoga philosophy and/or reading this book? Specifically, what must you do (abhyāsa) or let go of (vairāgya) to get the most out of your study?
- What prevents you from establishing a daily meditation practice? What helps you in establishing a daily meditation practice?
- Write down your definition of the three components of an established practice (YS 1.14).
  - ~ How are you doing with regard to each?
  - ~ How do you think about that third component of practicing properly and with devotion?

- Consider abhyāsa and vairāgya as making the choices that take one farther down the path of yoga. Think of abhyāsa as what you need to do to say "yes" to your practice, and think of vairāgya as what you need to let go of or say "no" to. Make two columns labeled "yes" and "no" on a piece of paper. Then list specific actions to take under each.
- What parts of your life have more readily faded away as you've continued on the journey of yoga? What other things do you still need to let go of?

KEY TEACHINGS FROM PART V

- Śaktipāta involves the initial and subsequent awakenings that propel one on the path of yoga.
- Adhikāra relates to the degree to which a student is prepared, ready, and interested in receiving practices and teachings.
- The circumstance wherein one is spontaneously enlightened is known as anupāya, or "no method." The texts make it clear that this applies to an extremely small percentage of people.
- Students require yogic methods, or upāya, appropriate to where they are on their path of yoga.
- The core means to yoga is balancing regular practice with dispassion. (YS 1.12)
- Practice is established when done for a long time, without interruptions, and in the proper fashion—even reverently. (YS 1.14)

PART VI

How the Yoga of Meditation Works

Part VI is the crux of the book, describing how meditation works to align with the highest Sourceplace and refine your being. It starts with the story of the Churning of the Ocean, a metaphor for the practice of yoga. Then several aphorisms from the *Yoga Sūtra*, which outline how meditation addresses saṃskāric habit patterns, and some of the results of that are explored. Also discussed is the prevalent teaching of the *guṇas* and how meditation creates a more illumined awareness/*sattva buddhi*. Then we spiral back to the concepts of vikalpa-saṃskāra and bhāvanā, reflecting on how meditation affects understanding and yields greater insight into anything we turn our attention to.

CHAPTER 38

The Churning of the Ocean

One of the most famous and important core myths from India is that of the Churning of the Ocean. Its teachings are relevant not only to the practice of yoga, but also to life in general, and how to live your yoga.

As with many myths in the tradition, there are different versions from different sources. Several are from the Purāṇas, the literature that gathers together the many stories of the tradition. This particular one also appears in the great Indian epic, the *Mahābhārata.* The story, Churning of the Ocean, is embedded within a much longer narrative, so we will be dropping into the middle and extracting an abbreviated version of this story known as the Samudra Manthana or Sāgara Manthana. *Samudra* and *sāgara* are both words for the ocean, and *manthana* means "churning." Let's begin by enjoying the story; then we will reconsider some of the components with respect to its teachings.

Once upon a time, the *devas* and *asuras*—the gods and anti-gods (demons)—who usually were at odds with each other—realized they needed to work together to obtain the nectar of immortality, which resided in the ocean. To obtain the nectar, they had to churn the ocean to bring it forth.

To do so, they upended a mountain to use as the churning stick. They stuck its top into the ocean with a great tortoise as a base. Around that, they wrapped the snake named Vāsuki to use as a rope. (Vāsuki is the snake depicted in images of Śiva.) After some negotiation, the asuras took the snake's head, and the devas took its tail. They churned and churned and churned, yet the nectar was not emerging, and they became a little discouraged. Viṣṇu was summoned to help, and he gave them a pep talk that re-energized them to continue churning.

Finally, a great variety of treasures began to emerge from the ocean, including the crescent moon, the sun, the goddess Śrī (or Lakṣmī), a white horse, a great gem, and an albino elephant with four tusks. As these things emerged from the ocean, they were claimed and distributed in various ways to both the devas and the asuras. For example, Śiva adorned his hair with the crescent moon.

As the gods and demons continued to churn, what began to emerge was a viscous, deep-blue, radioactive-like substance that could paralyze the world with its vapors. This was a poison called *kālakūṭa* or *halāhala*. The substance was extremely noxious and somehow had to be dealt with to keep the poison from polluting the world. As in many of these stories, when things got difficult, Śiva was called upon to deal with the problem. Some accounts say he drank the poison; others say he put his finger in it and absorbed it that way. In either case, so that the world would not be obliterated by the poisonous substance, Śiva held it in his throat, where it was transmuted. The poison turned his throat blue, and this is how Śiva got his name Nīlakaṇṭha. *Nīla* means "blue," and *kaṇṭha* means "throat." This is one of Śiva's names: the Blue-Throated One, Nīlakaṇṭha.

Once the poison was dispensed with, the churning resumed, and several other things emerged from the ocean, including a wish-fulfilling cow. Finally, the physician of the gods emerged, holding a pot in which the nectar was held. The story goes on with more shenanigans between the asuras and devas, but we'll end it here and consider what it teaches us about the journey of yoga.

Part of the backstory of the tale is that the gods needed the demons to obtain the nectar, so they had a shared goal. Neither could do it alone, so they put aside their differences in service of a greater reward. There's a lot to think about in just that, especially regarding how society functions—or not! Gods and demons can be thought of as different parts of ourselves: we all have angelic and demonic qualities within us. Or, they can be thought of as different types of habit patterns, saṃskāras, which are pushing and pulling us in different directions. These different impulses are within us, and the question is: How can we work with them?

As the energy of the churners waned, Viṣṇu gave them a pep talk to keep the churning going. Viṣṇu represents all the people in your life—parents, friends, coaches, teachers—who serve to encourage you on the path of yoga and/or in life in general. This is a role of Viṣṇu, who always tries to restore the order of things. The lesson here is that when tired, discouraged, or when the going gets tough, we often need someone to give us encouragement or whatever is needed to take the next step. This is true especially on the path of yoga, which can be challenging at times. And sometimes that helpful person is yourself—remember that you are every character in the story.

One way to interpret the overall story is as a metaphor for the practice of meditation. The ocean is consciousness, which is churned as we practice. Often we practice and practice and nothing seems to be happening, and we might even want to stop. Hopefully we continue, perhaps with some encouragement from a teacher or someone else who is our Viṣṇu. We may begin to experience some of the fruits, or treasures, that emerge from the practice. There may also be challenges and "poison" that arise. We, as Śiva, must be able to hold and transmute that poison. It is part of the process. In the story, it is only after the poison has been emitted that the nectar emerges.

In the practice of yoga āsana or meditation, like the churners, we may want to quit after trying for a while. Sometimes this occurs after experiencing some of the benefits or treasures of the practice. Some people think the treasures they've received are enough, and there isn't more that they need. Or sometimes, when the poison comes up, many people decide that is the time to quit. They think it's too hard or that the practices aren't working, when in fact they *are* working precisely as they should. The poison that arises is exactly the junk that we need to work through and move beyond to experience healing and wholeness. Unfortunately, some people want only the jewels of the practice without experiencing the inevitable poison.

When we do yoga, whether the physical āsana practice or meditation, there's a naturally occurring cleaning-out of all that obstructs us: the saṃskāras, all the old crud from previous actions. On the physical level, āsana can take us to the sticky places, physically or psychologically—or both. When moving in āsana practice, we come up against physical limitations. These can be patterns in the body established from lack of movement, from holding ourselves in particular ways, from old injuries, or for any number of reasons. Working through these limitations can be challenging and even painful at times, yet hopefully we eventually receive the joy of more ease in the body. In āsana practice, we may also have to deal with old, reactive psychological patterns.

Likewise, when the mind is moved inwardly in meditation practice, we encounter whatever blocks us. The muck is invariably stirred up. Sometimes this process is so mild we don't even notice it, like we may not notice the effects of a gentle stretch or feel a soft breeze on our skin. At other times during that inward turn, the cleaning out of saṃskāras will be registered in various ways at the surface of awareness.

When meditating, we might begin to feel agitated physically, emotionally, or mentally. Or, we might simply start having thoughts. That's why it is completely normal for thoughts to arise during meditation: it's part of the process. The thoughts are likely unrelated to what is being encountered and cleaned out at the depths, so there's no need to analyze them. The thoughts or agitation that arise during meditation are a byproduct of this natural cleansing of awareness when moving from the surface to the depths to contact the deepest layers of our self, toward a greater awareness.

While going through this process, there's a danger that the poison will spill out into the world, which was the concern of those churning the ocean. When experiencing agitation or stuff coming up in practice and daily life, we may be tempted to lash out or otherwise project the poison onto others. Instead, as yogis, we must be Śiva and transmute that poison within ourselves rather than polluting the world with it.

A word for the nectar is *amṛta. Mṛta* means "death," and with the *a* negating that, it is called the nectar of immortality. It is also called *soma*, which is found in many different contexts in the tradition. For example, soma is a mysterious substance heralded in the Vedas, an ambrosia of sorts. There is much to say about soma, but for now, soma can be thought of as an energy that aids healing. And the story, Churning of the Ocean, teaches us that practice will inevitably yield this healing energy if we stick with it.

As we move along the path of yoga, doing our practices, at times there will be delight/ānanda, health, and healing. But remember, the nectar/amṛta emerges only after the poison has been dealt with. And truthfully, sometimes what we think is poison is actually nectar, once it is held and transmuted. We may have an experience that at the time seems like the worst thing to happen to us, but when we look back on our life we realize it was the impetus for change, growth, and healing. This was my experience of turning to yoga after a heartbreak. It turned out to be the greatest blessing of my life. **Sometimes practice yields beautiful experiences and results, and other times it is challenging. Yet ultimately the nectar of healing yields an alignment with the Highest, leading to a beneficial refinement of one's entire being, as well as life as a whole.**

This story can also teach us about the practice of svādhyāya/self-study in both the sense of studying the texts and of studying ourselves. The process of studying the texts can feel like poison sometimes. It can be challenging and exasperating. Yet when we persevere, hold it in awareness with the practice of bhāvanā, sit in a place of confusion, stay with it, and write what comes out, the nectar of increased understanding can appear. Similar things happen when exploring aspects of our personal lives that are challenging.

It is Śiva who is the god powerful enough to take in the poison and transmute it. In doing so, it turns his throat blue. The throat is the center of language and speaking one's truth. There's a lot to say about the power and role of language in Tantra, but for now, know that transmuting the poison that arises within and that *must* be dealt with, aligns you with the Highest and refines your individuality. Then what emerges in awareness and in words will begin to reflect a greater Truth.

In some versions of this story, Śiva comes in the form of Sadāśiva, who is associated with mantra, a tool in sādhanā. Mantras can be used for meditation. They can be recited internally or out loud in the practice called *japa*. Japa (which emerges from the throat) is a powerful tool for transmuting energy.

Finally, I love that one of the things that emerges from the act of churning the ocean is the wish-fulfilling cow. As my practice has progressed, it is my experience that my wishes—my desires and intentions/saṃkalpa—become more auspicious and aligned with the Highest. And my wishes actually start to manifest, sometimes in ways that I could never have imagined.

REFLECT AND EXPLORE

- Contemplate any aspect of the Churning of the Ocean story that speaks to you.
- How are you every character in this story? For example, consider the role of Viṣṇu on the path of yoga and life. Who has been your Viṣṇu? How have you been Viṣṇu to others?
- What treasures have emerged from your practice(s)? Consider the practices of āsana, meditation, and any other practices you do.
- How have you experienced poison arising in your practice, and how have you handled it?
- How have you eventually noticed more healing or joy after a "poisonous" experience?
- Consider this story as a metaphor for social upheaval, challenge, and change. What does it teach us?

CHAPTER 39

The Process and Effects of Meditation

The Churning of the Ocean story is a metaphor for how meditation works. When we meditate, the ocean of consciousness is churned, and from that, various gifts and poisons arise. One of the misconceptions about the path of yoga is that it is all "light and love," but as the story indicates, there will be many times when poison rises to the surface. The challenges we must confront are exactly what must be dealt with to refine awareness and align with the Highest. Remember Gaṇeśa, or Vighneśvara, as the Lord of Obstacles. The tradition explicitly acknowledges that there will be challenges and that we will need to call upon this quality of the Highest to confront, negotiate, and resolve everything that obstructs access to the highest within ourselves, so that eventually the nectar can emerge.

In this chapter, some sūtras from the *Yoga Sūtra* that describe how the practice/abhyāsa of meditation works to remove the problematic saṃskāras and shift our state of being are examined. In doing so, we will continue to consider some of the misconceptions around the path of yoga. This chapter covers quite a few teachings with depths of meaning and philosophical nuance, but to start they are presented at an introductory level to begin to understand how yoga works.

Remember that the citta-vṛttis are the thoughts and feelings in everyday awareness that guide behavior and have consequences for your life experience. They are the result of those underlying saṃskāras, the latent impressions laid down by previous actions/karmas that activate current behavior.

In popular culture, karma is thought of as something bad that happens to us, as in "bad karma," but karma is simply the result of our actions, good and bad. When I first studied Classical Yoga, I learned that all thoughts should be stopped (YS 1.2), and I thought that all saṃskāras were bad, in line with the general renunciate thrust of the *Yoga Sūtra.* Yet Patañjali acknowledges that some saṃskāras are useful on the path of yoga. In sūtra 1.5, he says the citta-vṛttis are of two types: *kliṣṭa* and *akliṣṭa*, afflicted or unafflicted, detrimental or nondetrimental. This sūtra suggests that **the karmas, saṃskāras, and citta-vṛttis can be a help or hindrance on the path of yoga.** Again, we are approaching these teachings to understand their implications for how yoga works, without attending to philosophical details. The main point for now is that saṃskāras, karmas, and citta-vṛttis can be either problematic or useful as one moves along the path.

YS 1.5 *vṛttayaḥ pañcatayaḥ kliṣṭa-akliṣṭāḥ*
vṛttayaḥ: fluctuations [of mind] (as in YS 1.2)
pañca-tayaḥ: fivefold
kliṣṭa: afflicted, painful, or detrimental
akliṣṭāḥ: non-afflicted, not painful, not producing suffering
There are five types of [citta-]vṛttis, and they can be detrimental or not.

At the beginning of chapter 2 of the *Yoga Sūtra* (the chapter on sādhanā/practice), Patañjali outlines *kriyā-yoga*, a yoga of action (YS 2.1). In the following sutra (YS 2.2), he describes how this yoga works to refine one's being in two ways. First, it helps attenuate the kleśas/impediments; second, it serves to cultivate samādhi, the deep state of meditative absorption. As considered in chapter 30, the primary kleśa is avidyā/ignorance (YS 2.4). Some call it spiritual ignorance, not knowing who you are beyond the surface of life. This is yet another way the tradition explains how the true Self is concealed. YS 2.2 says that yoga helps address the root obstructions to the heart, the kleśas, and yoga/meditation also creates samādhi. Remember that samādhi is a series of progressively deeper and immersive states of awareness resulting from the practice of meditation.

YS 2.2 *samādhi-bhāvana-arthaḥ kleśa-tanū-karaṇa-arthaś ca*
samādhi: state of meditative immersion
bhāvana: cultivating, causing, bringing about
artha: meaning, purpose
kleśa: affliction, impediment
tanū-karaṇa: attenuating, making weak
artha: purpose
ca: and
The purpose [of kriyā-yoga/the yoga of action] is samādhi/ meditative immersion and attenuating the kleśas/afflictions.

This is exactly why meditation is an effective way to create changes at the surface of life by directly addressing these underlying mechanisms of the kleśas and saṃskāras, which prompt us toward feeling and acting in particular ways based on past actions/karma. It is very hard to get to the root of the saṃskāras by working only with the surface mind and behaviors. Through meditation, you go deeper than the surface to the saṃskāric seeds and burn them up, so they will no longer sprout.

In the garden of our lives, if there are weeds that need eliminated, it takes some effort to pull them out. Sometimes we have to dig deep to get at the root. But if the plant has fully matured and gone to seed, and if any seeds from that plant have been allowed to remain, they will sprout when the conditions are right. So **working on the surface of life with the saṃskāras can be effective to some degree, but meditation helps burn up the seeds of saṃskāras and attenuate the kleśas, the root hindrances.**

This is the teaching of the *dagdha-bīja*, the burnt seed, which is alluded to in several places in the text (See, for example, YS 2.4). These seeds can be latent, just waiting for the right conditions to sprout, as in the gardening analogy. When the mind finally comes to rest in meditation, the seeds of saṃskāras are burnt up and can no longer sprout.

In the *Yoga Sūtra*, meditation is emphasized as *the* method for knowing our true selves. The process of meditation acts on the deepest layers of individuality to remove (burn up) the saṃskāras and attenuate the kleśas, clearing a pathway to the true Self. YS 1.47 says that in the deepest states of samādhi, awareness is clarified, revealing the inner Self.

YS 1.47 *nirvicāra-vaiśāradye-adhyātma-prasādaḥ*
nirvicāra: a state of samādhi without any thought
vaiśāradye: lucidity, clarity, pure flow
adhyātma: inner Self
prasādaḥ: clarity, purity, luminosity
In the lucidity of nirvicāra-samādhi, there is clarity of the inner Self.

When you meditate, several things happen simultaneously that serve to shift and refine awareness, thus supporting the recognition/pratyabhijñā of the deepest Self. When turning the mind inward during meditation practice, awareness starts to traverse from the surface layers to the subtler layers. With repeated practice the habit pattern of moving into deeper places inside is cultivated. You are creating inward-moving saṃskāras. **Meditating establishes the saṃskāra/habit pattern of moving awareness from the surface to deeper layers, to the deepest part of oneself.**

As you move deeper into meditation, you also move away from the surface activity of the mind—those choppy waves at the surface of awareness—into the quieter depths. As the mind calms down, you may notice that the breath and the nervous system settle, which has all sorts of positive effects on your overall mental and physical health. Eventually, the mind completely rests in a state of samādhi, absent of any thought.

Patañjali goes on to say in Sūtra 1.48: from this state of awareness comes truth-bearing wisdom. This can be thought of as the underlying Truth of Reality. Truth here isn't simply some factual knowledge, it is the fundamental Truth of revelation, an awareness that there is nothing that is not Śiva (nāśivaṃ vidyate kvacit). The seer/draṣṭṛ is fully present (YS 1.3).

This deep state of yoga yields the wisdom that is the opposite of avidyā/ignorance. That is, you gain the knowledge of the deepest Self. So there is a direct experience of that Truth rather than just an intellectual understanding. And that leads to seeing the truth in a lot of different ways. **One obtains the highest knowledge regarding the nature of reality, and this will lead to insight into the nature of many different**

things (YS 1.48). This insight is what helps one make smart choices in life. It helps one respond more gracefully, and it supports the processes of svādhyāya/self-study, vikalpa-saṃskāra/refinement of understanding, and bhāvanā/contemplation, among many other effects.

YS 1.48 *ṛtaṃ-bharā tatra prajñā*
ṛtaṃ: truth
bharā: bearing
tatra: that, there
prajñā: wisdom, the highest knowledge and insight
There is truth-bearing wisdom in that state [of samādhi].

The experience of steeping awareness in the deep spaces of consciousness creates a different type of saṃskāra. YS 1.50 teaches about two types of saṃskāras. There are those more conventional saṃskāras discussed at length in previous chapters. Then there are the saṃskāras born of that truth-bearing wisdom referred to in YS 1.48. Sūtra 1.50 basically says that this latter type of saṃskāra, which arises from the experience of this flash of wisdom, acts to obstruct other saṃskāras. So **the practice of meditation creates obstructor saṃskāras that don't activate awareness with citta-vṛttis like other saṃskāras. Instead, they put a damper on the outward-moving saṃskāras, even destroying them. (YS 1.50)** With continued practice, this has the effect of eliminating the influence of those old saṃskāras/subliminal activators we're carrying around from previous life experiences. And this is a continuing and reiterative process.

As practice continues, more and more of the problematic saṃskāras are burnt up and cleaned out. As indicated in the Churning of the Ocean story, the poison has to be extracted before the amṛta/nectar is released. Many times the removal of the poison may not even register in our surface awareness, and at other times smoky residue from the burning of the saṃskāras may be experienced. At times on the path of yoga, we may feel agitated or otherwise disquieted as these old saṃskāras are churned up. In general, this is not a conscious process with some clear cause and effect specific to particular saṃskāras. We simply might find ourselves feeling "off," and that is the time to turn to Viṣṇu, in the form of a teacher or a wiser part of ourselves, to remind us to keep going with the practice, because ultimately the amṛta/nectar will emerge.

YS 1.50 *taj-jaḥ saṃskāro 'nya-saṃskāra-pratibandhī*
tat: that [truth-bearing wisdom]
jaḥ: born
saṃskāra: subliminal impressions/activators
anya: other
saṃskāra: subliminal impressions/activators
pratibandhī: obstructing, preventing
Saṃskāras born from that [truth-bearing wisdom] obstruct other saṃskāras.

At the same time we're burning up problematic saṃskāras, our meditation practice produces the obstructing or inhibiting saṃskāras (YS 1.50). A commentary on the *Yoga Sūtra* says that these blocking saṃskāras enhance the experience of samādhi, creating more of the wisdom saṃskāras, which block the others, and so on. As well, remember that meditation helps establish the habit of moving awareness internally. All of this eventually leads us to have fewer citta-vṛttis and experiencing more calm during meditation. The obstructer saṃskāras are a way that our awareness is reorganized. In this way, awareness is slowly clarified. This clarity of awareness is known as *sattva buddhi*, which is explored in the next chapter.

REFLECT AND EXPLORE

- Review the aphorisms and teachings from this chapter.
  - ~ Contemplate any of the teachings you feel drawn to or find challenging.
  - ~ Describe how you have experienced these teachings.
  - ~ How do these teachings relate to how you approach the practice of yoga?
- Consider how the teachings relate to the Churning of the Ocean story.
- If you have a meditation practice, how have you noticed the release of old patterns and/or a greater clarity?

CHAPTER 40

The *Guṇas* and *Sattva Buddhi*: Clarifying Awareness

The teaching of the *guṇas* is prevalent throughout the yoga world. *Guṇa* means "strand" or "quality." **The guṇas are three primary qualities, or threads, that make up the fabric of the world, including individual awareness**, as part of that manifest world. Everything in relative reality is some combination of these qualities. **The three types of guṇas are *sattva, rajas,* and *tamas.* Sattva is luminous, harmonious, intelligent, and pure. Rajas is active, fiery, energetic, and passionate. Tamas is inertia, dull, heavy, and dark.** Sometimes the state of sattva is described as equilibrium, suggesting that sattva is a balanced state of rajas and tamas. Given that yoga is about joining or finding the balance, it makes sense that the balance of rajas and tamas is sattva.

Applied to our individuality, the guṇas can describe different physical and psychological modes of being. Rajas is very energetic, even aggressive; tamas is sluggish and dull; and sattva is calm and compassionate. So again, one might argue sattva is the balance of the other two extremes. Many of us find ourselves bouncing from one of these extremes to another. In some periods of my life, I have been quite tamasic: very lazy, eating heavy foods, drinking alcohol, and so on. At other times I have been super rajasic, especially when stressed and overcommitted. Then I work nonstop, drink too much caffeine, and can be very short and irritable with people. Everything in existence, including us, is some combination of these three qualities. Feeling endarkened, concealed or disconnected—maybe even depressed—is tamasic. Feeling agitated, distracted, or being pulled out into the world, is rajasic. And feeling connected and light is sattvic.

Ultimately the guṇas are another way of considering how to live your yoga. Examining how the guṇas work to facilitate (or not) cultivating a connection with the Heart and living life from that place, is a critical part of the yogi's journey. This is one approach to self-care.

Coming back to my own example, if I am feeling tamasic, tired, or sad, I cannot be productive or creative. So how can I generate just a little more rajas to find the sattvic balance? In general, for me this is addressed through my physical body, by making sure I am getting enough rest and exercise and clarifying my diet.

On the other hand, when night rolls around, I occasionally find myself hyped up and way too rajasic. Sometimes this is bodily, like from too much caffeine, but it can also be mental: too much news or social media, for example. So I know that I need to monitor the intake of these substances as my day progresses.

Sattva can be cultivated at all the levels of life, including the body and the mind, as already suggested. Ultimately, however, we must cultivate sattva in the buddhi, that part of citta/mind that is the individual light or soul, close to the highest Self. So "self-care" is ultimately about taking care of this place of the heart inside. This agenda of maximizing sattva is taught in many texts, for example in the *Bhagavad Gītā* and also in Patañjali's *Yoga Sūtra*. And yoga, particularly meditation, is a primary means of cultivating sattva. For example, YS 1.47 (see chapter 39) says that steeping in the deep state of samādhi yields clarity of the innermost self. **During meditation, one penetrates to quieter, clearer states of awareness. Then individuality is suffused with sattvic clarity, and life unfolds from this clearer place.**

Many of us create sattva physically through diet and exercise. For example, we create a more sattvic body by eating foods that are more sattvic. The practice of yoga āsana can contribute to a more sattvic condition in the body-mind. Also, consider what is taken in mentally through the senses. For example, what we read and watch: is it more sattvic, more rajasic, or more tamasic? (Remember PH 5: Awareness contracts around objects of perception.) And YS 1.47 indicates that the deep state of samādhi in meditation infuses the innermost self with this quality of sattva/lucidity.

So one agenda of meditation is specifically and purposefully geared toward creating sattva buddhi through the burning up of saṃskāras and infusing the innermost self with the luminous quality of the Highest.

More clarity in the buddhi yields less reactivity and more ability for mindfulness, being present to what is actually happening rather than activating and enacting deleterious saṃskāric patterns.

REFLECT AND EXPLORE

- Write down your definition of the three guṇas.
- How do you see the guṇas manifesting in each of the levels in your life? How do you work with them? Specifically consider:
  - The physical: How do different substances (like food, alcohol, caffeine) affect your physical well-being, your overall energy, your digestion? How is your sleep affected? What is the effect of moving the body (or not)?
  - The mind: How is your mind affected by these different substances? Also consider what you bring into your mind: what you view or listen to via electronics, books, art, etc. How do all these "inputs" affect your overall state of being? For example, do you feel foggy, clear, sad, agitated, or centered?
- How do the guṇas impact the choices and actions you make in your life?

CHAPTER 41

Refinement of Awareness and Spontaneous Insight: *Vikalpa-Saṃskāra* and *Bhāvanā* Revisited

At this point, it will be useful and interesting to spiral back to the notions of vikalpa-saṃskāra and bhāvanā to reiterate how the process of aligning and refining uplevels our life. For this discussion, I am indebted to my teacher Paul Muller-Ortega, who has uniquely brought these teachings forward. (His seminal article on this topic is cited in appendix IV).

Previously we discussed the notion of vikalpa-saṃskāra, primarily as it relates to conceptual understanding. We learned that when we study and work with the teachings, understanding becomes clearer, more refined. In addition, with practice, the general field of awareness becomes more refined, and that clarity itself aids in understanding. These are both aspects of vikalpa-saṃskāra. As we're discussing in this part of the book, the process of meditation in particular refines our whole being, leading to this refinement of our awareness field, including thoughts.

The engine here is all the practices that refine awareness, but primarily the practice of meditation. Through practice, awareness itself becomes more sattvic/purified. So the field into which we place anything about which we wish to have greater insight has also undergone vikalpa-saṃskāra/refinement. With access to these clearer and deeper layers of awareness, anything placed into that space can be seen more clearly. This increased ability to more directly perceive the truth (YS 1.48) is how the contemplative practice, bhāvanā, becomes successful. The deeper we penetrate in meditation, the more wisdom will come forward when a teaching is placed in our awareness for contemplation.

Meditation establishes that pathway to the deepest Self, which will impact everything we do, including bhāvanā. As awareness itself is more refined, we are better able to penetrate into the meaning of the teachings. **The more refined one's general state of awareness becomes through practice, the more successful the svādhyāya/self-study and bhāvanā/contemplation practices will be, as the process of vikalpa-saṃskāra/refinement is also supported.**

As awareness becomes more and more refined, and as the access ramp to Source is more available, the processes of vikalpa-saṃskāra and bhāvanā get sped up. The ability to receive insights that previously required more analytical or contemplative work begins to arise spontaneously in real time, and seemingly out of nowhere. Thus the ability to both think and act in an aligned and refined way is more available on a moment-by-moment basis. We have greater access to that wisdom in our daily lives. This is why some of the yogic masters are called ṛṣis/seers—because of their access to this wisdom. In short, through our practices, awareness becomes less contracted, everything becomes less concealed to us, and the revelations naturally flow. You may have already had a glimpse of this.

Have you noticed how sometimes you feel in the flow and connected, and able to say and do the right thing? At other times, however, things feel clunky, and you put your foot in your mouth and say something stupid. Later, after shifting into a less contracted place, it comes to you how to handle the situation better. As awareness is refined through practice, there are more experiences of being in the flow and fewer experiences of disconnection.

As we move along the path of yoga, the practices churn up agitation or poison and we may think of a perfect comeback or some way to zing someone that reflects or perpetuates more contraction. It is important to remember that at the surface of life, we and others are relatively limited beings and that sometimes what arises in awareness may still be unclear or limited because it comes from a less than perfectly clarified state of awareness. I mention this as a way to introduce some humility, as we must stay open-minded and acknowledge that our perspective may have limitations that can lead to more or less accurate conclusions.

Yet, we do get clearer as those limitations are removed and dust is cleaned off our heart. One reason we are exploring vikalpa-saṃskāra and bhāvanā more deeply now is to acknowledge that the teachings may be unclear to us for a whole variety of reasons. But if you continue to honor them by doing the practices of svādhyāya, bhāvanā, meditation, and all the rest, you *will* get clearer. And this is the process of vikalpa-saṃskāra.

REFLECT AND EXPLORE

- If you have a meditation practice, how have you noticed an increase of insight and understanding over time?

KEY TEACHINGS FROM PART VI

- Sometimes practice yields beautiful experiences and results, and other times it is challenging. Yet ultimately the nectar of healing yields an alignment with the Highest, leading to a beneficial refinement of one's entire being, as well as life as a whole.
- The karmas, saṃskāras, and citta-vṛttis can be a help or hindrance on the path of yoga.
- Working on the surface of life with the saṃskāras can be effective to some degree, but meditation helps burn up the seeds of saṃskāras and attenuate the kleśas, the root hindrances.
- Meditating establishes the saṃskāra/habit pattern of moving awareness from the surface to deeper layers, to the deepest part of oneself.
- One obtains the highest knowledge regarding the nature of reality, and this will lead to insight into the nature of many different things. (YS 1.48)
- The practice of meditation creates obstructor saṃskāras that don't activate awareness with citta-vṛttis like other saṃskāras. Instead, they put a damper on the outward-moving saṃskāras, even destroying them. (YS 1.50)
- The guṇas are three primary qualities, or threads, that make up the fabric of the world, including individual awareness.
- The three types of guṇas are sattva, rajas, and tamas. Sattva is luminous, harmonious, intelligent, and pure. Rajas is active, fiery, energetic, and passionate. Tamas is inertia, dull, heavy, and dark.
- During meditation, one penetrates to quieter, clearer states of awareness. Then individuality is suffused with sattvic clarity, and life unfolds from this clearer place.
- The more refined one's general state of awareness becomes through practice, the more successful the svādhyāya/self-study and bhāvanā/contemplation practices will be, as the process of vikalpa-saṃskāra/refinement is also supported.

PART VII

Enlightenment

In the journey of yoga, we've considered how individuality arises from the ocean of Consciousness, and then how we can get stuck in the eddies—in saṃsāra—in which we have forgotten the Source and live our lives captivated by the surface drama.

Part VII deals with a concept that is central to the tradition and the focus of the journey, yet it is hard to describe, wherein we break the bonds of limitation to rest in the heart of who we are. In the following chapters, we discuss various ways the tradition describes this indescribable state, including the teaching that there are progressive stages in the journey beyond those outlined in Classical Yoga. The last chapter addresses the state in which we live fully in the world while liberated: *jīvan-mukti.*

CHAPTER 42

Stages of the Journey

As I've already mentioned, it is common to think of revelation or enlightenment as a switch that gets turned on: from that moment, the light pervades. Yet for most of us, the experience of enlightenment is more like a journey toward that all-pervasive light. Remember how the malas/impurities were described as dust or veils over the innermost Self? For most people, the journey is a gradual and progressive removal and unveiling of all that obscures the Heart.

The journey of yoga has different stations or stages, called *bhūmis*. Movement or progress in most aspects of life occurs with a sequential unfolding. Sometimes the movement is hard to discern in the short term. Yet we plant a seed, and under the right conditions, it sprouts, grows, bears fruit, and produces more seeds. And all of the stages are astonishing, *vismaya*. I'm always amazed to see the seeds I planted in the garden move through the mysterious process of sequential growth. Likewise, I've been joyfully amazed and full of wonder at the sequential unfolding of my journey of meditation.

SS 1.12 *vismayo yoga-bhūmikāḥ*
vismaya: wonder, amazement, astonishment
yoga: yoga
bhūmikāḥ: steps, stages
The stages of yoga are amazing.

The stages of yoga are amazing, says SS 1.12. The teachings of different lineages describe different stages and milestones along the way and argue about what the ultimate state of enlightenment is. The details of this are beyond the present scope and, practically speaking, less important until we approach these places in our own awareness. Nonetheless, this will be briefly considered in the context of what is discussed in this book.

Remember that Patañjali defines yoga as stopping all the thoughts (YS 1.2). Ultimately this requires achieving a state of samādhi that is completely without any thoughts or concepts, known as *nirvikalpa* or *nirbīja samādhi* (YS 1.51). Because this is a state beyond conceptual thinking, it is difficult to describe. It's hard to even register this space in awareness because when we're experiencing it, subjectivity is dissolved. It's an extremely internalized state of awareness wherein one is completely withdrawn from the material world and all thoughts have stopped/nirodha.

Recall that the *Yoga Sūtra* gives us the teaching that when the mind is stilled (YS 1.2), the Seer abides (YS 1.3). **Traversing the path, creating a sattva buddhi and purifying the saṃskāras, dispels ignorance and our luminous essential nature is revealed. This is a state of Self-realization.**

Different streams in the tradition, with their different philosophical predispositions, name these states in various ways. The *Yoga Sūtra* uses the term *kaivalya* (See, for example, YS 2.25), which means "aloneness." It is aloneness in the sense that the true self has been separated from all the impurities of our ordinary being. This represents the removal of ignorance/avidyā and realization of the Self. It is likened to cleaning the dust off the mirror into which we look, so that we can see ourselves.

Recall that in the Tillai Forest, Patañjali received the teachings of Classical Yoga, but Vyāghrapāda asked for more. That "more" is reflected in Tantra's further elaboration of the nature of reality, of Consciousness, and the progressively higher states of awareness moving toward recognition of *caitanyam ātmā* (SS 1.1). Consciousness is the Self. The Self is Consciousness.

Tantra views the deep states of samādhi as a stage on the path to further states of awareness, wherein one realizes that they are nothing but Śiva and that there is nothing that is not Śiva. So, there is a close-eyed experience of revelation in meditation, which expands to

an open-eyed experience of everything as absolute Consciousness. One can penetrate beyond the surface appearance of things—beyond the waves dancing on the ocean—to see the oceanic Source alive and present in everything.

Remember, we are not moving somewhere foreign, but into the depths of our own Heart. Nonetheless, as we move along the path of yoga through these stages and states, it can be disorienting. That's why a teacher-guide is so important to help us understand where we are and how to further negotiate the path of yoga.

REFLECT AND EXPLORE

- How have you experienced stages in your journey of yoga?

CHAPTER 43

The Expanded State of Consciousness

The venerable text of the *Śiva Sūtra* provides a sūtra that encapsulates the teachings in this section. SS 1.5 acknowledges that point at which the light turns on in a flash. Some tipping point has occurred. This sūtra says the upsurge is Bhairava, a name for Śiva. In a flash, there is an opening—an upsurge—of awareness that I Am Śiva.

SS 1.5 *udyamo bhairavaḥ*
udyamo: upsurge, flash, opening
bhairava: a name/form of Śiva
The upsurge is Bhairava [Śiva].

Sūtra 13 from the *Pratyabhijñā-hṛdayam* expands the understanding of recognizing the Self. You may notice that this sūtra is the inverse of PH 5, which we considered in chapter 27. Recall that this earlier sūtra describes manifestation, how the expansive state of the heart (cetana) contracts to become individual awareness, the mind/citta. Here in Sūtra 13, we see that an inward turn of awareness allows for a return to that expanded state (cetana), an awareness of the Heart, a full knowledge (parijñāne) of who we are. This knowledge is sometimes described as a sense of expansion into the fullness of ourselves, *pūrṇa-ahaṃ*, or "I am full." The specific methods/upāya to facilitate the inward-facing turn (antarmukhī-bhāvena) through progressively deeper states of consciousness must be received from a qualified teacher.

PH 13 *tat-parijñāne cittam-eva antarmukhī-bhāvena cetana-padādhyārohāt citiḥ*
tat: that [the pañca-kṛtyas/five acts]
parijñāne: full knowledge
cittam-eva: mind itself
antarmukhī-bhāvena: through inward-facing
cetana: uncontracted or expanded Consciousness
padādhyārohāt: ascending to the state
citi: absolute Consciousness
When one fully realizes that [one is the enactor of the pañca-kṛtyas/five acts of Śiva], through inward movement the individual mind ascends to expanded consciousness and becomes Consciousness.

PH 13 starts with "When one fully realizes that. . . ." "That" in this sūtra refers to the five acts/pañca-kṛtyas (covered in chapter 26), and specifically an awareness that you, as Śiva, are the enactor of the pañca-kṛtyas. Recall that PH 9 (covered in chapters 31 and 32) indicates that the covering of the malas leads to limited awareness and delusion about one's powers. PH 13 says that **the inward-turning practices of yoga illuminate an awareness that you, at essence, are creating, sustaining, and dissolving experience. Also, you take part in concealing and revealing the heart. Recognizing this, you become the Heart (Citi).** You know your true Self.

That may sound like a bit of a word salad, which is why some traditions simply do not try to explain this profound experience of recognizing the Heart. And, as we have discussed, any description lands in the student's awareness to the degree that they have the ability/adhikāra to understand, which is dependent on where they are on their individual journey. However, the Tantric tradition reveres both knowledge and language, so even though difficult, it seeks to articulate an understanding of the aim of yoga, called by many names.

It is the practice of yoga, particularly meditation, that pivots awareness into the depth to uncover the heart of who we are. We just need to recognize the heart that is always there. Naṭarāja's arm that occludes the heart points to his graceful upturned foot of revelation/anugraha. When we come to this recognition of the true Self, ignorance about who we are is diminished. Previously we thought the individual life wave was enacting our lives. We think we are in control and that we are the doer (remember the kārma-mala). In this sūtra we recognize that we are the ocean that is generating the waves. We understand that Śiva is performing the five acts *as us*. The individuality (ego, personality) is not in control. We experience a shift in self-identity. And indeed, our whole perception of the world is shifted.

This discussion highlights the arc of the yogic journey. We started with the "highest first," a vision of the unlimited Absolute reality, which is none other than our very Self. Then we learned how that Highest reality contracts, becomes covered over, and manifests individuality into this material world. We then considered how the journey of yoga helps us uncover our hearts and move from a place of concealment to a place of revelation.

The traditions of yoga use many words to describe this indescribable goal and state of yoga. I struggled with what to call part VII of this book and settled on the word *enlightenment* because it's one most of us have heard and have an impression of. Different lineage streams speak of this state of awareness with different words: pratyabhijñā, nirvāṇa, mokṣa, enlightenment, liberation. These lofty terms make it seem distant and unattainable. Yet as we've considered, it is close—it is as close as our hearts. The Divine is within us, *is* us. It is the light by which we see. It is inside and around us. We are It. We are the ocean of Consciousness. Realizing this, we experience oneness and understand that we are Śiva and that there is nothing that is not Śiva. We experience the heart of who we are.

The yogic journey is just that: a journey. It has its ups and downs, pauses and accelerations, and sometimes side trips. Truly it is a journey that never ends, even as we make progress toward greater awareness. We are using the metaphor of the yoga path as a journey, but it is important to note that we don't have to go somewhere to get something we don't already have. Revelation/anugraha or recognition/pratyabhijñā is simply becoming aware of who we are at essence. However, if we fail to register that essence, it is like it's not there.

Many of us begin with an experience of some sort of awakening, which hopefully leads us to seek out a teacher, teachings, and practices to move us farther along the journey. As we've seen, the journey is a process of aligning with the Highest and refining our very being, uncovering the heart of who we are.

It may come initially as a glimmer or a flash, a momentary glimpse, or an awakening that, when nurtured through practice, becomes a full-blown experience of expanded awareness. Ultimately all that conceals the heart is attenuated, and we are led to the revelation that we are nothing but Śiva. We recognize who we are at essence. We understand that we are more than our surface lives, history, and personality. We are not separate. We are Consciousness itself.

This is a profound and important step on the path. But according to Tantra, understanding "there is nothing that is not Śiva/nāśivaṃ vidyate kvacit" means that we are aware not only that *we* are Śiva—but so is all of the manifest world.

REFLECT AND EXPLORE

- Contemplate the concept of spiritual liberation.
  - ~ How would you describe it?
  - ~ How have you experienced it?
  - ~ How do you think of the journey?
- Consider how you create more or less revelation or concealment in your life.
- Practice and note your experience(s): Observe how you are the performer of the pañca-kṛtyas/five acts at the different levels of being.
  - ~ Watch your breath and how it moves through you. Where does the breath come from? Consider the breath as a divine pulsation moving through you.
  - ~ Observe your thought process. Watch how thoughts arise (creation), persist for some time (maintenance), then dissolve (dissolution). Notice the moment before a thought: the space from which a thought arises.
  - ~ Similarly observe your actions. Notice the moment when the impulse to act arises into awareness before you act.

CHAPTER 44

Jīvan-Mukti: Living While Liberated

***Jīvan-mukti* means "living while liberated." It indicates that one can be liberated while in the body and live in the world in that liberated state.** This is in contrast to some philosophies that assert that full liberation occurs only at death. So this concept further distinguishes the Tantric householder practice, reiterating that the practices and their results can be applied and experienced by those who have productive lives in the world. In fact, the yogic practices enhance life in ways we will be exploring in this and the following chapters.

The prerequisite for jīvan-mukti is *mukti*, a word the tradition uses for spiritual liberation, recognizing that you, and everything else, is nothing but Śiva, as we just considered in chapter 43. When this awareness permeates our entire waking life on a moment-by-moment basis it is known as *jīvan-mukti.*

Again, we often think that liberation is an on-or-off experience, but for most people, it is a process in which we have momentary revelations with progressive and increasing overall clarity. We might have a flash of recognition that pervades awareness during meditation and that even persists for some time afterward, then slowly fades. When the experience no longer fades and we're firmly established in that place at all times, that is jīvan-mukti.

Sūtra 16 from the *Pratyabhijñā-hṛdayam* speaks to jīvan-mukti and ties it to the experience of cit-ānanda, consciousness and bliss, or the bliss of consciousness, two of the pañca-śaktis/five powers we considered in chapter 25. This sūtra says that jīvan-mukti is the experience of the bliss of Consciousness, even as we experience life as embodied beings.

PH 16 *cit-ānanda-lābhe dehādiṣu cetyamāneṣv api cidaikātmya-pratipatti-dārḍhyaṃ jīvan-muktiḥ*
cit: absolute Consciousness
ānanda: bliss
lābhe: attainment
deha: body
ādiṣu: and so on
cetyamāneṣu: perceivable
api: even
cit-aikātmya: identical or one with Consciousness
pratipatti: attaining, ascertainment
dārḍhyaṃ: firm, stable, steady
jīvan-muktiḥ: liberation while embodied
When the bliss of the Highest is attained, along with a steady perception of the body and everything as Consciousness, this is liberation while embodied.

Jīvan-mukti is predicated on the stabilization of the awareness and recognition that everything is Consciousness/Śiva/Cit/Citi. This is a full experience and understanding of "*caitanyam ātmā* (SS 1.1)," and all the other teachings of the "highest first." Jīvan-mukti isn't a matter of feigning liberation while going about ordinary life. Instead, it is something that flows naturally from the state of mukti.

In his commentary on PH 16, Kṣemarāja suggests a way of working with and extending the experiences of oneness into everyday life. For example, we may experience a sense of heightened awareness during or after practicing yoga āsana or meditation. When emerging from practice, Kṣemarāja suggests staying present and aware in that space of transition called *vyutthānu*. This can allow us to progressively retain the expanded state as we move into daily life. (This teaching is more fully addressed in PH 19).

What is it like to live in this state of jīvan-mukti? It is truly the lived experience of nāśivaṃ vidyate kvacit ("There is nothing that is not

Śiva.") **One is endowed with an ability to penetrate beyond the surface presentation into the heart of all things to recognize each and everything in the universe as Consciousness.** And we do so even as we fully experience embodied life. So, amid our daily activities, one can still maintain a continuous awareness of the Heart that pulses through everything.

REFLECT AND EXPLORE

- Contemplate the concept of jīvan-mukti.
- Practice and note your experience(s): Stay present during the transition from practice (vyutthāna) to "ordinary" daily activities.

  ~ What makes it easier or more difficult?

KEY TEACHINGS FROM PART VII

- The stages of yoga are amazing. (SS 1.12)
- Traversing the path, creating a sattva buddhi and purifying the saṃskāras, dispels ignorance and our luminous essential nature is revealed. This is a state of Self-realization.
- Tantra views the deep states of samādhi as a stage on the path to further states of awareness, wherein one realizes that they are nothing but Śiva and that there is nothing that is not Śiva. So, there is a close-eyed experience of revelation in meditation, which expands to an open-eyed experience of everything as absolute Consciousness.
- The inward-turning practices of yoga illuminate an awareness that you, at essence, are creating, sustaining, and dissolving experience. Also, you take part in concealing and revealing the heart. Recognizing this, you become the Heart (Citi). (PH 13)
- Jīvan-mukti means "living while liberated." It indicates that one can be liberated while in the body and live in the world in that liberated state.
- One is endowed with an ability to penetrate beyond the surface presentation into the heart of all things to recognize each and everything in the universe as Consciousness.

PART VIII

Embodying the Emerging Yogic Qualities

Part VIII concerns several teachings particularly relevant to how the journey of yoga is applicable to living life in the highest possible way. First is the concept of *saṃdhāna*, alignment with Source, and the teaching of Capture the Fort, a metaphor for how yogic riches are available when one aligns with the Highest. Next discussed is how yogic virtues spontaneously emerge as we move farther on the path. The explanation of embodying yogic qualities begins with judgment as a positive capacity. Then the overarching concept of svātantrya/freedom is presented, followed by the teaching of "cultivating the opposite." The directive that future suffering is to be avoided is presented, with an example and summary of how to apply the teachings in this book in everyday householder situations. Finally, the famous *brahma-vihāras* are given as an extended example of embodying yogic qualities.

CHAPTER 45

Capture the Fort and *Saṃdhāna*: Aligning with the Highest

Śiva Sūtra 1.5, discussed in chapter 43, describes the state of expanded awareness as an "upsurge." Here, the following sūtra 1.6 indicates that when one aligns with the power or energy of the Source, here called the *śakti-cakra*, then the apparently separate, surface reality dissolves, and one experiences that everything is Consciousness. With this awareness, the sense of separation dissolves and one's individuality is saturated with the upsurge of qualities of the Highest.

SS 1.6 *śakti-cakra-saṃdhāne viśva-saṃhāraḥ*
śakti: power, energy
cakra: wheel, multitude, collective
saṃdhāna: union, joining, bringing together
viśva: universe
saṃhāraḥ: dissolution, withdrawal
Aligning with the wheel of śaktis, the [separate] universe dissolves.

Critical for us on the journey of yoga is the concept of *saṃdhāna*, which roughly translates as "alignment" and can be applied on all levels of existence. All of the practices, subtle or more gross, serve to effect the alignment with Consciousness itself. This alignment/saṃdhāna with the source of everything in the universe, the śakti-cakra, sets in motion an unfolding of the highest qualities of Consciousness within our individual consciousness. Then at the level of the mind and our actions, we can consciously choose to embody this alignment, saṃdhāna. **Aligning with the highest Sourceplace allows the power of the Absolute to flow through one's individuality, yielding shifts in awareness that reflect the highest and most auspicious reality.**

Maharishi Mahesh Yogi often gave a teaching that illustrates this, known as Capture the Fort. He would say that one may want the treasures of a territory—its gold or silver mines, for example. To receive each of the individual riches one could try to capture each mine individually. He taught that a much more efficient and effective strategy is to capture the fort that controls the entire territory. **With access to that which rules over all the treasures, one has access to everything in the territory.**

This is a great metaphor for an approach to embodying yogic qualities. For example, one could try practicing compassion or truthfulness as individual practices. Or one could "capture" the Sourceplace that rules over all of these qualities, the heart of everything. Then these qualities will naturally emerge.

REFLECT AND EXPLORE

- Contemplate the teaching of saṃdhāna and how it relates to your journey of yoga.
- Contemplate the teaching of Capture the Fort.

CHAPTER 46

Yogic Qualities as Emergent Qualities

Anyone exploring yoga and spirituality learns about its many edicts, all the ways yogis are supposed to be as spiritual practitioners. For example, in the *Yoga Sūtra*, the *yamas* and the *niyamas* are the first two limbs of the famous aṣṭāṅga/eight-limbed system (YS 2.29). They include qualities like nonharming, truthfulness, nonstealing, cleanliness, and more. Elsewhere in the *Yoga Sūtra* are listed several attributes to cultivate on the path of yoga, such as joy, equanimity, faith, and strength (YS 1.20 and 1.33). These are treasured attributes of the path of yoga.

As I began studying the texts in my early days as a yoga practitioner, I earnestly tried to cultivate in my daily life the qualities I read about. I imagined myself embodying various attributes, much like the New Age notion of visualizing some outcome one wishes to manifest. However, if one works only on the level of the relative surface existence, success may be relatively limited.

Consider that these treasured attributes are innate capacities of the heart that may be blocked or veiled to some degree, so success in cultivating these qualities is directly correlated with the clarity of awareness and the ability to access the highest within. A more potent and effective means of manifesting them is to "capture the fort" of the heart—that which rules over everything else. **As one becomes more aligned with the Highest and refines awareness, innate capacities of the heart begin to naturally emerge and flow.** Churning the ocean of awareness in meditation allows the jewels of yogic virtues to spontaneously arise.

Since these qualities are actually already within us, it is simply a matter of unleashing them. As discussed, the process of yoga eliminates and shifts our habitual patterns/saṃskāras and they no longer guide behavior. As awareness becomes more clear and lucid—more sattvic—the sattvic responses these virtues represent will naturally arise. These positive characteristics can be thought of as emergent qualities. They naturally emerge as the practices move us farther along the path to greater awareness and clarity.

Like many things in yoga, cultivating these virtues is a bit paradoxical as they are both the result of practice, and they are practices in and of themselves. The world desperately needs each of us to embody these qualities, so it is good to cultivate them to whatever degree possible. This is in line with the discussion of PH 5 in chapter 29, regarding how awareness contracts around objects of perception. The more we consciously bring these attributes into awareness, the more our being will be colored by them.

These qualities are dharmic—they help hold things together on the surface of life. As we cultivate these virtues, they create more positive saṃskāras and fewer negative saṃskāras as we proceed along the path, as they begin to arise spontaneously more frequently. Most importantly, they have a positive effect on our own lives and on the world at large.

This present discussion is relevant to the mysterious yogic powers or accomplishments, known as *siddhis*, discussed in the third chapter of the *Yoga Sūtra*. One way to think of the siddhis is as capacities that can be accessed once we've risen to full awareness of the innermost Self. Also related is the idea previously discussed that spontaneous bhāvanā becomes more prevalent as one moves along the path of yoga. This can be experienced as heightened intuition and increased perception of reality at its depths.

REFLECT AND EXPLORE

- How have you found positive qualities of the heart arising along the path of yoga?
  - ~ Do you find them easier to cultivate over time?
  - ~ Do you observe them spontaneously arising?

CHAPTER 47

The Role of Judgment

Something one hears quite often in the contemporary yoga scene is "Don't be so judgmental." This has some level of truth, but quite often it's used inappropriately. In fact, the ability to make judgments is not only a human tendency but a gift. We're always making judgments, probably due to an evolutionary impulse to evaluate whether something in the environment is going to eat us or if it's something we'd like to eat. We are always scanning our surroundings and making flash judgments about safety and threat. This expands to judgment of good and bad and the value of things; ultimately it aids us in making wise decisions.

From this perspective, judgment is useful for us. One needs it to effectively function in the world, and an increased ability to do so enhances householder life. We need to judge whether the skillet is too hot to handle, the food is spoiled, or whether some particular course of action will be of benefit. And the broader concept of *viveka*, or discernment, is highly valued in the yoga tradition. So good judgment is an emergent quality as considered in the previous chapter. **The increased ability to be discerning and use good judgment is a hallmark of progress on the path of yoga.**

Judgments are used to discern what is problematic, bad, or unacceptable in the world. At a societal or political level, for example, we use judgment to evaluate a person or policy and decide whether the associated words, actions, or likely results are uplifting, true, useful, and good—or whether they're false or detrimental, and therefore problematic. In general, we need to use our judgment and then set boundaries around words and actions that are harmful, untruthful, and damaging.

This is by no means easy! It is a human tendency to quickly judge something as good and then attach to it. Likewise, when judging things as bad, there is a tendency to push them away. These are two of the kleśas/hindrances outlined by Patañjali in the *Yoga Sūtra* (YS 2.3). We must be aware of how judgment is operating in our lives, since thoughts are the result of innate human tendencies and saṃskāric patterning.

Judgment isn't necessarily bad, just like the citta-vṛttis aren't all bad. Judgments are simply thoughts that are more or less accurate and refined. One must learn to discern when thoughts are aligned with the Highest and when they are detrimental saṃskāric patterning. Yoga sādhanā clears out the obstructions to the wisest Self so spontaneous judgments eventually become more accurate.

REFLECT AND EXPLORE

- Notice how often you use your capacity of judgment. Does it feel like a gift or a hindrance?
- When is judgment a good thing, and when is it problematic?

CHAPTER 48

Enacting Freedom: *Svātantrya*

Recall this fundamental teaching from the beginning of the *Pratyabhijñā-hṛdayam* (highest first!): "Consciousness in her freedom brings about everything in the universe" (PH 1). The highest Absolute reality as the ground of being manifests relative reality out of its own freedom. The power of freedom, the *svātantrya-śakti*, is considered the highest form of the power of Consciousness. (Svatantra as an attribute of the Absolute was covered in chapter 21.) Here, what svātantrya/freedom means for the embodied yogi is discussed in more detail.

Svatantra is usually translated as "free" or "independent," but remember another interpretation of this word is "self-weaving." I love this definition, as it invokes the image of our lives as a piece of cloth or a quilt that we create over a lifetime. So the question becomes: What do you want the quilt to be like? All the thoughts and behaviors weave what becomes the fabric of your current life and, the tradition says, future lives.

As a fundamental quality of the Absolute, *svatantra* means that the Highest is completely unlimited, independent, and absolutely free. And out of that freedom, It dances everything into existence. Human beings are the result of that dance. As a wave on the ocean of Consciousness, we also have a fair amount of freedom, though not the unlimited freedom of the Absolute itself. As relative beings, by virtue of being embodied, we are more or less limited depending on our embodied form, social circumstances, progression on the path of yoga, and so on.

As discussed, the tradition indicates the various ways the highest Consciousness becomes limited as individuality is manifested, including the malas/coverings and the saṃskāras that serve as activators of thoughts, feelings, and behaviors. And remember, the tradition asserts the fundamental limiting condition is ignorance. One way to think of avidyā/ignorance is "not-knowing" that we are limited. We think we are free, when in fact we are driven by unconscious saṃskāric patterning.

One term the tradition uses for a realized being is *siddha*: an adept, seer, or an accomplished or perfected yogi. One attribute of such a being is svātantrya/freedom. SS 3.13 says that when one has accomplished a state of realization, svātantrya is achieved. As one moves toward this state of realization, progressively less limitation and more freedom are experienced.

SS 3.13 *siddhaḥ svatantra-bhāvaḥ*
siddhaḥ: is achieved
svatantra-bhāvaḥ: state of freedom
[When one is established in] the state of [realization], freedom is achieved.

We gain what my teacher Paul Muller-Ortega calls "the ledge of freedom," a resting place on the journey where one can pause and consciously choose the next step. Oftentimes we are scrambling rather haphazardly up the mountain of life without pause, contemplation, or even direction. We just keep going without any self-reflection. **Moving along the journey of yoga, a place to pause and gain some perspective is accessed. This ledge of freedom allows one to survey options and consciously choose the next steps.** The practice yields expanded awareness, which gives us access to this ledge of freedom from which to make the most conscious and aligned choice possible.

The ability to pause and mindfully assess a situation before responding is like that moment at the beginning of the *Bhagavad Gītā*, when Arjuna pauses to consider what the heck he is doing before commencing with a war. In that pause, he consults Kṛṣṇa, who represents his highest Self. He exercises his freedom to mindfully choose the highest course of action.

In everyday life, choices are often made unconsciously. We might not understand that we are even making a choice or that there are different options. We just mindlessly carry on, often out of personal habit or prescribed social convention. For example, we always brush our teeth or commute to work in a certain way, without even thinking about it. With a pause, we can see how habitual ways of thinking and general mindsets are being activated.

Many times when facing challenging situations, we yearn to go back to "normal," which essentially means enacting old behavioral patterns. That may not necessarily be bad, but each moment is an opportunity to pause and evaluate whether "normal" is the highest way of being for everyone involved. There is an opportunity to access the ledge of freedom and consciously examine these patterns. Then, out of freedom, we can choose how to be. Or, we can unconsciously allow the old patterns to dominate and reiterate, which affects not only our personal lives but society at large.

Svātantrya is an overarching attribute of the Divine, allowing for all of the powers and actions of the Highest to unfold. We think of freedom as a birthright, but it isn't about the ability to do or enact anything without recourse. Ultimately this can lead to bondage on so many levels. **As embodied beings, svātantrya/freedom is being free of the bonds of unconscious, habitual, saṃskāric patterns so that one acts consciously from the highest accessible place, bringing the greatest possible alignment to any given situation.**

I once had a teacher who suggested I consider whether or not every one of my actions would lead me farther along the path of yoga. In some ways, this is a really heavy teaching, because it puts responsibility for our lives squarely on us and requires constant mindfulness. It means that we each are responsible for how we weave the fabric of our lives. In each moment, there is a choice to create a more aligned, integrated, and joyful life out of freedom—or one can choose misalignment, disintegration, and suffering.

REFLECT AND EXPLORE

- Contemplate the concept of svātantrya. How do you see it playing out in your life?
- To what degree do you feel free? Consider your thoughts, feelings, and actions.
- What inhibits you from feeling free? What encourages a feeling of freedom?
- Are there circumstances in which you unconsciously limit your freedom of choice and/or expression?
- Practice and note your experience(s): For some period of time (it could be a day, a week, a month), pause as you move from one activity to the next and notice the impulse to think or act or feel a certain way. Ask yourself:

  ~ am I considering all my choices?

  ~ what aligns me with the Highest?
- Practice and note your experience(s): Observe yourself negotiating challenging circumstances. How are you enacting freedom, or not?

CHAPTER 49

Pratipakṣa-bhāvana: Cultivating the Opposite

A common misconception about meditation is that it makes life easier. However, even as the practice of yoga works to thin out, and eventually burn, negative saṃkāras/subliminal activators, we may find ourselves assailed by negative impulses. Life will continue to come at us with both challenges and blessings, but through the increased clarity that sādhanā yields, we are better able to more gracefully respond in ways reflective of our highest intention and the highest Self. And in Sūtra 2.33, Patañjali gives a way that meditation practice can help deal with the remaining impulses: *pratipakṣa-bhāvana*, cultivating the opposite.

YS 2.33 *vitarka-bādhane pratipakṣa-bhāvanam*
vitarka: supposition, dubious knowledge, doubt
bādhane: binding, harassing
pratipakṣa: opposite
bhāvana: cultivation
When assailed by negative thoughts, cultivate the opposite.

Even though the *Yoga Sūtra* traditionally outlines a renunciate path, this sūtra is particularly relevant for householder yogis. When out in the world, as opposed to being sheltered in an ashram, cave, or forest, householders are likely to find themselves in challenging situations simply because that's how life is, or due to personal baggage. Either way, there is an opportunity to shift.

I have to admit that when I first encountered the notion of pratipakṣa-bhāvana, I approached it rather naively, thinking that whenever something negative occurred to me, I would simply visualize the opposite. There is some degree of efficacy to that, but ultimately we need to go deeper to the seed from which the negativity sprouts: the kleśas and the saṃskāric and karmic residue. As well, all the practices comprising sādhanā can be cultivated to work synergistically, creating the conditions for pratipakṣa-bhāvana. Therefore, there are three interrelated ways pratipakṣa-bhāvana works to counteract negativity. **Pratipakṣa-bhāvana/cultivating the opposite includes cultivating states of awareness through practice that naturally contain the opposite quality, working with the surface thoughts and emotions, and enacting other aspects of sādhanā that address negativity.**

The word *bhāvana* in YS 2.33 is key; it comes from the verbal root *bhū*, "to become." In this context, bhāvana can be thought of as a state of being. Through practice, we cultivate a state of awareness that supports and spontaneously creates the positive types of thoughts, the akliṣṭa citta-vṛttis. These beneficial counteracting states come naturally from our heart space.

Pratipakṣa in this sūtra literally means "the other wing." Tying this back into the core teachings of the *Yoga Sūtra*, remember the definition of yoga in YS 1.2: Yoga is calming the mind. Then, YS 1.3 says, the seer abides in its true nature. Meditation practice allows one to quiet the mind, moving into deeper levels to contact the essence, the seer, the draṣṭṛ. When we don't move deeper, we end up identifying with all the surface fluctuations, as YS 1.4 says.

So the situation described in YS 1.4 can be thought of as one wing or one way of being, in which one stays enmeshed in the surface activity of the citta-vṛttis, caught in the samsāric eddies of the external drama of life. In contrast, to whatever degree one cultivates more clarity (sattva buddhi) to contact the Heart, as conveyed in YS 1.3, then the other wing is strengthened. So through practice, states of awareness that already contain the opposite quality of being are cultivated, allowing ready access to that state.

Quite simply, pratipakṣa-bhāvana works as the result of meditation, which is primary in supporting this process of yoga in a variety of ways.

Meditation helps weaken reactive patterns, so negativity is less likely to arise. At the same time, meditation creates an expanded awareness that allows for an increased capacity to work with whatever manifests in our life. In general, the ledge of freedom is more accessible and one gains a greater perspective as the "other wing" is cultivated.

As well, simultaneously, one can work on the surface with the thoughts and emotions. So when negativity arises, consciously decide to not reinforce it. This requires the ledge of freedom, enough mindfulness to notice what arises in the awareness field, and then exercising svātantrya/freedom to choose what to reinforce. Regarding YS 2.33, the primary commentary indicates that the continued choice of indulging in negative thoughts is like a dog licking its own vomit. There's a fine line between allowing oneself to notice, feel, and experience the so-called "negative" emotions, and dwelling too long in those emotions, which can lead to reinforcing the negativity and prolonging suffering. The ability to negotiate this line is enhanced by practice.

What I've noticed in myself is that when the negative thoughts arise, I have the ledge of freedom to observe them from a more expanded state. Almost instantly, the negative thoughts are followed by an opposite, more positive impulse, given the space I have created through my practices. The ledge of freedom allows me to choose how to be in that situation in a manner that is more aligned with the Highest.

Another way to address negativity is to utilize all of the different practices comprising sādhanā. Sometimes the practice of bhāvanā can be useful by contemplating and writing about problematic issues that arise, yielding increased clarity. Āsana, *prāṇāyāma*/breath work and japa/chanting are excellent means to shift energy in the body-mind. The practice of svādhyāya/self-study helps us understand the whole journey of yoga and how our sādhanā works so we can put experiences into perspective.

It is important to remember that this is an unfolding process. As long as any of the obstructing saṃskāras, kleśas, or karma remain, the *vitarka-bādhane*/negative thoughts that YS 2.33 is addressing, will inevitably arise. Though we continue to experience challenging emotions, the expanded and refined state of awareness created through yoga practice makes it much less likely those emotions will take hold and keep us captive for long periods.

REFLECT AND EXPLORE

- Consider any persistent negative thoughts you have.
  - How do you experience and enact pratipakṣa-bhāvana?

CHAPTER 50

Future Suffering Is to Be Avoided

This book has addressed many ways the heart is obscured, be it ignorance or cloaking mechanisms such as the malas. The texts of the tradition explain that as a result of these obscurations, human life invariably dishes up some form of suffering. By the very nature of coming into the world, humans can feel limited, contracted, or somehow incomplete—less than our optimal self. Many are pulled toward yoga precisely because of a sense that there is more to life and seemingly inescapable suffering.

Remember what Patañjali says about the saṃskāras/habit patterns and kleśas/impediments as part of the underlying psychophysical makeup. He indicates they may be intermittent or dormant, or they may become activated (YS 2.4). So in a sense, as householders moving into potentially stimulating scenarios, we have the opportunity to consciously work on the activated saṃskāras, while at the same time our sādhanā works to address all of the saṃskāric residue.

YS 2.16 says in very straightforward terms: **Future suffering is to be avoided.** I used to think this sūtra was rather silly because of course one should avoid suffering. But it is not about simply avoiding challenges in life. Aversion/*dveṣa* is one of the kleśas/obstacles to practice (YS 2.3). It *is* about living in a way that minimizes suffering. And the journey of yoga involves the mechanisms for doing just that, particularly all the teachings discussed in this part of the book, including the naturally arising emergent qualities, increasing discernment, enacting freedom, and cultivating the opposite. All of these and more serve as aids in avoiding future suffering.

YS 2.16 *heyaṃ duḥkham anāgatam*
heyam: to be avoided
duḥkham: sorrow, suffering, pain
anāgatam: not yet come, future
Future suffering is to be avoided.

Primary is the alignment/saṃdhāna with the Highest to access a deeper wisdom to guide our actions. To "capture the fort," we must first cultivate the practices that go to the root of who we are. Meditation practice burns those saṃskāric seeds so they can no longer sprout. In addition, the inward-turning saṃskāras are developed, which are akliṣṭa and don't produce suffering. And they increase the ability to move inward, allowing access to that place of wisdom more readily on a moment-by-moment basis.

As well, when we meditate, the saṃskāras for meditation are created. So, for myself, I get up in the morning, make some tea, and go to my cushion. It is a habit. When I don't meditate, I feel "off," like I've forgotten to brush my teeth. Each morning I allow the citta-vṛttis to settle and traverse into the deeper layers of my being in meditation. I bathe in the luminosity of the Self. Then my day unfolds with more ease and less suffering.

What is outlined in this book about the journey as embodied humans on the path of yoga gives us a framework for continuing to refine and align. For example, remember the karma-saṃskāra-citta-vṛtti cycle outlined in chapter 33. Everything you do, everything that happens to you (karma), creates a saṃskāra, a residual trace that activates the citta-vṛttis (thoughts or emotions) to act in ways that reinforce the saṃskāras, and so on. By paying attention, you will see how this plays out on every level of life: your diet, physical activities, relationships, how you drive, your sādhanā/practices, and so on. And again, some of these patterns can be useful/akliṣṭa, but others are detrimental/kliṣṭa.

As we've discussed, the practice of meditation helps to attenuate the negative saṃskāras, progressively refining and aligning every aspect of being. But until one is thoroughly refined, residual saṃskāras will activate.

Yet the practices of yoga create a ledge of freedom from which to work with the activated saṃskāras, as they activate thoughts prompting action on the surface of life. This process at first may need to be slowed down and worked with consciously, then it gradually becomes more automatic. It is important to consider how to work with this cycle as it emerges in everyday situations, as life is comprised of a long thread of moments, which weave together to create more or less alignment and refinement.

To make this very concrete, let's say I'm at a party and I'm offered some wine. Repeatedly in the past, I've had wine at parties, laying down the saṃskāra, and when that saṃskāra is activated I have the thought: drink some wine. Now, I take the sacred pause and ask: Is the wine going to move me toward a greater connection with my heart? Sometimes it has seemed so: a glass of wine to chill out, relax, and let go of some stress.

If I choose to have the wine, I get a nice buzz and again have the opportunity to drink more wine—it's a party after all! The saṃskāra was imprinted from the karma—the action of drinking—so the thought/citta-vṛtti again arises: drink another glass. Then here comes another choice point: an opportunity to exercise my svātantrya/freedom. I need to pause on my ledge of freedom and listen to my Heartself, rather than my saṃskāric impulses. I know that in my case, less wine is better.

Earlier in my life, I hadn't figured this out. Many people unconsciously think alcohol is a way to avoid suffering, feel good about themselves, and so on, and therefore choose to continue to drink, perhaps to excess. But I began to connect the dots, see the relationship/sambandha between drinking and how I feel the next few days. With the greater mindfulness developed through my practices, I noticed a subtle sense of cloaking over both my mind and my heart. Repeated drinking can build toward feelings of depression and disconnection from my Heartself. As my being becomes more refined through many years of practice, disconnect is less acceptable.

What's so tricky is that when the effects are delayed, it is hard to connect the dots, to see the pattern. This situation could play out like this: after a night of having a few drinks, I feel a bit sad or generally "off" the next day or later in the week, and I want some relief from that feeling. So the citta-vṛtti arises from the underlying saṃskāra created by the action of drinking alcohol. The impulse arises to drink since it seemed to lift me up a bit before. If I choose to act on the impulse, it can ultimately lead to more feelings of depression and the pattern can be repeated. And all of this can unfold unconsciously, leading to the formation of a habit pattern or even addiction.

Just to be clear: I am not making a moral argument about the use of alcohol. I'm simply sharing an example of this process. One reason it's a good example is that there's a history of alcoholism in my family, so I likely have a propensity toward addiction, some sort of genetic saṃskāra. I have worked with this propensity by channeling it into habits that support my highest saṃkalpa/intention to recognize and channel the absolute Consciousness. I began yoga with a very rigorous habit-forming practice that was so much healthier than alcohol or drugs. I learned how to turn addictive tendencies into good habits.

So when a saṃskāric pattern produces a thought or feeling/citta-vṛtti to act habitually, pause and consider if this citta-vṛtti is akliṣṭa/useful or kliṣṭa/detrimental and remember that future suffering is to be avoided (YS 2.16). The ledge of freedom gives us a larger perspective of who we are. Our identity is aligned with the highest Self instead of only the surface thoughts and situations. As well, the ledge of freedom gives space to watch what is happening on a moment-by-moment basis and to more freely choose acts that are most likely to refine our individuality and life, as well as align us with the Divine, instead of creating or reinforcing bad habits that produce suffering.

It is a very pragmatic consideration: how sādhanā/practice supports our householder life. The process I've outlined in my personal example is based on the teachings of yoga outlined in this book. It isn't some type of magical thinking wherein one wishes or prays for something to manifest and simply waits for it to happen. The ability to manifest anything is dependent on many factors we've discussed. Sometimes we expect dramatic experiences in our practice, but often what's happening is a slow process of clarifying awareness, creating sattva buddhi. This may not be consciously experienced in any given meditation session. But over time, sādhanā creates a field of awareness in which refinement and transformation of our being occur on all levels of life. All of this allows us to avoid future suffering.

REFLECT AND EXPLORE

- Sometimes it is easier to see the patterns that create suffering in others. What patterns have you observed in others?
- What patterns can you see in yourself?
- What do you do to avoid future suffering?

CHAPTER 51

Brahma-Vihāras: Qualities for Clarity of Mind

This last chapter in this part regarding emergent yogic qualities explores YS 1.33 in order to further examine how yoga supports our lives and allows us to shift the world around us. From the beginning of my studies of the *Yoga Sūtra*, I have been enamored of this teaching, which lists exquisite qualities of being and suggests how they can be applied in situations we might encounter.

This aphorism first lists four qualities to cultivate on the path of yoga: maitrī (friendliness or love), karuṇā (compassion), muditā (joy), and upekṣā (equanimity). These virtues are also heralded in Buddhism as the *brahma-vihāra*s. The next part of this sūtra lists four types of people: sukha (happy), duḥkha (suffering), puṇya (virtuous) and apuṇya (nonvirtuous).

This sūtra suggests that cultivating (*bhāvanātaś)* the four qualities toward those four types of situations one might encounter, yields greater clarity of mind (*citta prasādanam*). Specifically, it suggests one should cultivate friendliness or love toward those who are happy, compassion toward those suffering, joy toward those with virtue, and equanimity toward nonvirtuous or evil people. So this sūtra gives a technique for creating clarity in consciousness by giving some tools to work with in relationships. As well, YS 1.33 can be thought of as describing qualities that naturally emerge given a more refined awareness.

YS 1.33 *maitrī-karuṇā-muditā-upekṣāṇāṃ sukha-duḥkha-puṇya-apuṇya-viṣayāṇāṃ bhāvanātaś-citta-prasādanam*
maitrī: friendliness
karuṇā: compassion
muditā: joy, gladness
upekṣā: equanimity
sukha: happiness
duḥkha: sorrow, suffering, pain
puṇya: virtue, meritorious
apuṇya: vice, demeritorious
viṣayāṇām: concerning or regarding object
bhāvanātaś: cultivating attitude
citta: mind, awareness
prasādanam: purification, clarification
The mind becomes clarified by cultivating [or alternately: A clarified mind yields] an attitude of friendliness, compassion, joy, and equanimity toward happiness, pain, virtue, or vice.

As I have contemplated this sūtra, it seems that its list of qualities starts with what is easiest for us to do and moves to what is most difficult. The first two, maitrī/friendliness and karuṇā/compassion, are relatively easy because they often arise spontaneously. Most well-adjusted people find it easy to be friendly and loving when they encounter happy people. Likewise, compassion/karuṇā often naturally arises toward those who are suffering/duḥkha.

The third quality, muditā/joy, may naturally arise in the face of someone who is puṇya/virtuous. For example, when someone performs a beautiful dance or makes a piece of art, we are joyful about that. If someone excels at a sport or a child performs a difficult piano piece, we naturally applaud their accomplishment, joyfully celebrating their virtuosity. However, at times when faced with someone else's success, instead of feeling joy, we might experience jealousy. So at times, that third pairing of extending muditā/joy toward someone else's accomplishment can be a challenge.

The last listed quality is the one many people find quite difficult: upekṣā/equanimity toward the apuṇya/nonvirtuous person. *Upekṣā* is often translated as "equanimity," which usually leads to the question: What does equanimity mean? *Equi* means what you might think: "equal" or "same." And *animus* indicates "mind," so equanimity can mean "even-mindedness."

Upekṣā is sometimes translated as indifference or even apathy, which seems inaccurate, as it comes from the verbal root *īkṣ*, which means "to see or look." Literally, *upekṣā* can mean "overlooking"—not in the sense of ignoring, but as in "taking a broader view," like at a scenic overlook. Where I live in the western United States, there are often scenic overlooks—pullouts on the side of the road where you can see the big view of the area, get the big picture, a greater perspective. Sometimes a pause is needed to step back from a situation to gain a higher perspective. Often, when thinking someone has behaved badly, we don't know the whole story or the entire context or big picture of where that other person is coming from.

Some may argue that it is absurd to consider equanimity toward those who seem truly evil. But remember: there is nothing that is not Śiva. So although the reality of the situation on the surface of life has to be dealt with, the way we deal with it—the attitude we bring to it and our saṃkalpa/intention—can profoundly affect the result. Though it is challenging to keep perspective in a heated moment when upset, triggered, or stressed out, one simple way to find perspective is to remember the teaching of the "highest first," cultivating an intention of aligning with the highest in any given situation.

Another strategy to cultivate upekṣā/equanimity toward those who behave badly is to remember that we often do not know the big picture. For example, many people who are abusive learned that behavior during their childhood from the adults in their life. That doesn't excuse the behavior, but a wider perspective might help us understand how someone comes to behave badly. That, in turn, may lead toward greater equanimity and maybe even compassion.

A good place to start cultivating these qualities is toward ourselves, as everyone has times when they're happy, sad, virtuous, or nonvirtuous. When suffering/duḥkha, can we give ourselves some karuṇā/

compassion? When we've behaved badly/apuṇya, can we foster a bit of upekṣā/equanimity? Can such behavior be put in perspective? For example, it's helpful to understand that making a mistake doesn't make us a bad person.

To practice cultivating these virtues, we can begin by consciously noticing our reactions when meeting these different situations. For example, in the case of someone else's success, what saṃskāric pattern habitually arises? We have the choice to continue to reinforce it or not, to the degree the ledge of freedom has been established. Though it is hard to stop a thought once it has arisen, we can choose to change the channel. It isn't a matter of stuffing or ignoring that thought; it's a matter of laying down a new pattern as with pratipakṣa-bhāvana/cultivating the opposite in YS 2.33. When we make the choice and act, that pattern/saṃskāra is established. When repeated, that action becomes a habit. So it is important to ask: What do we want our habit patterns to be like?

Many of the teachings we've considered through our svādhyāya/study can be useful in these situations. For example, understanding how the malas and other mechanisms of concealment work to occlude the heart allows for more karuṇā/compassion for ourselves and others and puts things in perspective/upekṣā. And all the practices work to remove the obscurations and clarify awareness/sattva buddhi. The contemplative practice, bhāvanā, can be particularly useful. When something like jealousy arises, bhāvanā could help uncover and eventually dissolve the source of this pattern. So it can be worked with through practice while acknowledging that at times we might need some additional help from a valued friend or a therapist.

The major point here is to act consciously and skillfully, from the highest place possible in the moment. In YS 1.33, Patañjali is suggesting to cultivate these virtues as a means to calm the surface agitation so one can move to a deeper level of awareness. When choosing to respond with positive qualities, we create more positive saṃskāras/habit patterns while at the same time a more sattvic buddhi/clarified awareness arises. So over time, this leads to a positive citta-vṛtti-karma-saṃskāra cycle, which will aid in surface life while at the same time refining the depths of awareness. We have to start connecting the dots of how the thoughts, feelings, and actions play out in our lives.

And remember, word order is important in these pithy sūtras, and the first word in YS 1.33 is *maitrī*/love. The practice of meditation aligns us with our very own Heart essence (*hṛdaya*). Exercise freedom/svātantrya to pause and connect, then choose to respond from that Sourceplace of love. When we can do this, it will shift our world.

REFLECT AND EXPLORE

- Consider each of the virtues listed in YS 1.33, as well as the types of people listed.
  - ~ Give a real-life example of each, preferably from your own life.
  - ~ How do they manifest in your life?
  - ~ What encourages or discourages their occurrence?
- Practice and note your experience(s): Pick one of these qualities to consciously cultivate for some period of time (it could be a day, a week, a month) and note your experience(s). Repeat this with other qualities.
- Practice and note your experience(s): For some period of time, cultivate these qualities toward yourself.
- Do you always experience joy for another's virtuosity, or does jealousy sometimes arise? How can you work with this?
- How do you think about upekṣā/equanimity? What helps you find a greater perspective?

KEY TEACHINGS FROM PART VIII

- Aligning with the highest Sourceplace allows the power of the Absolute to flow through one's individuality, yielding shifts in awareness that reflect the highest and most auspicious reality.
- With access to that which rules over all the treasures, one has access to everything in the territory.
- As one becomes more aligned with the Highest and refines awareness, innate capacities of the heart begin to naturally emerge and flow.
- The increased ability to be discerning and use good judgment is a hallmark of our progress on the path of yoga.
- Moving along the journey of yoga, a place to pause and gain some perspective is accessed. This ledge of freedom allows one to survey options and consciously choose the next steps.
- As embodied beings, svātantrya/freedom is being free of the bonds of unconscious, habitual, saṃskāric patterns so that one acts consciously from the highest accessible place, bringing the greatest possible alignment to any given situation.
- Pratipakṣa-bhāvana/cultivating the opposite includes cultivating states of awareness through practice that naturally contain the opposite quality, working with the surface thoughts and emotions, and enacting other aspects of sādhanā that address negativity.
- Future suffering is to be avoided. (YS 2.16)

PART IX

Change Consciousness and Change the World

The final part of the book begins with the deity Hanumān, as he teaches about skillful means and serving with devotion. Then the teachings of *dharma* and *svadharma* from the *Bhagavad Gītā* are considered, along with a definition of *yoga* from the text: yoga is skill in action. We revisit our intention/saṃkalpa, and consider how the journey of yoga is a spiral in which we continuously circle back to issues and topics at new levels as awareness and understanding is refined, and how aligning with the Highest amplifies our lives as emergent yogic qualities are embodied. We finish with the vision that as we each change consciousness, we can change the world.

CHAPTER 52

Hanumān and Devotion to Service

One of the most intriguing of the Hindu deities is Hanumān, known for his dedication to service and devotion to the Divine. He figures prominently in the great Indian epic, the *Rāmāyaṇa*, as an ally to the main character, Prince Rāma, and is often pictured opening the cave of his heart to reveal his beloved Rāma and Sītā (Rāma's wife).

One of the many wonderful stories about Hanumān starts when he is young. One day he sees the sun shining in the sky and it looks just like a big, juicy, ripe fruit. Being a strong and young god, Hanumān leaps for the sun. This angers the gods, for how can there be life without the sun? The god Indra hurls a thunderbolt at Hanumān, which breaks his jaw. This is how he gets his name, which means "one having a distinctive jaw."

Indra's thunderbolt knocks Hanumān unconscious and sends him hurtling toward Earth. At the last minute, his father, Vāyu, scoops up Hanumān and sets him down. Vāyu, god of the Wind, is angered, and he withdraws *prāṇa*, the air and life force from the earth, and everything begins to suffocate. Now the gods have a different problem. To appease Vāyu, the god Brahmā heals Hanumān, and the other gods bestow upon Hanumān many gifts in the form of yogic powers/siddhis.

Many of us probably have stories like this from our youth, when we acted without reflection. Hanumān simply leaps for what he wants, without any consideration of the consequences or of what he really wants—or why. It's a story about not looking before you leap and about rushing to act without pausing first.

As he grows, Hanumān learns how to harness his tremendous power—particularly in service of the Divine. The lessons of his youth teach him about stepping more gracefully into the flow, and the story reminds us that everyone makes mistakes. The question is whether we learn, like Hanumān, to become more skillful in our actions.

Hanumān's greatest desire is to be in service of the Divine, and as this story exemplifies, in his childhood and youth he learns to be more skillful in applying his substantial power. One of his siddhis/powers is that of *kāmarūpa*. *Kāma* means "desire" and *rūpa* means "form"—so Hanumān can make himself into any form he desires. He is a shapeshifter.

In the *Rāmāyaṇa*, Hanumān displays this ability on several occasions. After Rāma's beloved Sītā is kidnapped, he and his brother, Lakṣmaṇa, wander the forest disguised as ascetics looking for Sītā. The forest prince, Sugrīva, is concerned about these two characters wandering in his forest, so he sends Hanumān to investigate. Hanumān exercises his power of shapeshifting and takes up the appearance of a Brahmin (a person of a priestly caste). As Hanumān approaches and honors Rāma and Lakṣmaṇa, Lakṣmaṇa notes Hanumān's sweet speech and they all become friends. In this way, Hanumān is then able to become an ally in the service of Rāma, an embodiment of the Highest.

Later in the epic, when Hanumān discovers where Sītā has been held captive, he finds her distressed and considering suicide. He shifts into a less intimidating form—a small monkey—and sits in a tree, observing. Hanumān knows he must act quickly, yet he pauses to consider carefully how best to approach Sītā. After consideration, he decides to sweetly and softly sing the story of Rāma's exploits. Sītā, though initially fearful of the monkey, is delighted by his words and they connect through further conversation.

These stories of Hanumān teach us so much about our lives as householder yogis. On a daily basis we must fulfill many roles: as family members, as professionals, as community members, and so on. Like Hanumān, we are shapeshifters, changing our demeanor, language, and so on, depending on the situation, to be most effective. And it is important to be skillful as one does this.

There are many occasions in life when we were more or less skillful, even when our desire is pure. I found this out during my first year of graduate school at a midwestern university. At twenty-one, I was feeling a bit rebellious and looked like the California Deadhead hippie I was. Both the faculty and other graduate students had trouble taking me seriously, so much so that I ended up leaving after a year. I transferred to a different graduate school and decided to take another approach, shapeshifting to present myself more conservatively and as a serious student, much like Hanumān approaching Rāma and Lakṣmaṇa in the forest. I found I was accepted much more readily and ranked at the top of my class. Eventually it didn't matter if I wore my blazer or my tie-dyes; I had made the connection successfully.

This isn't a teaching about changing to please others. It is about fulfilling our heart's desire, the highest saṃkalpa/intention, and being skillful in the pursuit of that desire. Following desire to its core, ultimately we want to be of service in some way and offer our unique gift to the world. And, in fact, each of us already changes into different ways of being in life when approaching the roles of employee, boss, friend, teacher, student, spouse, sibling, child, or parent. To be of the greatest service in each of these roles, skill is required to find a way to connect in order to offer our gifts. Hanumān teaches about the utility of skillful means, of aligning intention with the Highest, and of serving with devotion.

REFLECT AND EXPLORE

- Make a list of the different roles in your life.
  - How is your heart's desire reflected in each?
  - Can you think of more skillful ways to approach some of these roles?
  - Does it help to remember your highest intention/saṃkalpa?
- When Hanumān finds Sītā, he pauses to watch and contemplate the right approach. Can you think of instances in life when this could be useful?
- Practice and note your experience(s): In a difficult situation, pause to contemplate the right approach.

In many ways, Hanumān represents the consummate yogi. He has gained yogic powers/siddhis, including that of shapeshifting. As yogis receiving the gifts of practice, we become empowered by them. Some people and yogis use the power they've gained for their own personal benefit, which has led to the downfall of many teachers and has caused many of the problems inherent in society. Like Hanumān, other yogis and people in the world choose to use their power in service/*sevā*. The beautiful thing about Hanumān is that he is so clear that he's serving the Highest. He always holds Rāma and Sītā inside his heart, and his association with Rāma, an incarnation of Viṣṇu, indicates his commitment to dharma/duty.

CHAPTER 53

Dharma and *Svadharma*: Righteous Conduct

Remember that the first word of any text is said to be of special significance and reflects the "highest first." In the case of the *Bhagavad Gītā*, the first phrase is *dharma-kṣetre*, "the field of dharma," referring to the field on which the battle is taking place. It represents life in its many levels and domains, where all the challenges encountered in the course of a lifetime play out. So in a sense, the entire conversation between Kṛṣṇa and Arjuna is about how to live our dharma in all the many facets of life.

Dharma is often translated as "sacred duty," "law," or "righteousness." It comes from the verbal root *dhṛ* "to hold, make firm, nurture, and sustain." **Dharma can be thought of as that which sustains or holds things together. It is often defined as "duty" and carries connotations of ethics, justice, goodness, and virtue.** There is really no one English word that captures the nuance of the concept of dharma.

Kṣetra literally means "field." At the level of the individual, this can be thought of as one's field of awareness. So dharma-kṣetra is the individual consciousness; it is where we grapple with our dharma, which is exactly what Arjuna is doing in the *Bhagavad Gītā*, with the help of Kṛṣṇa. On the battlefield are two opposing sides, one of which is considered more righteous, or dharmic, than the other. The war has come about in order to restore dharma/righteousness. And metaphorically there are parts of ourselves struggling with what is dharmic in the many situations in life.

The field can also be thought of in a larger way, as any domain in which we operate. This could be our family or spiritual community, our profession or workplace, or society at large. This concept, in particular, applies not only to our individual lives but also to upholding and nurturing society as a whole. Dharma is what sustains society. It is that which is uplifting and leads to the greatest collective good. The *Bhagavad Gītā* challenges us, from its very beginning, to consider deeply how our actions align with righteousness, and how we uphold righteousness in a misaligned world.

Arjuna and Kṛṣṇa are standing on the field of dharma, and metaphorically these characters are two parts of ourselves and the field is the inner topography of consciousness. Arjuna is experiencing a battle within himself, trying to understand what his duty is and what will hold things together, create alignment, and serve the highest. And for each of us as embodied beings, the whole world is the dharma-kṣetra, the field where we discover and enact our dharma, minute by minute, day by day, year by year.

During their conversation in the *Bhagavad Gītā*, Kṛṣṇa refers to Arjuna's svadharma. You may recall that *sva* means "self," so *svadharma* is one's own particular dharma. Our own duty. In more modern times, svadharma has been described as one's purpose in life. What must you do to create greater alignment within yourself and in the world? How are you helping to hold things together?

Kṛṣṇa reminds Arjuna that his svadharma is that of a warrior. (See, for example, BG 2.31 and 2.33). In the context of this story, Arjuna's dharma is to uphold righteousness in society through his actions as a warrior. The whole premise of the *Bhagavad Gītā* is Arjuna questioning this, as he is not happy about facing an opposing army comprised of people he is connected with. But the concept of dharma dictates that upholding society requires him to do his duty as a warrior. As part of a lineage of nobility, he has received a great deal of privilege, and with it comes certain responsibilities. Yet he must make his own choices about what he believes is righteous, so he is not doing what someone else thinks is his dharma. In the course of the conversation, Arjuna is coming to understand his *sva-dharma*, his own dharma.

In many societies, even today, there are fairly strict roles, so this teaching could be challenged when it is used to oppress or "keep people in their place." For example, in societies where women's roles are traditionally restricted, women are extremely challenged to live their own dharma. They may have to confront societal prescriptions to enact what is truly their svadharma, in terms of what is more nurturing and sustainable.

It is interesting to think of the story of Vyāghrapāda and Patañjali in this context of svadharma. Recall that Patañjali initially sought to give the same offering of flowers he saw others making to the liṅga in the Tillai Forest. Ultimately, he discovered that his offering was different because he was of the earth, not the trees. I know for myself early in my career, I tried to follow the examples of other yoga teachers who developed a large following and traveled around giving workshops. It took me a while to discover my svadharma was a different model of teaching.

Modern society seems to have so much freedom and so many options that it can be overwhelming to understand what is most dharmic. That's why the yogic practices are so important in contemporary society as a way to connect to the essence as a guide, our Kṛṣṇa self, to discover our gifts, and to become clear on what is dharmic in each situation and in life as a whole.

Dharma operates on all levels of life simultaneously. Throughout the *Bhagavad Gītā*, Kṛṣṇa teaches that yoga is not about becoming a renunciate or withdrawing from familial and societal duties and responsibilities. Instead, dharma is about being actively present to the opportunities life offers for sustaining the world, for upholding dharma in society and nature, and for inner growth, including what nurtures us individually and what connects us to our highest purpose.

In his commentary on the first verse of the *Bhagavad Gītā*, the great Tantric sage Abhinavagupta cites a text that says the highest dharma consists of the realization of the Self by means of yoga. Abhinavagupta is saying that to be dharmic we start with the Self, refining ourselves through the practice of yoga, which aligns us with the Highest. Then we are pulled spontaneously to create alignment on societal and global levels. When we do the practices and begin to realize the Heartself, our essence, it is easier to see the connection of all things, and quite naturally actions begin to unfold in a way that reflects dharma in all of our activities.

As Kṛṣṇa repeatedly teaches, each action is an opportunity to assert dharma. Sometimes it is fulfilling the duty of a role in life—for example a warrior, teacher, spouse, or parent. Sometimes dharma is about making the best choice in a challenging situation, one that perhaps we would prefer to avoid altogether. Sometimes it is about remembering what we uniquely have to offer in a given situation: our own dharma/svadharma. And as Abhinavagupta reminds us, sometimes dharma is about doing what aligns us with the highest Self.

Kṛṣṇa teaches that to create dharma in the world, we must act. We must consider how every decision, every action, contributes toward sustaining the righteous integrity of connection with the innermost self. And our actions should also help sustain and hold together society and the planet in the highest possible way.

REFLECT AND EXPLORE

- Write down your definition of dharma, then contemplate.
- Given your definition of dharma, how is it reflected (or not) in your actions?
- Consider the idea of dharma on its many levels, including your duty in society, to your individual self, and to your highest Self. What does dharma mean in these different contexts?
- When have you faced a conflict like Arjuna, wherein your individual desires conflicted with what seems best for society? How can you best negotiate such a circumstance in the future?
- Consider dharma as what holds things together.
    - How does this relate to yoga practices, especially meditation?
    - What does this mean for householder life?
- Contemplate the term svadharma.
    - What does it mean for Arjuna?
    - What does it mean for you?
- Practice and note your experience(s): For some period of time (it could be a day, a week, a month), mindfully consider whether each of your actions is dharmic.

CHAPTER 54

Yoga Is Skill in Action

Among my favorite teachings from the *Bhagavad Gītā* is "Yoga is skill in action" (BG 2.50). I love it foremost because it acknowledges that there is no avoiding action. The guru Kṛṣṇa points out that you can't not act. You must act. Action is necessary in this world, at the very least one must act to maintain the body (BG 3.8). And like us, Arjuna is not a renunciate, he is a householder. He is a warrior.

Arjuna's questions suggest that he would perhaps prefer to withdraw to a cave and avoid the battle he faces. But if you think about it, making a choice to *not* do something in particular is actually making a choice to do something else. Hiding one's head in the sand in an uncomfortable situation amounts to withdrawing and surrendering rather than acting skillfully.

What does it mean to act skillfully? Skill has the sense of more than just talent. It is something that is honed and refined through practice. Any skill requires practice/abhyāsa, and that practice yields knowledge of how to act skillfully. Remember how the path of knowledge has two components. First is intellectual knowledge, jñāna, like what one might receive from this book or the texts. In many domains of activity, it is extremely important to create intellectual knowledge through study. But the second component of knowledge is also very important: experiential knowledge, vijñāna.

Skill in action involves summoning both intellectual knowledge, jñāna, and deep experiential knowledge, vijñāna, to respond from the highest place in any given situation. As Abhinavagupta noted, this involves knowing the Self, accessing our Kṛṣṇa self. This is knowledge of who we are inside, beyond all the surface definitions in life. It is a knowledge of that sourceplace deep within.

Kṛṣṇa gives several ways to create that knowledge of the Self. One that's very clearly laid out in the *Bhagavad Gītā* is meditation. (See BG chapter 6). Through the yoga of meditation, one comes to a place of *sama-darśana* (BG 6.29), which literally means "seeing the same." Sādhanā eventually yields the awareness that we are all one, from the same Source, related to the teaching that "there is nothing that is not Śiva." So first, the journey of yoga involves an awareness that everything comes from the same essence, which eventually leads to the ability to consciously experience that on a moment-by-moment basis.

At the same time, through the practice of yoga, particularly meditation, one comes to know and connect with the Heart and the deepest wisdom within. As we establish that connection daily with practice, a pathway is created, an access ramp, so that in any given situation the wisest self can be summoned as a guide to the most skillful action. This may require a conscious pause to consider the highest action, as in the opening of the *Bhagavad Gītā*. In this way, we act from our hearts, in service of the Highest, gaining an increased capacity to reflect dharmic/ right action into the world. This is the yoga of skill in action.

REFLECT AND EXPLORE

- Consider situations in life when you were more or less skillful.
  - ~ How could you have been more skillful?
  - ~ What have you learned from your mistakes?
- Consider any particularly sticky relationships or situations in your life right now.
  - ~ What is your most auspicious desire in this situation?
  - ~ How might you most skillfully move in that direction?

CHAPTER 55

Refinement of Intention: *Saṃkalpa* Revisited

As we come to the final chapters of our journey together in this book, how to end is as perplexing as how to begin—because, of course, there is no end. In so many ways, we're still at the beginning, and the journey continues. As indicated earlier, many aspects of the journey of yoga involve a spiral wherein one circles back again and again to issues and topics. In doing so, awareness and understanding are increasingly aligned and refined. Each time we spiral back, it is at a higher, deeper, or more refined level. You may have noticed this strategy was used in this book with several topics that were addressed in an increasingly deeper way along our journey. In fact, this is happening right now, with saṃkalpa/intention.

Recall the last of the pañca-kṛtyas/five acts, and how all things come to an end with saṃhāra/destruction. But remember, saṃhāra can be thought of as reabsorption and can lead to transformation. What is no longer of service is allowed to dissolve in favor of a new creation or understanding. Often what is thought of as an ending becomes the beginning of a new phase of the journey.

So now/atha, let's spiral back to the concept of saṃkalpa, as a way to represent and unfold the process of imbibing and enacting all of the qualities of yoga we wish to embody. Saṃkalpa is often translated as *intention*, but it is associated with will and desire as well. As discussed in chapter 3, saṃkalpa/intention makes conscious, and sets in motion, the desires we wish to manifest.

REFLECT AND EXPLORE

- Review your saṃkalpa for reading this book. (See chapter 3).
- How did your intention manifest, or not?
- Did you find your intention revised, expanded, or changed during your journey with this book?
- Consider your part in enacting your intention through the pañca-kṛtyas/five acts.
  - What or how did you create, maintain, and dissolve during this journey?
  - What was revealed?
  - What remains concealed?
- How did your intention relate to the highest will/icchā-śakti?

Let us remember the foundational teaching of "highest first." We always begin with the Highest. And in the context of saṃkalpa, the highest intention must be remembered as a guide on a moment-by-moment basis, so that any action is the best one is capable of in any given moment. What is most important? What is your purpose/svadharma? How do you want to live your life? Who do you want to be? What do you want to create? It is critical to keep your eyes on the prize.

Reviewing and reconsidering your contemplations and experience is enacting sambandha/making the connection, as discussed in chapter 10. In the many aspects of life, we must learn to connect the dots between intention, action, and their consequences. This goes not only for saṃkalpa, but for the myriad yogic qualities, many of which were considered in this book. The world so desperately needs more people who have the capacity to bring forth these qualities, including maitrī/lovingkindness and karuṇā/compassion. The ability to embody these qualities arises automatically through the refinement and alignment that comes from engaging the practices. However, consciously reflecting and adjusting both our behavior and our saṃkalpa will yield an even greater effect.

SS 1.19 *śakti-saṃdhāne śarīrotpattiḥ*
śakti: power, energy
saṃdhāna: union, joining, bringing together
śarira: body
utpattiḥ: arising, producing
When aligned with the *icchā-śakti* (Divine will) one has the power to shape embodied reality.

SS 1.19 speaks to how aligning with the icchā-śakti/the will of the Highest allows creativity to flow forth, which refines and shapes our embodied life. **When intentions are aligned with the Highest, what manifests is a reflection of the Highest. The power/*śakti* of the ocean of Consciousness supports and amplifies the individual life wave, enhancing life on all levels.** The greatest successes will emerge from tapping into the deepest and most auspicious desires.

As we've discussed, the process of sādhanā connects us with the Highest so that the individual will is aligned with the will of the absolute Consciousness, the icchā-śakti. Again, this is why it is so important to pause and reflect. When one's intention has not manifested, why is that? Have you enacted will/icchā, knowledge/jñāna, and action/kriyā? Or perhaps your saṃkalpa was not refined, not aligned with the Highest. Perhaps it came from the more limited aspects of individuality, like the still-cloaked Arjuna, acting from fear or old saṃskāric patterns.

Manifesting our heart's highest intention is facilitated by the journey of yoga outlined in this book. First, through sādhanā, we must align with the Highest and refine our individual awareness in order to receive the impulses of the Śakti. Then we must actively continue to consult the highest, like Arjuna pausing to consult Kṛṣṇa, and hear what the Highest has to offer by way of refinement. This is the sacred pause in which we engage freedom to act from the highest. And finally, it is important to reflect on our actions and whether they served the Highest. Do they take you farther from the intention, or is it supportive of it? All of life provides increased opportunity for bhāvanā/contemplation and vikalpa-saṃskāra/refinement, which results in further refinement of awareness, intention, and action.

REFLECT AND EXPLORE

- Looking back on the journey of this book, consider any of the following.
  - ~ What was offered that you were able to receive?
  - ~ What did you learn?
  - ~ What can you do better?
- Are there dots you need to connect in your life?
- What's next? What do you intend to do with any new information you've learned through this journey of yoga?

CHAPTER 56

Change Consciousness, Change the World

From the first time I encountered the idea of embodiment as a gift of the Divine, I was enthralled. A place deep inside said "yes!"—even more so with further studies, and even more as I began to practice meditation and experienced its life-enhancing effects. Due to my meditation practice, I learned to traverse into deeper layers of my self and to refine my being by creating a more sattvic buddhi and eliminating what was blocking my heart. This created a clearer pathway, and as my alignment and resonance with the Highest strengthened, I noticed that the positive yogic qualities I'd been reading about started percolating spontaneously from the depths into the surface of my life. All of this happened very naturally as a consequence of choosing to create a daily practice of meditation.

I would be remiss if I did not issue a word of caution before closing. It can be easy to think that we, or someone else, are enlightened—that the peak of the yogic journey has been attained—when in fact that may not be the case. All of us, including those who are teachers, must continually check in not only with the highest Self, but with teachers and the teachings in order to guard against veering off the path and into delusion. It is imperative to hold both ourselves and our teachers to the standards indicated in chapter 13 and appendix III, which discuss teachers and gurus.

Sometimes those on the path of yoga are accused of being selfish and self-absorbed. Indeed, we do garner personal benefit and experience the healing effects of practice. Ultimately, however, increased alignment with the Source from which everything manifests, śakti-cakra-saṃdhāne (SS 1.6), allows us to bring these qualities into our world, our lives, our relationships, and our work. In doing so, we begin to shift the world around us.

That is not to say there isn't work to be done on the surface of life. As community members, we must continue to work to correct all the ills of society through laws, social programs, and all resources available. We must also protect and improve the natural environment for all beings on Earth, each of which is a precious embodiment of the Divine. The *Bhagavad Gītā* teaches a yoga of action. After the conversation with Kṛṣṇa, Arjuna steps onto the battlefield to do his dharma, and accompanying him is Kṛṣṇa, the Highest, who will support Arjuna in all his actions. Consider how serving in the world to create more dharma—holding things together—is facilitated when more and more people are connected to their hearts so that the impulses of love and compassion are the ground from which they operate.

Householder practitioners have the opportunity and responsibility to harness their increasingly clarified awareness and power in service of uplifting their own lives and for the sake of society and the planet as a whole. I know this sounds grandiose, but this is my highest vision. I have experienced it unfolding within myself, and I've seen it manifest with my cohorts and students. I wrote this book because I truly believe this. It's a grand claim, but the assemblage of outcomes is even grander.

This book uses the metaphor of the journey, understanding this is all a process. It requires our participation, one step at a time. This isn't something magical that emerges out of nowhere—although as it emerges, it can be experienced as magic. A sequential journey has been laid out, beginning with the highest vision of who we are underneath the sheaths and layers of our being. We have explored that which cloaks the highest Self and described the process by which sādhanā, the body of yogic practices, enables us to return to our very own clear hearts.

The yoga journey starts by taking the first step, then taking the next step, and continuing step by step. For most people, the key component to unlocking the process is sādhanā, which requires, first of all, adhikāra/studentship. There must be willingness and receptivity to receive the necessary practices and teachings as guides onto the path and to help in the journey. Getting this far in this book is testimony to your adhikāra, but reading this book is not enough. Reading about any activity does not accomplish the activity—though of course one will learn something (jñāna). Ultimately, one must do the practice of meditation to experience the results (vijñāna). To move further, a teacher is likely necessary, so refer to the information in appendix III on finding a teacher, and explore the resources in appendix IV.

Sādhanā yields greater freedom from habitual patterning and allows one to more consciously choose to move from the place that is most aligned with the Source, the śakti-cakra. We are better able to make the right choices and know what is right/dharmic. And it becomes painful—even impossible—to do the nondharmic thing. We are also better able to align intention/saṃkalpa and our will/icchā with the will of the Highest. It happens on a moment-by-moment basis in each now/atha. Harmonizing/saṃdhāna with the Highest brings more positivity into the world. A life unfolds that reflects and embodies the qualities this world needs most, including love, compassion, wisdom, and righteousness/dharma. A misunderstanding of meditation is that it is about "navel-gazing" or about transcending and leaving the world. This may be true for some, but as householders, our dharma/duty is to use the gift of embodiment in service of the Highest.

Like Naṭarāja, we can dance gracefully in our lives, holding ignorance at bay, grounded in the sourceplace of the Heart. Through sādhanā, the clear, stable, grounded aspects of Naṭarāja are established. It is from this basis we can meet the challenges of life and dance the wild dance of embodiment in a grace-filled way. We become clearer about how we are creating, sustaining, and dissolving our lives, as well as about how we participate in the concealment and revelation of our very own hearts.

Capturing the fort of the innermost Heartself, all of the riches under control of that heart begin to spill out into our lives. We experience greater clarity and can see and understand reality at deeper and higher levels. The māyīya-mala, the cloak of differentiation, begins to dissolve, yielding the experience of the connectedness of everything and the increased understanding that approaching anyone without love in our hearts yields only more pain and suffering. Furthermore, as we understand that there is nothing that is not Śiva, we are unwilling to do harm and are naturally drawn to a life of service in some capacity. Working on our individuality, cleaning out the saṃskāras and addressing our karma, we become conduits for the Highest, which has positive effects on our lives and for the lives of others. But there is more than what is happening at the surface, our work as yogis affects multiple layers of reality.

When I was a little girl there was a popular song called "Good Vibrations." The clear and Heart-centered person emits these good vibrations. Although to some this may sound silly, most of us have experienced it in someone whose presence feels good to be around. Somehow their energy, their vibration, uplifts us. This is precisely why it is important to keep good company. And remember the story of Śeṣa/Patañjali, who felt the vibrations of Viṣnu after returning from seeing Naṭarāja dance. And we've all experienced the opposite, the bad vibes and negativity, which are potently spewed out in some sectors of our society, now and in the past.

Both the positive and negative vibrations are experienced locally through contact with our family, co-workers, neighbors, social media, and so on. And even more so in larger groups. Coming together blends and amplifies the vibrations. As these amplified vibrations are created, they begin to affect the collective consciousness. Depending on the nature of those vibrations, it can be good or bad. Experiencing the good vibrations is why people enjoy gathering together in workshops, retreats, festivals, and events of different types. And then some folks seem to relish coming together to increase negativity.

Coming back to the Churning of the Ocean story, think of the ocean as our collective consciousness, and what emerges from that churning is the collective karma generated over the millennia of human existence, both positive and negative. Remember that poison was generated, but also the healing substance of amṛta emerged. The poison had to be transmuted by Śiva, the consummate yogi. And who is Śiva in this interpretation of the story? Śiva here can be thought of as the yogis, all the practitioners (in any tradition) who come together in various ways to move into the deepest layers of reality, into the Heart, and release the healing amṛta for the benefit of the collective consciousness.

The planet itself and our collective consciousness are desperately in need of healing. All one needs to do is look at the news on any given day to understand that on the societal level pain and suffering persist. The residue of planetary strife is embedded in the body of the collective. Many times in history humanity has approached a tipping point, and somehow we've been brought back from the brink, somehow the poison has been transmuted. Now it is our turn to contribute to this upliftment. Ultimately, as more and more people move in the direction of the Heartself, the energy of the planet will shift. In this way, **as we change consciousness, we change the world.**

So while the journey of yoga is beneficial to individual practitioners, and to their family and larger community, there's an even larger context that can be addressed. We as yogis have the power to help with the transmutation of the collective karma, as well as working to create the amṛta to begin to heal our collective consciousness. And it all starts with each of us stepping onto the path, finding a guide to take our hand, and lead us toward our deepest Heart.

REFLECT AND EXPLORE

- Consider the idea of amplification of vibrational energy in the group context.
  - ~ What do you think about it?
  - ~ How have you experienced it?
  - ~ What can you do to contribute?
- Contemplate the teaching that changing consciousness can change the world.
- After reading this book, people have commented that they want to read it again. One reading provides the map, the initial lay of the land, and then they are ready to spiral back again and dive deeper through more svādhyāya/study and increase their understanding/vikalpa-saṃskāra. You may want to do this. And in that next reading, maybe do more of, or different, contemplation questions.
- Or you may simply want to look back and review your writing, remembering and expanding the prior thoughts and insights.
- Reconsider your personal path of yoga. Look at your practice and its results. Connect the dots/sambandha. What is your next step? Perhaps you are ready to find a teacher of meditation. If so, set that intention and follow through. Perhaps you already have a practice and you simply need to begin again. So sit down and do the practice. Perhaps you would like to explore in more detail some of the teachings: the recommended texts and resources in appendix IV give plenty of options.

KEY TEACHINGS FROM PART IX

- Dharma can be thought of as that which sustains or holds things together. It is often defined as "duty" and carries connotations of ethics, justice, goodness, and virtue.
- Skill in action involves summoning both intellectual knowledge, jñāna, and deep experiential knowledge, vijñāna, to respond from the highest place in any given situation.
- When intentions are aligned with the Highest, what manifests is a reflection of the Highest. The power/śakti of the ocean of Consciousness supports and amplifies the individual life wave, enhancing life on all levels.
- Householder practitioners have the opportunity and responsibility to harness their increasingly clarified awareness and power in service of uplifting their own lives and for the sake of society and the planet as a whole.
- As we change consciousness, we change the world.

APPENDIX I

List of Key Teachings

Introduction: Welcome to the Journey of Yoga

- Study is an iterative process in which teachings are considered again and again to discover nuance, deepen comprehension, and understand their application.
- Although myths may not literally be true, they teach a greater truth. When studying the stories of the tradition, consider yourself to be every character in the story.
- Meditation is a process wherein awareness is turned inward to penetrate beyond the surface toward your essence—the heart of who you are.
- Sādhanā is an assemblage of practices utilized over time as one moves along the path of yoga and meditation.
- It is important to have personal contact with a qualified teacher to teach the practice, explain how the practice works, what to expect, and for support on the journey.

Part I: Beginning the Journey

- Now let us study the teachings of yoga. (YS 1.1)
- There are many yogas.
- Saṃkalpa/intention makes conscious, and sets in motion, the desires one wishes to manifest.
- The seed contains the potential for the tree.

Part II: Preparing for the Journey: Foundational Concepts

- There is a general contrast between two paths of yoga: the nivṛtti, or renunciate path, and pravṛtti, the householder path.
- The path of yoga requires an intellectual understanding, jñāna, as well as an experiential understanding, vijñāna.
- Traditionally, svādhyāya refers to recitation and study of the yogic texts, but it can also refer to a mindful exploration of everyday life, as well as the innermost Self.
- Vikalpa-saṃskāra is the refinement of understanding, including both understanding of the teachings and the refinement of the place of awareness from which that understanding arises.
- The practice of bhāvanā presumes a willingness to consider the teachings seriously and to work with them, allowing their wisdom to saturate awareness, so that anything that seems impenetrable begins to soften, sprout, and reveal itself.
- The one primal guru that is Consciousness itself appears in many forms. Human teachers who can access this Consciousness act as conduits for the highest knowledge.
- Guru can be thought of in three ways: the external teacher, the teachings themselves, and the highest Self.
- Each of the gods is a representation of some aspect, attribute, or flavor of the Highest.

PART III: The Nature of Consciousness

- There is a Sourceplace that is the ground of being, which pulsates everything into existence as part of Itself.
- Individual life waves arise from the ocean of Consciousness.
- The oceanic sourceplace is called the "Absolute Consciousness." It creates all of the waves of existence, known as "relative" reality.
- Reality is different at different levels.

- "Highest first" asks one to turn toward the Highest in the first moment of an endeavor and in each moment throughout life.
- Everything emanates into existence from Source, including you. You are not separate. You are Consciousness.
- The Absolute Highest Consciousness is known as "transcendent," and its manifestation is known as "immanent." The paradox is that the transcendent Consciousness is also immanent in everything.
- At the level of the highest reality, the absolute Citi is completely free.
- The tradition proclaims, *nāśivaṃ vidyate kvacit*: There is nothing that is not Śiva.
- Śiva-Śakti is both the absolute stillness of Consciousness as well as the unlimited potential of power and creativity.
- The pañca-śaktis/five powers are: cit/Consciousness, ānanda/bliss, icchā/will, jñāna/knowledge, and kriyā/action. They are different aspects of the potency of Consciousness.
- The pañca-kṛtyas/five acts are sṛṣṭi/creation, sthiti/maintenance, saṃhāra/dissolution, tirodhāna, vilaya, or nigraha/concealment, and anugraha/revelation or grace.

Part IV: Human Manifestation and the Human Condition

- The mind/citta is a manifestation of the Highest/Citi. Indeed, it is a gift that allows one to maximize householder life and to contact the highest Consciousness.
- The mind is saturated with whatever one turns attention to.
- Ignorance leads to a fundamental confusion. Instead of experiencing the atma/Self, which is eternal, pure, and joyful, one identifies with the surface self (the an-ātma or "not-self"), which is transitory, impure, and painful. (YS 2.5)
- Limited knowledge is bondage. (SS 1.2)

- The malas are what cover, conceal, and limit the pure, full, and free Consciousness. There are three types of malas: the āṇava-mala, the māyīya-mala, and the kārma-mala.
- A saṃsārī is one who experiences saṃsāra, including suffering, and transmigrates from one lifetime to another due to karma.
- Yoga is accomplished by calming the movements of the mind. Then one sees the deeper true Self, like stilling waves on a lake. Otherwise, one remains identified with the thought patterns, which are like waves on the lake. (YS 1.2–1.4)
- There can be a repetitive cycle when the citta-vṛttis prompt action, thereby creating karma, which lays down the saṃskāra, which causes more citta-vṛttis, and so on.

Part V: First Steps on the Path

- Śaktipāta involves the initial and subsequent awakenings that propel one on the path of yoga.
- Adhikāra relates to the degree to which a student is prepared, ready, and interested in receiving practices and teachings.
- The circumstance wherein one is spontaneously enlightened is known as anupāya, or "no method." The texts make it clear that this applies to an extremely small percentage of people.
- Students require yogic methods, or upāya, appropriate to where they are on their path of yoga.
- The core means to yoga is balancing regular practice with dispassion. (YS 1.12)
- Practice is established when done for a long time, without interruptions, and in the proper fashion—even reverently. (YS 1.14)

Part VI: How the Yoga of Meditation Works

- Sometimes practice yields beautiful experiences and results, and other times it is challenging. Yet ultimately the nectar of healing yields an alignment with the Highest, leading to a beneficial refinement of one's entire being, as well as life as a whole.
- The karmas, saṃskāras, and citta-vṛttis can be a help or hindrance on the path of yoga.
- Working on the surface of life with the saṃskāras can be effective to some degree, but meditation helps burn up the seeds of saṃskāras and attenuate the kleśas, the root hindrances.
- Meditating establishes the saṃskāra/habit pattern of moving awareness from the surface to deeper layers, to the deepest part of oneself.
- One obtains the highest knowledge regarding the nature of reality, and this will lead to insight into the nature of many different things. (YS 1.48)
- The practice of meditation creates obstructor saṃskāras that don't activate awareness with citta-vṛttis like other saṃskāras. Instead, they put a damper on the outward-moving saṃskāras, even destroying them. (YS 1.50)
- The guṇas are three primary qualities, or threads, that make up the fabric of the world, including individual awareness.
- The three types of guṇas are sattva, rajas, and tamas. Sattva is luminous, harmonious, intelligent, and pure. Rajas is active, fiery, energetic, and passionate. Tamas is inertia, dull, heavy, and dark.
- During meditation, one penetrates to quieter, clearer states of awareness. Then individuality is suffused with sattvic clarity, and life unfolds from this clearer place.
- The more refined one's general state of awareness becomes through practice, the more successful the svādhyāya/self-study and bhāvanā/contemplation practices will be, as the process of vikalpa-saṃskāra/refinement is also supported.

Part VII: Enlightenment

- The stages of yoga are amazing. (SS 1.12)
- Traversing the path, creating a sattva buddhi and purifying the saṃskāras, dispels ignorance and our luminous essential nature is revealed. This is a state of Self-realization.
- Tantra views the deep states of samādhi as a stage on the path to further states of awareness, wherein one realizes that they are nothing but Śiva and that there is nothing that is not Śiva. So, there is a close-eyed experience of revelation in meditation, which expands to an open-eyed experience of everything as absolute Consciousness.
- The inward-turning practices of yoga illuminate an awareness that you, at essence, are creating, sustaining, and dissolving experience. Also, you take part in concealing and revealing the heart. Recognizing this, you become the Heart (Citi). (PH 13)
- Jīvan-mukti means "living while liberated." It indicates that one can be liberated while in the body and live in the world in that liberated state.
- One is endowed with an ability to penetrate beyond the surface presentation into the heart of all things to recognize each and everything in the universe as Consciousness.

Part VIII: Embodying the Emerging Yogic Qualities

- Aligning with the highest Sourceplace allows the power of the Absolute to flow through one's individuality, yielding shifts in awareness that reflect the highest and most auspicious reality.
- With access to that which rules over all the treasures, one has access to everything in the territory.
- As one becomes more aligned with the Highest and refines awareness, innate capacities of the heart begin to naturally emerge and flow.

- The increased ability to be discerning and use good judgment is a hallmark of our progress on the path of yoga.
- Moving along the journey of yoga, a place to pause and gain some perspective is accessed. This ledge of freedom allows one to survey options and consciously choose the next steps.
- As embodied beings, svātantrya/freedom is being free of the bonds of unconscious, habitual, saṃskāric patterns so that one acts consciously from the highest accessible place, bringing the greatest possible alignment to any given situation.
- Pratipakṣa-bhāvana/cultivating the opposite includes cultivating states of awareness through practice that naturally contain the opposite quality, working with the surface thoughts and emotions, and enacting other aspects of sādhanā that address negativity.
- Future suffering is to be avoided. (YS 2.16)

Part IX: Change Consciousness and Change the World

- Dharma can be thought of as that which sustains or holds things together. It is often defined as "duty" and carries connotations of ethics, justice, goodness, and virtue.
- Skill in action involves summoning both intellectual knowledge, jñāna, and deep experiential knowledge, vijñāna, to respond from the highest place in any given situation.
- When intentions are aligned with the Highest, what manifests is a reflection of the Highest. The power/śakti of the ocean of Consciousness supports and amplifies the individual life wave, enhancing life on all levels.
- Householder practitioners have the opportunity and responsibility to harness their increasingly clarified awareness and power in service of uplifting their own lives and for the sake of society and the planet as a whole.
- As we change consciousness, we change the world.

APPENDIX II

A Selective History of Yoga

It is important to note at the outset that specific historical dating of yoga is both problematic and controversial. This is in part because most of the teachings and stories were initially oral, then later collected and codified over many centuries. More important is to understand the general order of the texts: which are oldest, which followed from earlier texts. As well there was a great deal of overlap in lineages and philosophical schools. In this section, I mention some of the major texts and schools from the tradition, with an emphasis on placing the teachings in this book in their historical context.

The many streams of yoga have often been subsumed under the label "Hinduism." The origin of the term *Hindu* has varied historical roots, but it evolved to describe those people on the Indian subcontinent who were not Sikh, Jain, Buddhist, Christian, or Muslim. In contrast to these listed religions, Hinduism has no unifying founder, though it may claim some foundational unifying themes. Nonetheless, within the realm of this general Hinduism category there's a wide variety of underlying philosophical presuppositions and practices.

When was the beginning of yoga? It depends on what you call "yoga." You may have heard claims that yoga is five thousand years old. That estimate is based in part on small statues and seals found in the Indus Valley, in which human figures seem to be in meditative postures. These are dated around 3000 BCE. However, there is controversy over whether these depictions are shamanic figures, which were represented in many cultures during that time, or whether they specifically portray a yogi.

The first "texts" in India are called the *Vedas*. The word *veda* literally means "knowledge." These are generally dated around 2000 to 500 BCE. For much of their history, the Vedas were passed down through generations by people who memorized and verbally recited them. The Vedas don't talk about yoga per se, they're generally hymns of worship and ritual. One way I've heard this explained is that they reflect how life was during these ancient times, when just surviving was a challenge. The rituals were conducted by priests acting as intermediaries to appease the gods and bring good fortune. There is a sense of exchange: if you do the ritual, some good will come. For example, items are offered into the fire in exchange for worldly boons.

Although there really wasn't anything called "yoga" in these texts, there seemed to be yogis on the periphery. There are mentions of *munis*, the "silent sages," alluded to in the earliest of the Vedas, the *Ṛg Veda*. The term *yoga* appeared in the later texts collectively called the *Upaniṣads*. Since they follow the Vedas, philosophically this knowledge is also known as the Vedānta, which means literally "the end of the Veda." The word *upaniṣad* means "to sit near," as in sitting near one's teacher.

There are more than two hundred Upaniṣads, but ten to twenty are considered to be the "principal" Upaniṣads, and there are many translations readily available. Some estimate the earliest Upaniṣads date from 600 BCE, with later ones composed into the medieval era.

It is in the Upaniṣads that the first use of the term *yoga* appeared (See, for example, the *Taittirīya Upaniṣad*), as well as the mention of yogic practices. There is a clear shift away from the sacrificial rite of the Vedas, which some saw as inferior, to the more philosophical and mystical discourse revolving around a quest for the ultimate reality, called Brahman.

During these early periods, there was a rise in the notion of asceticism: withdrawing from life in order to transcend suffering. In the early Upaniṣads and early Buddhist and Jain teachings, the ritual of the Vedas became more internal and something the individual could do, compared to the Vedic Period, in which priests acted as intermediaries. There was a sense that power was created by withdrawing and concentrating one's energy. One becomes empowered with a more direct access to the Absolute, or Brahman.

Around the fifth to the fourth century BCE, the two great Indian epics emerged. The first is the *Rāmāyaṇa*, which involves many characters, including Rāma, Sītā, and Hanumān. The second great epic is the *Mahābhārata*, which is the longest poem in the world. It is the story of the Pāṇḍavas and Kauravas (two related families) which details their rivalry, exploits, and war. The influential *Bhagavad Gītā*— "The Song of God"—is actually a section of the *Mahābhārata*. The *Gītā* contains some of the earliest teachings of yoga and summarizes much of what was extant at the time. Many of the stories from the Indian tradition are contained in these epics, as well as in many other texts.

In the period from 500 to 400 BCE, Sāṃkhya became codified. It is one of the more influential streams of Indian philosophy, which has been incorporated into, and refined by, many of the later streams. Sāṃkhya can be thought of as the metaphysical infrastructure of the *Yoga Sūtra*, and you also find early accounts of it in the *Bhagavad Gītā*. Literally, *sāṃkhya* means "enumeration" or "counting." It begins with two basic principles. The first is *puruṣa*, the innermost self, and the second is *prakṛti*, which is matter. *Sāṃkhya* describes how the material world evolves into twenty-four constituents, or ingredients, known as the *tattvas*.

This brings us to the author/sage Patañjali's *Yoga Sūtra*, which most scholars place between 100 BCE and 300 CE. Though Patañjali is not the founder of what came to be known as "Classical Yoga," he was the systematizer of it. The *Yoga Sūtra* text is based on the assumption that the goal of yoga is to unravel the confusion between spirit and matter, puruṣa and prakṛti. It is an ascetic text and also what is called a "dualist" approach: the goal being to withdraw from the material world of prakṛti in order to experience the completely separate and pure puruṣa.

Concurrent with the codification of Patañjali's writings and other streams of yoga, different forms of Buddhism began to crystallize. Buddhism has vast and varied teachings beyond the scope of this book. But it is important to note that one of the difficulties in studying the texts of yoga is that many of them are debating with Buddhism and other philosophical streams about particular technical points. So the history of yoga in its many streams is intertwined with Buddhism.

A very influential stream, Advaita Vedānta, arose in about 800 CE. *Advaita* means "not two" or "not dual," so this is a nondualistic school, in which the world is seen as arising out of Brahman, the Absolute, and the manifold appearances in the world are seen as an illusion. A proponent of this is the very influential teacher Śaṅkarācārya. Many of the early proponents of yoga in the West adhered to this school, and its themes remain dominant in many textual commentaries and in much of the yoga that is taught today.

Intertwined and emerging from all of this are the streams of Bhakti and Tantra. Bhakti is a path of love and devotion to a supreme deity.

There are many lineages within this tradition, which have different ways of enacting and experiencing loving devotion, as well as many gurus and forms of god to which devotion is expressed. This is reflected today in the popularity of *kīrtan(a)*, chanting praise or the names of god. Many of the early streams involved worshiping Viṣṇu, and especially the form of Kṛṣṇa. This teaching is reflected in the *Bhagavad Gītā* and in other textual and poetic sources.

There are many streams of Tantra, including Buddhist Tantra. In the Hindu tradition these include Kashmir Śaivism and Śrīvidyā, but there are many others, with widely varying philosophical assumptions and practices. In the West, Tantra has unfortunately become associated with sexual practices, which is a gross and unacceptable misunderstanding. (Some aspects of Tantra do involve sexual practice, but it's not necessarily a principal tenet.)

A root text of the Tantric tradition is the *Śiva Sūtra*, which was said to be revealed to the sage Vasugupta, a great devotee of Śiva, during the first half of the ninth century CE. Vasugupta was a native of Kashmir, and the text of the *Śiva Sūtra* became the inception point for what scholars later called Kashmir Śaivism.

Of importance to our studies is the great Tantric polymath, Abhinavagupta, who taught in Kashmir around 1000 CE. He wrote many commentaries and texts, but perhaps most notable is his *Tantrāloka* ("Light on the Tantras"), which critiques, refines, and synthesizes many of the streams of Tantra. Also important for our studies is his student, Kṣemarāja, who wrote a commentary on the *Śiva Sūtra* and also brought together the teachings of the Pratyabhijñā, or "Recognition" school, in his text, the *Pratyabhijñā-hṛdayam* ("The Heart of Recognition"), among many other writings.

In the ninth through twelfth centuries, Hatha Yoga emerged, which some characterize as a form of Tantra. *Hatha* means "forceful" and often involves an austere discipline of the body. Hatha Yoga has many variations; among them are some that emphasize an alchemical approach to transforming the body-mind.

With the rise of Islamic culture in northern India in the fourteenth century, many yogic teachings went underground, moved to other regions and/or completely disappeared.

What we call "yoga" and do in modern-day yoga āsana classes is very recent, and some argue that much of it came out of the gymnastics traditions brought to India by Europeans. Some call what is practiced in most yoga studios today "Modern Postural Yoga."

This very brief history gives a flavor of the unfolding of yoga philosophy, with emphasis on aspects covered in this book. It is important to know that our Western yoga culture today has been influenced by these many different streams of yoga, each with a different approach and assumptions, which led to different ways of practicing. Therefore, there is no *one* yoga: there are various streams that have emerged and intertwined and made their way to us through many sources. Each subsequent philosophy takes from the older texts that which they regard most useful and reinterprets it in line with its philosophy.

Several debates wind themselves through this long history that should be kept in mind. As indicated, the early practices were very ritualistic; later, the ritual became internalized with the development of the ascetic or renunciate path. (Though it must be noted that ritual is still a big part of many lineage streams.) From this emerged communities, including ashrams and monasteries for the renunciates, as well as wandering or forest-dwelling ascetics. So one debate contrasts the ascetic path with other paths of yoga for householders.

There are also approaches that are dualistic, in which spirit and matter are said to be completely separate, in contrast to nondualistic approaches that say everything is a manifestation of spirit. There is also a debate about whether or not the material world is, in fact, real or simply exists in our minds. Likewise, there are debates about whether there is something like God or Absolute Consciousness.

This is the long, diverse historical stream that any serious student of yoga must step into. As this summary indicates, there isn't just one yoga philosophy. Also, modern practitioners often receive information that mixes everything up. Wherever you are in your understanding, and wherever you begin now, is exactly perfect. From that place, we simply wade into the stream.

APPENDIX III

Choosing Yoga Āsana and Meditation Teachers

I would be remiss if I didn't offer some guidance for choosing a teacher. However, please be aware there is no straightforward answer: what follows are just general guidelines.

One of the best ways to find a teacher is via word of mouth, specifically from someone you know and trust. Popularity does not matter. In the marketplace of life, what's popular is not always the best thing for you. I also recommend interacting with a teacher's students and considering whether they are representative of who or how you want to be. And be sure to observe how the students embody the teachings.

As you consider teachers, it is useful to release expectations and be open, because the teacher may come in a way you aren't expecting. They may not look the way you envisage, or be in an assumed place. On the other hand, don't be naïve. Use your intelligence and discernment. And you should ask questions (like the ones indicated below) and listen carefully to both the content and demeanor of how the questions are answered.

You may want to try several teachers to discover different options, instead of settling on the one you first encounter. You may also want to interact with a teacher a few times, as one encounter may not represent what they are fully capable of. And remember, your initial reactions may not be the best indicators of a good "match." It could be that a teacher who pushes your buttons is exactly what you need.

Consider what you want in a teacher. You may want to consciously contemplate/do bhāvanā on this. If you have a yearning for the deeper aspects of yoga beyond the physical āsana, keep looking until you find someone who suits your needs. And in general, the best teachers will meet you where you are, rather than using a "one size fits all" approach.

Determine the lineage of the teacher. This is how the teachings are traditionally passed from teacher to student. This can verify that what the teacher is offering is authentic, has been tested, and is therefore effective. Beware of teachers who "do their own thing." They may be great, but often not. Ask who they've studied with in the past. Are *their* teachers reputable? Do you resonate with the teachings of those teachers?

How long have they practiced? I believe that no one should teach yoga āsana or meditation until they've practiced a *minimum* of five years. Years of practice are necessary to understand how the practice works, to have experience with the practice, and to digest it on many levels before being ready to teach. In the modern yoga scene, anyone with a 200-hour yoga teacher training can call themselves a yoga teacher, even if they haven't practiced or don't know very much about the tradition of yoga or meditation. If a student is only involved in the physical practice, this is more or less of a problem, since one can be physically hurt while studying with an unqualified teacher. But the risk is also great regarding meditation and other methods intended to penetrate into the depths of consciousness.

It's also important to discern whether a potential teacher is still currently studying. This is especially important for younger teachers, though it applies to everyone.

Essentially, I'm suggesting with these guidelines that the teacher has both jñāna/knowledge and vijñāna/experience. They should have practiced long enough to have a solid experiential basis as well as the foundational knowledge and understanding to guide you. Most likely this involves some type of training to become a qualified teacher. This is really important. It is one thing to have a practice; it is a completely other thing to be trained how to teach it.

Also consider whether the teacher practices what they preach. It is wonderful for a teacher to espouse lofty teachings, but do you see them embodying those teachings? Beware any teacher who teaches one thing but acts another way and/or somehow makes themself an exception to the teachings. It is especially important to know that the potential teacher is a regular practitioner. If not, again beware.

Consider the teacher's overall demeanor and whether you resonate with it. Are they humble or inflated? Do they embody qualities of patience, kindness, and intelligence? Are they inspirational and encourage you to be the best in your life? Why do they teach? Is it for you, the student? Is it for the greater good? Or do you sense they are seeking power or fame?

Asking these questions will hopefully filter out unqualified teachers, and how they answer will allow you to assess their character and your resonance with them. Any teacher who seems resentful about answering these questions is likely not a good choice. This will continue to be true as you study with any teacher. You always want to feel comfortable asking questions. If a teacher is not available to answer questions via some mechanism, steer away.

Again, these are just guidelines, and they can be tricky to determine. Ultimately you must rely on your inner guidance, though at some point, you might find you've made a mistake, or you may sense you've learned enough from that teacher. If you decide a particular teacher is no longer serving you, feel free to move on.

APPENDIX IV

Recommended Texts and Resources

For those interested in further study, the resources listed in this appendix represent a range of what is available, with a particular focus on topics relevant to this book, including translations of source texts, articles, websites, and the teachers I have most benefitted from. Many of the books have appeared in multiple editions and publishers, so I have omitted the specifics. Generally, any edition is fine.

Teachers

Below are three teachers of mine who have had the greatest impact on this book.

Paul Muller-Ortega, Blue Throat Yoga
BlueThroatYoga.com
Paul is a scholar/practitioner *par excellence.* The school of meditation he leads, Blue Throat Yoga, teaches deep Tantric practices as well as study of the tradition.

Douglas Brooks, Rajanaka
Rajanaka.com
Douglas is a wellspring of knowledge, especially about mythology. Many of the myths in this book came from him, and he teaches courses on many topics.

Christopher Wallis, Tantra Illuminated
TantraIlluminated.org
Christopher, or Hareesh, Wallis leads a Tantra-based school of practice and study. He is the author of several outstanding books (some listed in the following pages) and an excellent blog, and he offers many opportunities for learning.

Source Texts

Translations of Sanskrit texts are unavoidably filtered through the lens of the translator, so they differ regarding how well they reflect the original intent of the text. Because of this, I generally recommend that you refer to at least two translations of any text in order to compare different perspectives. I also recommend that you get at least one translation with a word-by-word translation so that you stay close to the original Sanskrit text.

Yoga Sūtra
(Note: All of the following books have a word-by-word translation.)

Edwin F. Bryant: *The Yoga Sūtras of Patañjali: A New Edition, Translation, and Commentary*
Bryant's version is by far the best translation as it includes summaries of the major commentaries. A warning: It is quite dense and very long.

Swami Satchidananda: *The Yoga Sutras of Patanjali*
Many people love this sweet translation, which is a readable, nonacademic version. Good as an introduction.

Georg Feuerstein: *The Yoga-Sūtra of Patañjali: A New Translation and Commentary*
This is a go-to for me, as it is succinct and precise. Includes verbal roots of words in the sūtras. Not an easy read, however.

B. K. S. Iyengar: *Light on the Yoga Sūtras of Patañjali*
Lovely for yoga āsana practitioners, as Iyengar relates it nicely. Also includes some great tables and background information. A nice balance between academic and readable.

SwamiJ.com: A useful website with information about many of the teachings covered in this book.

Pratyabhijñā-Hṛdayam

Christopher Wallis: *The Recognition Sūtras*
The best translation currently available, though it's somewhat academic and idiosyncratic. Includes a translation of Kṣemarāja's auto-commentary.

Swami Shantananda, with Peggy Bendet: *The Splendor of Recognition*
Highly readable, though it adds a lot of the author's perspective. General Tantric concepts are covered, and it has a word-by-word translation.

Jaideva Singh: *Pratyabhijñāhṛdayam: The Secret of Self-Recognition*
Includes Kṣemarāja's auto-commentary. Has a useful introduction to the underlying philosophy. Pithy, and a challenging read.

Śiva Sūtra

Jaideva Singh: *Śiva Sūtras: The Yoga of Supreme Identity*
A somewhat academic approach with a word-by-word translation that includes Kṣemarāja's commentary. Also includes a great introduction to the nondual Śaiva philosophy.

Swami Lakshmanjoo: *Shiva Sutras: The Supreme Awakening*
Somewhat accessible approach by a great modern master of Kashmir Śaivism.

Bhagavad Gītā

The *Bhagavad Gītā* is probably the most translated of the Indian classics, so there are many to choose from. Translations vary from more literal to being a vehicle for espousing the translator's spiritual agenda. Below are the ones I use most often.

S. Radhakrishnan: *The Bhagavadgītā*
Verse-by-verse translation, with a moderate amount of exposition.

Georg Feuerstein with Brenda Feuerstein: *The Bhagavad-Gītā, A New Translation*
Includes an excellent word-by-word translation. More technical than readable, it includes some supportive essays on related subjects.

Eknath Easwaran: *The Bhagavadgita*
Nice chapter summaries and very readable.

Other Books, Articles, and Teachers

The author's website is CindyLusk.com, which includes current offerings of yoga āsana, meditation, and a blog.

Tantra

Christopher Wallis: *Tantra Illuminated: The Philosophy, History, and Practice of a Timeless Tradition*
A most excellent introduction to a wide range of Tantric concepts, including those in this book.

Paul E. Muller-Ortega: "'*Tarko Yogāṅgam Uttamam*': On Subtle Knowledge and the Refinement of Thought in Abhinavagupta's Liberative Tantric Method" in *Theory and Practice of Yoga,* Knut A. Jacobsen. ed. 181–212, 2005.
A seminal and excellent article regarding the concepts of ignorance and knowledge, vikalpa-saṃskāra, and bhāvanā.

Paul Eduardo Muller-Ortega: *The Triadic Heart of Śiva: Kaula Tantricism of Abhinavagupta in the Non-Dual Shaivism of Kashmir*
A challenging but worthwhile study of the concept of the Heart. It includes a translation of Abhinavagupta's *Parātrīśikālaghuvṛttiḥ*.

Swami Shankarananda: *The Yoga of Kashmir Shaivism: Consciousness Is Everything.*
An excellent exposition of Kashmir Śaivism that weaves together teachings from several traditional texts.

Kavitha Chinnaiyan: *Glorious Alchemy: Living the Lalitā Sahasranāma*
An accessible and practical introduction to the Śrīvidyā tradition of Tantra.

André Padoux: *The Hindu Tantric World: An Overview*
As the title suggests, a somewhat scholarly but readable introduction to the history of Tantra.

Mark Dyczkowski has a number of books and additional resources at anuttaratrikakula.com.

Yoga Overview and History

Georg Feuerstein: *The Yoga Tradition: Its History, Literature, Philosophy, and Practice*
A classic introduction to the history and philosophy of the different branches of yoga.

James Mallinson and Mark Singleton: *Roots of Yoga*
A sourcebook on yoga organized by topic, including translated excerpts from many traditional texts.

Amy Vaughn: *From the Vedas to Vinyasa: An Introduction to the History and Philosophy of Yoga*
A down-to-earth and readable history of yoga, with summaries of the major philosophies.

Meditation

There are many modalities of meditation. Below are two resources I am personally familiar with and can recommend.

Neelakantha Meditation
BlueThroatYoga.com, founded by Paul Muller-Ortega
This is the lineage in which I practice and teach, so I highly recommend it.

Sally Kempton
SallyKempton.com
Meditation for the Love of It
A beautiful book introducing different varieties of meditation

Yoga: General Interest

Here's a sampling of books on yoga that I have found useful.

Bill Dorigan with Judyth Hill: *Finding the Midline: How Yoga Helps a Trial Lawyer Make Friends and Connect to Spirit*

Richard Freeman: *The Mirror of Yoga: Awakening the Intelligence of Body and Mind*

Christina Sell: *My Body Is A Temple: Yoga As a Path to Wholeness*

Sacred Chanting

Kirtan, or sacred chanting, was part of my awakening process, and it continues to help me connect to the divine. Below are resources I have personally benefitted from.

Shantala (Benjy and Heather Wertheimer): shantalamusic.com

Krishna Das: krishnadas.com

Deva Premal and Miten: devapremalmiten.com
Note: They have a lovely rendition of the *Oṃ gaṃ gaṇapataye namaḥ* chant given in chapter 14.

APPENDIX V

A Little Bit About Sanskrit

Anyone interested in studying the deeper teachings of yoga inevitably encounters Sanskrit, the primary language of the tradition. I have included source teachings in transliterated Sanskrit to authentically represent and honor the tradition. If you are not interested in the Sanskrit, it is fine to ignore it, since throughout this book the English equivalents are provided. However, a little knowledge about Sanskrit—even if at first it seems daunting—can take one a long way and will aid in understanding the teachings. Following are a few pointers.

- The original beautiful, flowy Sanskrit script with the connecting line on the top, is called Devanāgarī. *Deva* refers to the gods and *nāgarī* means "city," so Devanāgarī means "city or abode of devas, or gods." This book includes the transliteration or romanized version of the original Sanskrit, which looks like English letters with various diacritical marks such as lines, dots, and accent marks. It is important to note that there are a variety of transliteration schemes—a standard one is used in this book—but elsewhere may use different spellings due to some other transliteration scheme from the original Sanskrit.
- Familiarizing oneself with the Sanskrit alphabet and its pronunciation could be very useful. Pronunciation guides on the internet and in many books are readily available—almost every translation of the *Yoga Sūtra* or *Bhagavad Gītā* has one. Some of the letters in transliterated Sanskrit have pronunciations similar to other languages. But note that technically there are subtle variations on where the sound originates in

the mouth. The good news is that unlike other languages, including English, Sanskrit is phonetic: letters are pronounced the same in every word. Very briefly, here are a few simplified pronunciation hints.

- » **Vowels** are pronounced differently than an English speaker might expect. For example, the Sanskrit vowel *a* is pronounced like the English *u* in "nut," and the long *ā* is like the *a* in "calm." The Sanskrit *e* is pronounced more like the English letter *a* as in "day." For example, Deva is pronounced "Day-vuh." So, it's useful to check a pronunciation guide for the different vowels.
- » When the **sibilant "s"** has an accent mark over it (ś) or a dot under it (ṣ), it's roughly pronounced like the English "sh." Note that these may be represented as "sh" in transliteration schemes elsewhere. For example, *Śiva* is pronounced "Shiva" and *Śakti* is pronounced "Shakti."
- » **Sanskrit consonants** are sometimes pronounced similar to English. However, the Sanskrit letters *c* and *ch* are both pronounced like the English "ch." For example, *citta* is pronounced "chitta." The consonant *g* is always "hard" as in the English "go." The aspirated consonants, for example *gh, th, dh, ph, bh,* are pronounced with some extra aspiration, as in "log house." The *ṛ* is pronounced roughly like "ri," and elsewhere it can be transliterated that way.

- In Sanskrit, when two or more words come together, the letters at their meeting place change. For example, *saccidānanda* = *sat* + *cit* + *ānanda*. This is based on *sandhi* rules, which govern the meeting of letters—in compound words, and elsewhere. Don't worry about the specifics; just know that words and the letters within them will morph when joined with others. This is in part why some words are spelled differently in different places. For example, the sūtra/aphorism itself, the definitions of the component words, and a discussion of that sūtra may have slightly different spellings of the same root word.

- A lot of the grammar of the Sanskrit language is embedded in the words. For example, different endings are used for nouns to indicate gender, case, and number. Similarly, verbs have different conjugations to denote a variety of things, including tense, voice, and mood. This can account for some of the differences in words that have the same root meaning, as well as differences between the source text and in a discussion.

- A very useful way to approach the source teachings is to parse the original Sanskrit into the component parts to see the words within the words. Sometimes there is a dash inserted to delineate the different words in a compound word. For example, the first aphorism of the *Yoga Sūtra*, *atha yogānuśāsanam*, can be parsed into *atha yoga-anuśāsanam.*

- One of the traditional ways to understand Sanskrit words is to look at the etymology of the words—in particular, which verbal root is involved. The whole Sanskrit language is built from these verbal roots, and identifying the root word can be a very illuminating way to look at the meaning of a Sanskrit concept.

- The traditional texts contain a lot of technical language. This is unavoidable, and unfortunately the same word can mean something completely different depending on the context. And, of course, words and concepts have different definitions within the different schools in the long history of yoga. In the Sanskrit dictionary, a single word may have a whole column of meanings, some of which may seem contradictory. Then as the teachings are applied to modern-day life, at times the meaning will be stretched or reinterpreted. For example, consider the word *yoga*, and how many different ways that is defined. The glossary includes the definition(s) used in this book.

APPENDIX VI

List and Index of Textual Teachings and Stories

Bhagavad Gītā (BG)

Pratyabhijñā-Hṛdayam (PH)

PH 9 *cidvat-tac-chakti-saṃkocāt malāvṛtaḥ saṃsārī* Consciousness is covered by impurities due to the contraction of its powers and becomes a transmigrating soul. **Ch 31: 126f**, **Ch 32: 130**, 131, 185

PH 13 *tat-parijñāne cittam-eva antarmukhī-bhāvena cetana-padādhyārohāt citiḥ* When one fully realizes that [one is the enactor of the pañca-kṛtyas/ five acts of Śiva], through inward movement the individual mind ascends to expanded consciousness and becomes Consciousness. **Ch 43: 184f**

PH 16 *cit-ānanda-lābhe dehādiṣu cetyamāneṣv api cidaikātmya-pratipatti-dārḍhyaṃ jīvan-muktiḥ* When the bliss of the Highest is attained, along with a steady perception of the body and everything as Consciousness, this is liberation while embodied. **Ch 44: 188f**

Śiva Sūtra (SS)

SS 1.1 *caitanyam-ātmā* Consciousness is the Self. **Ch 19: 92f**, 125, 140, 182, 189

SS 1.2 *jñānaṃ bandhaḥ* [Limited] knowledge is bondage. **Ch 30: 125**

SS 1.5 *udyamo bhairavaḥ* The upsurge is Bhairava [Śiva]. **Ch 43: 184f**, 195

SS 1.6 *śakti-cakra-saṃdhāne viśva-saṃhāraḥ* Aligning with the wheel of śaktis, the [separate] universe dissolves. **Ch 45: 195f**, 237

SS 1.12 *vismayo yoga-bhūmikāḥ* The stages of yoga are amazing**. Ch 42: 181f**

SS 1.19 *śakti-saṃdhāne śarīrotpattiḥ* When aligned with the *icchā-śakti* (Divine will) one has the power to shape embodied reality. **235**

SS 2.6 *gururupāyaḥ* The guru is the means. **67f**

SS 3.13 *siddhaḥ svatantra-bhāvaḥ* [When one is established in] the state of [realization], freedom is achieved. **202**

Yoga Sūtra (YS)

YS 1.1 *atha yoga-anuśāsanam* Now let us study the teachings of yoga. **Ch 2: 18f**, 26, 32, 34

YS 1.2 *yogaś citta-vṛtti-nirodhaḥ* Yoga is restraining the movements of the mind. **Ch 6: 32f**, 44, 86-87, 119, 131, 133, 146, 149, 166, 182, 206

YS 1.3 *tadā draṣṭuḥ sva-rūpe-avasthānam* Then the seer abides in its essence. **33**, 60, 87, 132, 133, 146, 168, 182, 206

YS 1.4 *vṛtti-sārūpyam itaratra* Otherwise, there is identification with the citta-vṛttis [whirlings of the mind]. **132-133**, 206

YS 1.5 *vṛttayaḥ pañcatayaḥ kliṣṭa-akliṣṭāḥ* There are five types of [citta-]vṛttis, and they can be detrimental or not. **Ch 39: 166f**

YS 1.12 *abhyāsa-vairāgyābhyāṃ tan-nirodhaḥ* [The mind] is restrained through practice and dispassion. 34, **Ch 37: 149f**

YS 1.14 *sa tu dīrgha-kāla-nairantarya-satkāra-āsevito dṛḍha-bhūmiḥ* This [practice] is firmly established when it is cultivated for a long time, uninterruptedly, properly, and with reverence. **Ch 37: 150f**

YS 1.33 *maitrī-karuṇā-muditā-upekṣāṇāṃ sukha-duḥkha-puṇya-apuṇya-viṣayāṇāṃ bhāvanātaś-citta-prasādanam* The mind becomes clarified by cultivating [or alternately: A clarified mind yields] an attitude of friendliness, compassion, joy, and equanimity toward happiness, pain, virtue, or vice. 197, **Ch 51: 214f**

YS 1.47 *nirvicāra-vaiśāradye-adhyātma-prasādaḥ* In the lucidity of nirvicāra-samādhi, there is clarity of the inner Self. **Ch 39: 167f**, 173

YS 1.48 *ṛtaṃ-bharā tatra prajñā* There is truth-bearing wisdom in that state [of samādhi]. **168-169**, 175

YS 1.50 *taj-jaḥ saṃskāro 'nya-saṃskāra-pratibandhī* Saṃskāras born from that [truth-bearing wisdom] obstruct other saṃskāras. **169-170**

YS 2.2 *samādhi-bhāvana-arthaḥ kleśa-tanū-karaṇa-arthaś ca* The purpose [of kriyā-yoga/the yoga of action] is samādhi/meditative immersion and attenuating the kleśas/afflictions. **Ch 39: 166f**

YS 2.4 *avidyā kṣetram-uttareṣāṃ prasupta-tanu-vicchinna-udārāṇām* Ignorance is the source of the other [kleśas, or causes of pain], whether dormant, weak, intermittent, or activated. **Ch 30: 123f**, 166, 167, 209

YS 2.5 *anitya-aśuci-duḥkha-anātmasu nitya-śuci-sukha-ātma-khyātir-avidyā* Ignorance is confusing the transitory, impure, and painful not-self with the eternal, pure, joyful Self. **Ch 30: 123f**

YS 2.16 *heyaṃ duḥkham anāgatam* Future suffering is to be avoided. **Ch 50: 209f**

YS 2.33 *vitarka-bādhane pratipakṣa-bhāvanam* When assailed by negative thoughts, cultivate the opposite. **Ch 49: 205f**, 217

Other Stories and Teachings

Capture the Fort **Ch 45: 196**, 197, 210, 239

Churning of the Ocean **Ch 38: 159f**, 165, 169, 176, 197, 240

dagdha-bīja/burnt seed **167**, 169, 170, 173, 205, 210

Gaṇapati/Gaṇeśa **74-75**, 90, 165

Hanumān **Ch 52: 223f**

Highest First 73, **Ch 18: 90f**, 93, 95, 125, 186, 189, 201, 216, 217, 227, 234

Ledge of Freedom **202-203**, 207, 209, 211-212, 217, 239

nāśivaṃ vidyate kvacit/There is nothing that is not Śiva. **Ch 22: 99**, 168, 182-183, 186-187, 188, 189, 216, 232, 239

Naṭarāja **Ch 8: 43f**, 88, 95, 103, **Ch 26: 108f**, 118, 123, 131, 186, 239; see "Story of the Tillai Forest" below

Ocean and the Wave **Ch 17: 86f**, 96, 102, 108, 109, 112, 118, 123, 125, 127-129, 137, 179, 183, 186, 201, 235

Seed and the Tree xi, 1, 3, 25, **Ch 4: 26f**, 61, 70, 144, 181

Story of the Tillai Forest **Ch 7: 39f**, 47, 48, 71, 86, 108, 110, 141, 144, 182, 229, 240

Glossary and Index of Sanskrit Terms

As already noted, Sanskrit words have many meanings. This glossary includes definitions relevant to how words are used in this book. In some cases, the page numbers listed also include references to the English equivalent.

abhaya-mudrā: gesture or hand position of "no fear" 40, 41, **108-109**

Abhinavagupta: philosopher and sage from Kashmir 56, 69, 70-71, 229, 231, **253**

abhyāsa: practice 34, **Ch 37: 149f**, 165, 231

adhikāra: studentship; readiness, qualification, capacity and/or entitlement to receive a practice 41, 141, **Ch 35: 143f**, 147-148, 185, 238

ahaṃkāra: "I-maker," ego, sense of individuality **119**

ānanda: bliss 39, **105-106**, 162, 188, 189

anugraha: grace, revelation 68, **109-112**, 140, 141, 144, 146, 186

āsana: seat, posture xi, **2**, 28-30, 33-35, 37, 44-46, 48, 52, 53, 58, 62, 67, 86, 92, 139, 143, 147, 150-153, 161-162, 173, 189, 207, 253-254, 255, 256

aṣṭāṅga-yoga: eight-fold yoga outlined in Patañjali's *Yoga Sūtra* 20, 51, 197

atha: now **Ch 2: 18f**, 24, 26, 233, 239, 240, 254

ātma/ātman: highest Self, Consciousness within an individual **93-94**, 123-125, 168

avidyā: ignorance 67, 69, 110, 115, **Ch 30: 123f**, 127, 130, 131, 166, 168, 182, 186, 202, 209, 239

Bhairava: name or form of Śiva **184**

karma: action, the chain of action and their effects 129, **130**, **131f**, 165-167, 207, 210-211, 217, 239, 240-241

kleśa: impediment, hindrance, affliction, cause of pain **123-124**, 131, 166-167, 200, 206, 207, 209

kriyā-yoga: three-fold path of yoga outlined in Patañjali's *Yoga Sūtra* 20, 51, 166-167

liṅga: statue or form that is a symbol of Śiva as the formless Reality **39**-41, 43, 71, 110, 229

mala: covering, impurity, limitation (of three types: *āṇava*, *māyīya*, *karma*) 115, 125, **Ch 31: 126f**, 130, 131, 181, 185, 186, 201, 209, 217, 239

manas: information processing mind **119**, 134

mantra: sacred phoneme, word, phrase, chant, or hymn 40, 52, 163

Naṭarāja: Śiva as Lord of the Dance **Ch 7: 39f**, **Ch 8: 43f**, 80, 88, 95, 103, Ch 25: 108f, 118, 123, 131, 144, 186, 239

nirodha: restriction, control, restraint, cessation **32**, 33, 119, 120, 149, 151, 182

nivṛtti: path of renunciation and turning away from the world 23, 42, **Ch 8: 43f**, 86-87, 92, 106, 152, 166, 205, 229, 231, 251, 252, 254

pañca-kṛtyas: five acts of Śiva (*sṛṣṭi, sthiti, saṃhāra, tirodhāna/ nigraha/vilaya, anugraha*) 41, **Ch 26: 108f**, 118, 140, 185-186, 233

pañca-śaktis: five powers of Śiva (*cit, ānanda, icchā, jñāna, kriyā*) 23, **Ch 25: 105f**, 123, 188

paramparā: succession of teachers, lineage stream xiii, 20, 28, 30, 65, **70**, 73, 104, 182, 186, 250, 253, 256

Patañjali: compiler of the *Yoga Sūtra*; a part human form of the serpant Śeṣa xii, 2, 18-20, **Ch 7: 39f**, 44-47, 48, 86, 173, **252**, (see also *Yoga Sūtra* and Story of the Tillai Forest in appendix VI)

prakṛti: matter, creation, material world, nature 132, **252**

pratipakṣa-bhāvana: cultivating the opposite **Ch 49: 205f**, 217

pratyabhijñā: recognition 87, 140, 168, 182, 186, 188, 189, 253 (see also *Pratyabhijñā-Hṛdayam* in appendix VI)

sūtra: aphorism **6**, 49, 90, 93, 99, 265

svadharma: one's own dharma, purpose, or duty **Ch 53: 228f**, 234

svādhyāya: "self-study," recitation and study of the texts, mindful exploration of one's self 2, 3, 5-6, 8, 9, 16, 19-20, 26, 46, 49, **Ch 10: 51f**, 56, 57, 58, 60-63, 65, 68, 70, 71, 89, 144, 153, 163, 169, 175-177, 207, 217, 231, 256, 258, 264

svatantra: free, independent 74, 93, **95**, **Ch 21: 97f**, 117, 127, 141, 201-202

svātantrya: freedom 95, **Ch 21: 97f**, 105, 118, 127, **Ch 48: 201f**, 207, 209, 211, 218, 235, 239 (see also "Ledge of Freedom" in appendix VI)

tantra: a yogic tradition or a text from that tradition xii, **2**, 20, 39, 45, 46, 57, 67, 77, 80, 81, 82, 83, 85, 87, 90, 92-93, 95, 97, 99, 103, 104, 105, 106, 108, 120, 125, 127, 131, 146, 147, 148, 152, 163, 182, 185, 187, 188, **253**

upāya: method, means 16, 34, 46, **67**, 69, 86, 87, 141, **Ch 36: 146f**, 149, 167, 173, 184, 207, 217, 229, 256

vairāgya: dispassion, nonattachment 33, 34, **Ch 37: 149f**

vijñāna: experiential knowledge **Ch 9: 48f**, 60, 89, 147, 231, 239, 256

vikalpa-saṃskāra: refinement of one's understanding of the teachings, refinement of the place of awareness from which understanding arises 16-17, 18, 20, 49, 54, **Ch 11: 56f**, 60, 61, 62, 65, 69, 70, 71, 79, 89, 94, 107, 131, 133, 154, 163, 165, 166, 168, 169, **Ch 41: 175f**, 197, 207, 210-211, 212, 214, 233, 234, 235, 237

Vyāghrapāda: "tiger paws," a character in the Story of the Tillai Forest **40-42**, 46, 47, 71, 86, 144, 182, 229

About the Author

Cindy Lusk, PhD, was born in Morgantown, West Virginia, but grew up all over the United States and Europe as an Air Force brat. She completed a BA in psychology at the University of California–Santa Cruz and earned her doctorate in social psychology at the University of Colorado. She began studying yoga *āsana* with Richard Freeman in 1985, and she has studied and taught both Ashtanga and Anusara yogas. An avid student of yoga philosophy, Cindy has taught many courses and in yoga teacher trainings. Cindy began studying with Paul Muller-Ortega in 2009 and is an authorized teacher of Neelakantha Meditation. Her students report that her teaching is authentic, accessible, and applicable, as it allows them to deepen their understanding of yoga and of themselves, transforming their practice and their lives. You may find out more about her at CindyLusk.com.

www.ingramcontent.com/pod-product-compliance
Lightning Source LLC
Chambersburg PA
CBHW060904120626
46553CB00001B/204
9798989558605